# When Information Counts

## Grading the Media

*Edited by*
Bernard Rubin
Associates in Research for Public Reporting

Professor of Governmental Affairs and Communication
College of Communication and the Graduate School
Boston University

**Lexington Books**
*D.C. Heath and Company/Lexington, Massachusetts/Toronto*

*Library of Congress Cataloging in Publication Data*
Main entry under title:

When information counts.

   Includes bibliographical references.
   1. Mass media—United States—Addresses, essays, lectures. I. Rubin, Bernard.
P92.U5W47   1985      001.51′0973      85-29
ISBN 0-669-10163-X (alk. paper)

Second printing, July 1985

Published simultaneously in Canada
Printed in the United States of America on acid-free paper
International Standard Book Number: 0-669-10163-X Casebound
International Standard Book Number: 0-669-10162-1 Paperbound
Library of Congress Catalog Card Number: 84-40826

*For All Whose Ideas and Works Enhance the First Amendment*

# Contents

# Preface

Whe *hen Information Counts* is the fourth volume in a series of studies developed to enhance the First Amendment.[a] Consistent with the previous volumes, this book is composed entirely of original research articles by outstanding practioner-scholars, offering analyses of key communications subjects. The authors contributed on invitation of Associates in Research for Public Reporting, which was formed in 1983.

The enterprise began with a series of small panel discussions held over a three-month period to hammer out the questions that would receive research priority. The goal was to provide readers with representative and fair depictions of crucial mass media issues of our times. Individuals with expertise and practical mass media experience, who had already demonstrated leadership traits in the media arts and industries, were then asked to participate in a year-long effort. Contributors met to dovetail their topics so as to stimulate a wide range of perspectives and complete a picture of mass media problems and opportunities. The authors were then given the remainder of the year to complete their chapters.

Each of us has concentrated on a topic of transcendent personal and public importance. We all believe that, for working purposes, *information,* insofar as public interests are concerned, must be defined: Information stimulates the intellect so as to encourage education. It consists of relatable knowledge of social, political, or economic value that helps the individual see the real world and take action or make decisions accordingly. Information is the grist that sustains imagination, which is so vital when it is necessary to fill the gaps between the known and the unknown. Information is not mere data. It is the sum product of data that are evaluated and weighed to fulfill a perceived need for knowledge.

---

[a]Bernard Rubin, ed., *Big Business and the Mass Media* (Lexington, Mass: Lexington Books, D.C. Heath, 1977); Bernard Rubin, ed., *Questioning Media Ethics* (New York: Praeger, 1978); Bernard Rubin, ed., *Small Voices and Great Trumpets: Minorities and the Media* (New York: Praeger, 1980). These books were research products of the Institute for Democratic Communication, College of Communication, Boston University.

Therefore, we have concentrated on such questions as the following:

1. How well did the media inform the public about the facts?
2. Did the essence of critical developments get through to media consumers in ways that promoted explanations of what was of immediate concern and of general or long-term consequence?
3. Was the bias of media presenters influential?
4. Were motivations, forces in contention, key players, and scenarios treated with accuracy and objectivity?
5. In dealing with the mundane, was sufficient attention given also to the humane?
6. Was problem solving accorded as much time and attention as problem presentation?
7. How much sensationalism intruded into coverage of stories; how much of it was justified?
8. Were the powerless treated as fairly as the powerful?
9. To what degree are the media manipulated by artful politicians or governors from the public or the private sectors?

As researchers and evaluators, we have endeavored to relate the real to the unreal and to provide clues as to how mass media information helps determine the powers and alternative futures of democrats, demagogues, and dictators.

We have deliberately avoided any attempt to be encyclopedic in this volume. Rather, our objective has been to offer material that is indicative of the media environment in which we live and that points to ways and means for more valid reporting by our democratically inspired press.

The range of experiences of the contributors is very wide. Each author is a mass media practitioner-scholar of considerable standing. Most are well known for their work as reporters and critics. Some of them have displayed their talents in novels, and many are also active in more traditional scholarship and popular press enterprises. For example, Caryl Rivers, Roger Manvell, and Cecelia Tichi are respected for widely varied achievements.

Manvell's significant contributions include his many books on international film history, biographies of great artists of the legitimate stage, and on the malicious evolution of the Third Reich. For illustration purposes only, I cite *Films and the Second World War* (1975), *Ellen Terry* (1968), *The Hundred Days to Hitler* (in collaboration with Heinrich Fraenkel, 1974), and one of his novels, *The Passion* (1960).

Rivers' magazine articles on contemporary social changes appear frequently in such publications as *The Nation, Saturday Review, Rolling Stone, McCall's, New York Times Magazine, Glamour,* and *Ms.* She is a leading interpreter of the course of feminism as a movement in such works as *Beyond Sugar and Spice: How Women Grow, Learn and Thrive* (1979) and *Aphrodite at Midcentury:*

*Growing Up Female and Catholic in Postwar America* (1973). This fine journalist has also won acclaim for her novels, *The Mind Stealers* (1983) and *Virgins* (1984).

Tichi is best known for her considerable prowess in the field of literary criticism and for her seminal analysis of environmental reform, *New World, New Earth* (1979). Forthcoming is *The Harper American Literature* (with Donald McQuade et al.). In such journals as *American Literature and Genre,* she has written of the giants Longfellow, Melville, and Whitman. In recent years, she has turned her attention to studying the cultural impact of the press.

Clemens has concentrated on U.S.–Soviet relations, Second World governments and their politics, and international arms control, and he has lectured in Asia and Europe on those subjects and others. Among his works are *The Arms Race and Sino-Soviet Relations* (1968), *The U.S.S.R. and Global Interdependence* (1978), and *National Security and U.S.–Soviet Relations* (1982). His articles have appeared in *China Quarterly,* the *New York Times, The Times* of London, the *Christian Science Monitor,* and other prestigious publications.

Ralph Rosnow is one of the foremost scholars in behavioral research from the discipline of psychology. His many book-length studies include *Rumor and Gossip: The Social Psychology of Hearsay* (1976), *Understanding Behavioral Science* (1984), *Experiments in Persuasion* (with Edward J. Robinson, 1967), and *Introduction to Contemporary Psychology* (with Robert E. Lana, 1972). One dares not even try to single out key learned articles from the hundreds he has contributed; therefore, I am content to cite one of his latest, "Van Osten's Horse: Hamlet's Question and the Mechanistic View of Causality," in the *Journal of Mind and Behavior* (1983). Marianthi Georgoudi, Rosnow's co-author, has previously concentrated on explorations of the dialectics of social explanation.

Robert Montgomery and Loren Ghiglione have had long and eminent careers as media managers. Montgomery is an advertising tyro who has directed advertising-marketing efforts for a number of business organizations. For ten years from 1958 to 1968, he was manager of advertising for the Borg-Warner Corporation of Chicago, and he has run his own advertising agencies most successfully, with special personal interests in campaign consulting and community group assistance. At Boston University, Montgomery the professor developed Ad Lab, an innovative model for students studying commercial and nonprofit advertising practices. His publications range widely, from *The Presidential Campaign Handbook* (with Clifford Martel, 1975) to *Case Study of the Alaska National Communication Program* (with Kirby Upjohn, 1983) to *Public Relations for Public Schools* (1954).

Ghiglione is the editor and publisher of *The News* (Southbridge, Massachusetts) and president of Worcester County Newspapers of Massachusetts, and has been prominent in press organizations (president, New England Press Association; member of the Board of Directors, American Society of Newspaper Editors; founding member of the pioneering National News Council). Ghiglione edited

*Evaluating the Press: The New England Daily Newspaper Survey* (1974). Others of his publications are *Gentlemen of the Press* (1984) and *Improving Newswriting* (1982), and his essays on media topics have appeared in *Questioning Media Ethics* (ed. B. Rubin, 1978) and other books.

Deac Rossell, the coordinator of film of the Museum of Fine Arts, Boston, is the vice-president of the Ford Hall Forum and a journalistic critic of the popular arts whose work has appeared in such journals as *Esquire, Boston* magazine, *Parents Choice,* and the *National Catholic Reporter,* as well as in book-length studies.

Ann Rawley Saldich's recent book, *Electronic Democracy: Television's Impact on the American Political Process* (1979), carries on her communications analyses, and her articles have appeared in the *Columbia Journalism Review, InterMedia* (London), the *Irish Broadcasting Review,* and the French journal *l'Année 2000.*

T. Barton Carter, by training and interest, pursues subjects dealing with communications law, media, and the public interest. Carter's concentrations have led him to right-of-reply issues, cable television, impacts of computers, rights of privacy, and broadcast administration. In addition to his practical research for such organizations as the National Association of Broadcasters, he tends to business as the president of Tanist Broadcasting Corporation, licensee of WFAU/WKCG in Augusta, Maine.

Since 1979, Tenney Kelley Lehman has been the editor of *Nieman Reports,* the prestigious critique of journalism around the world published by the Nieman Foundation of Harvard University. She is also executive director of the foundation.

Bernard Rubin has been examining communications problems from governmental or political perspectives for more than thirty years. In his books and articles, he has explored the evolution and changing roles of the mass media in America, as well as problems of communications development on the international scene, particularly in the Third World. His books include *Political Television* (1967) and *Media, Politics and Democracy* (1977).

*When Information Counts* is intended to provoke the reader with its thoughtful analyses of controversial subjects. Our studies do not provide packaged, all-purpose answers to communications problems but readers will be better prepared to understand and deal with crucial issues when they are specifically informed about why and how social and political pressures increase because of mass media interventions. Our goal is to document and analyze the backgrounds to such issues as applicable to similar ones just over the horizon.

We all count on information that meets our selfish educational needs and connects personal concerns to the broader objectives of society as a whole. As individuals and as members of the body politic, the most important objective shared by thoughtful, caring people is the enhancement of democratic ways and means. The mass media of our day record, in one manner or another, achievements and failures in the struggles to perpetuate freedom where it exists and to bring it as a human right to those places where it never existed or has been driven underground. Information counts every day, from the moment we open our eyes.

The issue-centered, case-related chapters that follow elucidate developments that no member of our democratic community dares to ignore. Therefore, of the primary audiences for whom this book is intended, the general citizenry in search of specific knowledge about how mass communication enriches or frustrates society is especially important. Readers drawn to these explorations of education, of entertainment, and of signaling (alerts and warnings) will note that pedantry is downplayed and precision of analysis is stressed.

*When Information Counts* is also aimed at college and university students and their professors who are concentrating on communications topics in arts and sciences or on communications and journalism studies. The truly educated individual knows that theory and practice are not easily separated and that documentation is valid across fields. Thus, the seekers of useful data in history, sociology, literature, psychology, or political science will treasure situational evidence from the worlds of the mass media to the same degree that students of journalism, public relations, advertising, management, and marketing are obligated to be broadly trained in the humanities and the social sciences.

Our third primary readership is composed of professionals in communications and allied fields. Print journalists, public relations specialists, advertising and marketing experts, and their clients will find much of immediate pertinency in these pages. Broadcasters in radio and television, and their colleagues in the filmic arts and industries, will also be intrigued by the relevance of these studies to their work projects and their professional aspirations.

The fourth constituency represented and addressed by the contributors to this volume are the activists in law and government who are devoted to the perpetuation of liberty for the peoples of this great land and for the growth and encouragement of democracy on this planet. Their special concerns are central to this enterprise.

I thank my colleagues for their devotion and for their gentle treatment of the taskmaster at all times.

*Bernard Rubin*
Director, Associates in Research for Public Reporting
Wellesley, Massachusetts

# Part I
# Grounds for Concern

# 1

# Women, Myth, and the Media

*Caryl Rivers*

"Clouds of pessimism" hung over the Moscone Center, declared the political reporter, with a flourish of metaphor. The sun may have been shining brightly on the cool waters of San Francisco Bay, but in Medialand, all was in shadow.

The time was July 1984, and the Democrats had come together in the city where "little cable cars climb halfway to the stars." They were to choose a candidate who, they hoped, would travel upward in the polls as fast as the cable cars clanged up the northern California hills. Fifty percent of the delegates were women—the party had mandated that fully half the people who would elect the nominee were to be female.

The delegates were about to witness a historic event. Walter Mondale had just announced that Geraldine Ferraro was to be his choice for vice-president. For the first time in the annals of the Republic, a woman would be part of the team that topped the ticket. But in the wake of the Ferraro announcement, a squabble had broken out in the ranks of the Democratic National Committee (DNC). Looking toward Southern votes, the Mondale staff had announced that Bert Lance would be the New DNC head. Lance, the good-ole-boy from Georgia who had resigned from the Carter administration after questions were raised about certain bank loans, would replace California Charles Manatt.

Now, firing a native son on his own soil just before the convention opened was not one of the brightest political moves of the decade. So the press descended, eager as the Assyrians, coming down like a wolf on the fold.

It was the standard political squabble—insiders at each others' throats—and would be forgotten utterly by the press a few days hence. Few Americans cared a fig about who headed the DNC, but it was a story political reporters really understood—the back room boys going at each other.

To the women delegates, however, "l'affaire Lance" was simply a small pimple on the face of jubilation. Their mood could best be described as triumphant, joyous, elated. For the first time, one of their own was to vie for the spot "a heartbeat away" from the presidency. There were no "clouds of pessimism" wafting about the heads of Democratic women in San Francisco.

But, as often happens, the reality that many of the reporters saw was *male* reality. What counted was what the guys in the back room were doing. They simply did not see the same reality as did many of the delegates to the convention—the women. Many of these men had spent a lifetime not seeing women, so it was no surprise that it was happening again. In the media, the Invisible Man is often a woman. Those reporters who didn't see what was happening with the female delegates weren't being spiteful, weren't putting down women or trying to shore up the patriarchy. They simply didn't *see*. Because they weren't expected to. Because they never had. And that fact is perhaps more distressing than if the distortion had been wreaked with malice aforethought. After all, when people throw rocks at you, at least they acknowledge your presence. When you are invisible, it is as if you didn't exist at all.

This is the most important truth that women must grasp about the media—about newspapers and magazines and TV. Much of what they hear, see, and read is not a presentation of "reality." It is edited, filtered, preselected—usually through the mesh of the male perspective. It reflects a universe in which women are too often totally invisible—or just barely so. Walter Cronkite used to say, at the end of the CBS newscast, "And that's the way it is." He *should* have said, "And that's the way it is—as decided by a very small group of people, nearly all of whom are white, male, who make more than thirty thousand dollars a year and never take their own clothes to the cleaners."

And, when women *do* appear in the media, the image is more often than not strangely contorted. Much of what the media present as "objective fact" is in truth a mish-mash of myth and misinformation. This is no less so—or not much less—than in the days before the women's movement existed. Behind the headlines on such stories as "sex and the brain," "Premenstrual Syndrome," "math genes," "stress," and "superwomen" boils a steaming cauldron of mythology of which few journalists who write such stories are aware.

As Elizabeth Janeway points out so incisively in *Man's World, Women's Place,* every society invents myths about itself and then proceeds to act on those myths as if they were fact.[1] Mythmakers are usually small, powerful, elite groups; referenda are not held on popular mythology. In time, myth becomes indistinguishable from truth. Plato's cave dwellers, inhabiting a world of darkness, saw their shadows dancing on the wall in the firelight and thought it was the shadows that were real.

The people who can learn to manipulate social mythology are powerful indeed. One of the great inventions of the twentieth century was the studied, methodical engineering of myth for political ends. Aryan supremacy was an absurd, unscientific concept, but it still managed to plunge the entire world into war and madness.

But more often than not, the mythology that operates where women are concerned is of the unconscious rather than the programmed variety. One of these myths, with roots that go far back into history, is the myth of feminine weakness. Women are not as rational, as stable, as competent, as logical as men. (Thus, they are not to be trusted.)

In the nineteenth century, the conventional wisdom of the medical profession was that the brain and the reproductive organs could not develop at the same time. Women were to be kept away from rigorous intellectual activity to protect their ability to function as wives and mothers. Does this sound dated, old-hat? Indeed. But its residue can be found in intriguing places.

For example, Theodore H. White, writing in 1984 in the *New York Times Magazine* about the election campaign, looks askance at the women's movement, fearing it will lead to the "Balkanization" of American politics.[2] (Translation: When anybody other than white males get power, it's Balkanization.) White says that laws are necessary to protect women against "the hazards visited upon them by nature."

Is he speaking, perchance, of the vapors? Men die, on the average, some eight years earlier than women; they are much more likely to drop dead in the prime of life with a heart attack, to die of lung cancer, to get ulcers, to drink themselves to death. But would any journalist *ever* write of the "hazards visited upon men by nature"? When it comes to hazards, both women and men have their share, though women come off a little better. But the only weakness that is perceived is the female one.

It intrigues me that any piece of "news" that seems to document female instability vaults right into the headlines. Premenstral syndrome is a classic example. Here is a condition that, in its extreme form, affects only a tiny minority of women. Indeed, many women do experience physical symptoms before the onset of their periods, changes in mood among them. For most, it's a minor inconvenience. Most women do not go berserk, cause mayhem, or go after their lovers with a butcher knife. Why, then, did this syndrome get headlines all over the globe and its own thirty minutes on ABC's "Nightline," while more devastating medical problems get barely a mention?

Because the story validates a long-cherished myth about women—they are unpredictable, crazy creatures who are prisoners of their hormones. Men, of course, never go berserk and hack up their families, pick off pedestrians from a twenty-second-story window with a rifle, abuse children, or beat up little old ladies. Will "Nightline" ever do a story on testosterone poisoning?

The myth of female weakness also lurks behind much of what is considered to be "objective" reporting on scientific theory. In recent years, theories of biological determinism have become chic, especially sociobiology and "genes-and-gender" science.

Many sociobiologists dismiss culture with a nod and insist that just about everything we do is programmed into our genetic structure. Harvard's E.O. Wilson suggests there may even be a gene for religion. (A different gene, one wonders, for Orthodox or Reform Jews and for Baptists and Unitarians?)

Sociobiology's critics point out that much of this stuff is highly theoretical and simplistic; and sociobiologists tend to take wild leaps in their search for a theory that wraps everything up in a neat little package. But is is not the least bit surprising, and not at all accidental, that sociobiology became so trendy.

In a time of diminishing resources, how comforting it is to have a theory that says things are the way they are because of inevitable genetic forces. Forget Head Start. Forget the ERA. Forget affirmative action. Social justice is expensive and painful. Articles in the popular media in recent years have suggested that there are people with "criminal" genes. Don't waste money on rehabilitation. Rape and wife-beating and child abuse are natural genetic adaptations—so women and children just have to relax and enjoy it.

"Genes-and-gender" science and the game I call "musical hormones" are very much in vogue these days. Take, for example, the flap over "math genes."

Two scientists at Johns Hopkins University, looking at national math testing data, found that boys did very much better than girls.[3] This was nothing new; such results have been popping up for years. What was new was the scientists' interpretation of the data. They said that the gap was so large that it had to be due to some genetic differences, not just to culture. Headlines all around the country trumpeted that boys have better "math genes" than girls.

Critics, of course, attacked this interpretation. They found little solid evidence for such a statement, given the intense social pressure on girls to avoid math and the sciences. The Hopkins researchers cited special programs set up to help girls in math. But is it not a bit naive to expect that the existence of a few special programs over a relatively short time span would undo a deep cultural bias? The critics, of course, didn't get the same play in the press as the original story did. And the reference to "math genes"—as if they were fact, not disputed theory—keeps cropping up in the media. Its very persistence could mean that, slowly and quietly, programs to seek out and encourage talented young women in math and science will quietly choke and die, the victim of another bit of media mythology.

Sex differences sell. We are seeing a spate of stories about differences between male and female brains, about male and female hormones and behavior. This is new, very complex research, and there is great debate among scientists about the findings. But in the headlines, speculation becomes fact, theory becomes "gee-whiz" prose. As science writer Barbara Beckwith points out in her research on genes-and-gender science, this genre has been grist for the mill of a large range of magazines, from *Science* to *Cosmo*.[4] (Pack journalism being what it is, one cover story begets another faster than two bunnies in heat.) Most of the stories give short shrift to critics who say that connections between hormones and genes and behavior are tentative, and much of the speculation may turn out to be eyewash—just like the "science" of measuring the brain to discover who was smarter. Beckwith notes:

> Popular magazines use genes-and-gender theories as justification for keeping things as they are. The five most popular science magazines—Science Digest, Science '84, Discover, Omni and Psychology Today, have printed Genes-and-Gender articles, virtually ignoring the debate going on about the issue.

Oversimplifications abound in much of the "gee-whiz" coverage. One newspaper headline announced that brain differences were the reason there were few female geniuses. The article, about left-brain, right-brain differences, never gave the reader the notion that there might be another historical reason for the dearth of female geniuses. The fact that in the first two centuries of the Republic, women were not permitted through the doors of universities might have had some slight impact on their intellectual accomplishments.

"Gee-whiz" science stories tend to accept uncritically the latest—and most chic—authority the reporter has interviewed. An example comes from the *Playboy* series on sex differences, by Jo Durden Smith and Diane de Simone.[5] The writers detail an interview with a scientist who speculates that females, because of brain function, may be better than males in integrating verbal and nonverbal function. She says that this may be at the root of what we call female intuition.

The writers describe leaving the interview convinced that she is right:

"Female intuition!" says one of us as we walk outside into a bustle of students. "Men's difficulty with emotions!" says another. "In the brain!"

If these writers had been a bit more critical, they might have examined other explanations for the same phenomenon. Let's take a look at one, from another scientific discipline. Psychologist Jean Baker Miller in (*Towards A New Psychology of Women*) has another theory on "female intuition."[6] Miller points out that societies have two categories of people, the dominants and the subordinants, who behave in different ways. Dominants are powerful, and they assign to themselves the jobs that are high in status and material rewards. The less valued jobs are assigned to subordinants, who are encouraged to develop a certain cluster of traits—submissiveness, dependency, passivity. Subordinants quickly learn how to use this behavior for protective cover. Blacks often had to learn the shuffle and the "Yassuh, Boss." to survive. Women got very good at the "dumb blonde" and "clinging vine" routines. Subordinate groups, unable to make demands or reach openly for power, become experts at manipulation. They know much more about the dominants than vice versa, because their survival depends on it. They become highly attuned to dominants, able to predict reactions of pleasure or displeasure.

Miller writes:

Here, I think, is where the long story of "feminine intuition" and "feminine wiles." begins. It seems clear that these mysterious gifts are in fact skills, developed through long practice, in reading many signals, both verbal and nonverbal.

Women, says Miller, are aware early on that they have a duty to nurture: "I must care for those who are not me." Female socialization is akin to a Ph.D. in caring. I have both a teenage son and a teenage daughter. My daughter is deluged with teen magazines that tell her how to handle jealousy, friendships, her friend's feelings, her boyfriend's feelings, breaking up, making up—she is being schooled to manage emotions. My son gets absolutely no such advice from society. Boys grow up expecting women will manage emotions for them. No wonder they aren't very good at it.

So, is it hormones or training that accounts for behavior? The truth of the matter is that human behavior is a very complex affair—a tangle of biology and environment that is extremely difficult to sort out. To understand it, one must be able to examine elaborate sets of forces, acting in concert. The "reductionism" that often operates in the sciences makes this nearly impossible. It's like saying a car runs because of the spark plugs, and looking very intently at the spark plugs. You wind up knowing a lot about plugs, but not a lot about the engine. And "gee-whiz" science writing often falls prey to this fallacy.

It's important for women to understand all this because of the absolutely dismal history of the interaction between biological determinism and politics. It's a truism that biological theories of differences between the sexes and races are inevitably used against the group that doesn't have political power. Harvard biologist Jon Beckwith sees a chilling parallel between today's "genes-and-gender" fad and the popularization of the "science" of eugenics early in the century.[7] Popular science journals then ran such articles as "A Study of Jewish Psychopathy" and "The Racial Element in National Vitality," promoting the idea that social behavior was inherited. The *Saturday Evening Post* took up the cudgel as well. The result of this was to create popular support for sterilization and miscegenation laws and immigration laws that discriminated against Slavs, Jews, Southern Europeans, and other groups.

The genes-and-gender stories of today often are very slick; the bias is buried in jargon and pseudoscience. But they can indeed build popular support for slowing the drive for equality between the races and the sexes. For example, an *Education Digest* article, citing brain research, proposes setting up different learning sequences for boys and girls to "allow for their separate predispositions."[8] If that happens, guess who's going to get the good stuff and who's going to get the drek. Separate but equal? Not likely!

Many of the genes-and-gender articles appear, on the surface, to be somewhat evenhanded, since they seem to be saying that both boys and girls get a share of "good genes." Boys are good at math; girls are good at verbal skills and communication. This, they say, is the decree of nature and will always remain so.

Well, then, shouldn't we expect some action? Certainly women, with their marvelous intuition and their ability to communicate, will be immediately appointed to most ambassadorial posts. Surely they will get the lion's share of editing and writing jobs. They will be made tenured professors of literature. They will be made managers in major corporations, where their ability to communicate will doubtless boost productivity.

Don't hold your breath. Women will keep on getting the low-paid jobs in the day care center, in the elementary school, and in the typing pool—unless the drive for equal opportunity does not slacken. Remember, this is a society that hasn't even been able to pass the ERA. Women had better be on guard; they could be talked out of the rights they have won the hard way by people who say they haven't got the right genes or hormones or the right structure in the brain.

One thing we do know is that social change *does* change behavior. It didn't take thousands of years of genetic change to end slavery. It took an act of law. The quantum leap in performance displayed by American women in the 1984 Olympics came not as a result of any change in hormones but from Title IX, which insisted that money and resources be allocated to women's athletic programs. In the early 1900s, the "criminal class" was overwhelmingly white, often Irish, Jewish, Slavic. Now it's largely black, Hispanic, or other minority. Was there a sudden genetic chance among Jews, Irishmen, and Slavs? No—they just moved up and out of poverty, to be replaced by newer groups at the low end of the totem pole. Social justice doesn't have to wait for evolution.

The myth of female weakness, as we've seen, can be a powerful force in the distortion of reality. There's another, nearly as potent: the myth of female strength. (Illogical? Mythology doesn't operate by the rules of logic.)

Rooted deep in our culture is the notion that if women obtain political power, the world will go to hell in a handcart. To me, this is a peculiar notion. Given a choice, I'd rather have a woman's hand on the little red button than a man's. (Except for Phyllis Schlafly's. She'd blow up the world because some guy told her to. Or Margaret Thatcher's. Token women in a male game have to prove they are tougher than the guys. How about a receptionist from Queens?)

Not only will the world go awry if women have power, says the myth, but women themselves will suffer. This bogeyman runs through the women-and-stress stories that are popping up in the media these days like mushrooms. The advice in them is seductive, because it seems so sympathetic: "You poor dear, we don't want to see you harmed!" The scent of crocodile tears is overwhelming.

The message being beamed to women is that if they set their sights too high, they will start dropping dead from heart attacks, develop ulcers, hound themselves to early graves.

It's interesting to see that these warnings are nearly always aimed at women heading for high-prestige jobs. How often do you see a headline: "Watch out for the typing pool: It's a killer!" Not often. But it may be the truth.

The federally funded Framingham Heart Study shows that working women do not show increasing coronary symptoms—with one exception: women in low-level clerical and secretarial jobs. And a major study by Columbia University's Dr. Robert Karasek, an industrial engineer, shows that lack of decision-making power is a factor in coronary risk.[9] The truly lethal combination, his study shows, is high psychological demand and the little decision-making power.

Dr. Karasek and his colleagues indexed jobs according to the demand/control index. Many of the jobs in the high-demand/low-control quadrant were "female ghetto" jobs—sales clerk, telephone operator, waitress, mall worker, garment stitcher. Why aren't women being warned away from these jobs? Because society needs drones, that's why. Disturbing projections on the future of the work force show that it's not in the glamour field of high tech where the greatest number of jobs will be, but in the low-paid service sector of the economy.

Another bogeyman to emerge from the myth of female strength is the new darling of the feature pages: Superwoman. She's chairman of the board, a dazzling dresser and partygiver, but she always has time to dash home and read *Winnie the Pooh* to the kiddies and whip up a batch of nutritious, noncarcinogenic toll house cookies. It's an image that, on the surface, seems flattering, but in reality it's designed to scare "ordinary" women right down to their toes. The underlying message behind Superwoman is that a woman has to be more than a mere mortal to manage having both career and family. If you can't scare women away from achievement by saying it's going to make them sick, try another tack. Imply that only exceptional women can do it. And Superwoman does scare women off. When a student newspaper at Boston University did an informal poll of women students, asking whether they could manage home and family, most expressed serious doubts. These young women were ignoring the experiences of millions of real women around them—women who managed job and family but were not Superwomen—and listening to the siren song of myth.

The media inadvertently foster the Superwoman myth in stories about women with good jobs, because the emphasis is always on what such women accomplish, not on the way they manage or the trade-offs they make. As an author, I am interviewed fairly often, and there are times when I do not recognize the disciplined, dynamic, supercharged woman on the printed page. The stories do not mention that I never remember my dentist appointments, that my office looks like the town dump, or that my children say my home-cooked meals could inspire a TV show: "That's Inedible."

But the Superwoman image just seems too sexy for the media to loosen its grip. Recently, I was interviewed by a reporter who did an excellent story about how working women aren't Superwomen and how the image is harmful to women. But the headline stuck on the story was "Those Superwomen are real—and happiest!"

The myth of female strength also often means that when things go wrong, women will get blamed—mothers in particular. When a woman has a child, perhaps the best thing she can do is absolutely refuse to read any newspaper or magazine article with the word *mother* in it. You can bet she's going to catch hell for something.

In the fifties, when women stayed home, dutifully, and lavished their time on their children, they were blamed for destroying the kids' character. "Momism" became a national buzzword. Critics said that American POWs broke under torture in Korea because their mothers had spoiled them. (Maybe their mothers should have locked them in the closet for days on end, blindfolded, to prepare them for brainwashing.) When mothers went out to work, they were blamed for alienation, latchkey children, low SAT scores, drug abuse, teenage pregnancy, cavities, and the decline of American civilization. Mothers are the favorite scapegoat of the media; there is *no* way they can win.

In the foreseeable future, I believe we are going to see more and more of biological determinism and myth-as-science. The economic picture does not seem rosy; already a mean-spiritedness seems to be rolling across the land. Many Americans want to believe that people go to soup kitchens to save money or sleep on sidewalk grates for kicks. The time is ripe—perhaps overripe—for theories that buttress the status quo.

At the same time, a disturbing trend in the media grows apace. "Upscale" is the buzzword in publishing these days. Increasingly, information is becoming a commodity to be sold to the affluent. Magazines desperately try to purge their subscription lists of readers who are not the "Yuppies" advertisers adore. Best-bagel and boutique journalism spreads like a malevolent weed. Editors grow increasingly impatient with the notion of giving their upscale readers information that will make them uncomfortable. Stories about affirmative action, poverty, the mentally ill, the homeless are just not "sexy."

It's not only women, of course, who need to beware of such trends—but also men who are committed to the idea of a society where social justice is not a hollow phrase. Blacks, Hispanics, gays, Orientals—all will be affected directly by social mythology. As our society becomes increasingly Hispanic and Oriental, I await the new scientific findings about these groups. Will Hispanics be found to be overly "right-brained"—perfect for playing guitars and doing the tango, but for God's sake, keep them out of Harvard? Do Orientals lack "originality" genes? Maybe their SAT scores go off the scale, but everybody knows they're just great copiers.

The media constitute an enormously powerful force—for good or ill—in all of this. They can shift the rudder that steers us in one direction or another. But if both the practitioners and the consumers of journalism don't understand the forces to which they are subject, we are all in trouble. If they continue to believe in the illusion of "objective," value-free "news", if they can't detect the strong distorting current of mythology, we may sail our ship in directions that many of us do not wish to travel.

# 2

# The Baggage of Buzzwords; or, History's Revenge

*Cecelia Tichi*

merica is wasting away. A century of industrial pollutants is taking its toll, the media tell us, and the nation's health is in jeopardy. A 1980 book jacket banners the title, *Laying Waste,* and shows a chilling photograph of an average American worker.[1] He is a Postal Service letter carrier delivering mail to private homes. He looks at the camera—in fact, at us, the readers—from the face mask and respirator he wears on the job. His route is the infamous Love Canal area of New York, and his image is haunting.

The waste of Love Canal became a national scandal in the late 1970s. Newspapers and television reported the sad cycle of corporate pollution, community illness, officials' denial of problems or responsibility, media publicity, and belated cleanup and reparation. Love Canal may be behind us, but anxiety remains. Is the photograph of the postman the probable readout of our future? Will decades of environmental dumping turn "spaceship earth" against us? Is a postman in a gas mask the image of our struggle to survive in an American wasteland?

History, it seems, takes revenge in the 1980s. *Waste* becomes a rhetorical umbrella, a catchall term for environmental arrogance, shortsightedness, ignorance, evil. And waste is history's whiplash. We think of the nuclear industry, which in nearly forty years has not solved the problem of waste storage, let alone disposal. We think of Times Beach, Missouri, its roadways sprayed with waste oil laced with toxic chemical carcinogens. The residents are moved out. The federal government buys the entire town.

But scientists and environmentalists insist we cannot simply buy our way out of this wasteland. The territory is too vast. Whole forests from New England to Appalachia are sick. Urban areas, too. In northern New Jersey the toxic substances so foul the air, water, and soil that "The Garden State" becomes a grisly misnomer. In many parts of the nation the television weathermen warn when air quality is "unhealthy" and urge residents to remain indoors. Meanwhile, in the Boston garden suburb of Wellesley, Massachusetts, residents are warned that their drinking water contains unacceptably high levels of salt. For decades the roadways once cindered against winter's snow and ice have been salted—and now winter's safety becomes a public health hazard, since road salt has seeped into the town's water supply.

Waste, we learn, is a weirdly democratic term. Acid rain falls on rich and poor alike. Asbestos particles ride everybody's air. The city might be an atmospheric sewer, but the countryside can be a toxic "silent spring."[2] Waste is history's skull and crossbones.

What, then, of efficiency? In rhetoric, it is the contrary of waste. Logically, it ought to suggest a solution to social or environmental problems. Couldn't *efficiency* be one safe passage out of the wasteland?

It seems not. Oddly, *efficiency* is a term seldom heard in dialogue on the cleanup of air, earth, or water. Instead, it comes up in business contexts, its social meaning ominous. Hardly a week passes that the newspaper, newsmagazine, or television does not report on the dubious efficiency of the American worker. The very term haunts America because, it seems, efficiency has left us. It is a thing of the past. It departed our shores and reportedly took up residence in Japan and the Pacific basin. In the United States, corporate industries—steel foremost among them—close plants and lay off workers indefinitely, claiming they must down-size their operations. "Lean" becomes synonymous with "efficient." But the Japanese automobile imports, the Asian textiles and electronics mock us as history takes its revenge once again. "Made in America" sounds quaint, sounds bitter. *Efficiency,* like *waste,* is history's big stick, bruising and battering the contemporary American ego.

And why not? Japan looms as efficiency incarnate, its workers pictured in regimental rows doing callisthenics before their work shifts. Japanese workers, in fact, look like ideal industrial robots. On television they are shown in orderly formation, unfailingly respectful, uniform in clothing and attitude. They look enviably synchronized, and in a kind of amnesia we conveniently forget that such industrial efficiency was discredited in Charlie Chaplin's movie, *Modern Times,* and in Fritz Lang's *Metropolis.* Efficient, the Japanese get the job done. Their products bespeak a society whose very hallmark is efficiency. From Sony to Honda to Nissan, every Asian brand name finds us wanting. Has something gone terribly wrong in America? Isn't *efficiency* the world we have lost?

So it goes. *Waste* and *efficiency,* contrary terms, become contemporary American indictments. Guilt and blame concentrate in them. Rhetoric becomes history's scourge. Seldom, however, do we pause to ask about the values the two words signify—what long-held meanings are encoded in them. The large-print headlines—"Waste-Deep Spending," "Two from Air Force Tell Senate Panel About Wasteful Practices"—hurry us past the reflective moment.[3]

In the very tumult of the headlines, moreover, we scarcely pause to notice that *waste* and *efficiency* have a low-volume life of their own in American culture. In a quieter way, they are even more revealing of our values than is the high-decibel, high-profile media use of them. For in daily American life, *waste* and *efficiency* function persistently in the realm of buzzwords.

Buzzwords—they come and go like a low, vibrating hum. They appear in the press and surface in television commentary in cycles of popularity. They are terms taken so much for granted that writers, speakers, and listeners—which is to say all of us—neglect to ask what they might actually mean. In print and on-air, they seem harmless, these fashionable contemporary terms. But a case study of the prominent 1980s buzzwords, *waste* and *efficiency*, shows otherwise.

For *waste* and *efficiency*, like all buzzwords, prove treacherous because they block information, because on a subconscious level they invite nods of assent but never a moment's pause for thought or interpretation. Freighted with unexamined values, they function like advertisements. They become subliminal messages forming a barrier against those who do not, or cannot, participate in the values implicit in those words. In the 1980s these two contrary buzzwords, *waste* and *efficiency*, put two groups under stress in American life. Those who suffer are the economically disempowered and those struggling to maintain a responsible balance between personal and work lives.

It goes without saying that one cannot demonstrate the treachery of buzzwords without first locating them. Occasionally, when the example is egregious, the task is easy. When El Salvador's ultra-right-wing leader, Roberto d'Aubuisson, proclaimed his nation's 1982 elections as votes for "free enterprise," the *Boston Globe* denounced him as a figure "effective in his command of buzzwords."[4] To hear the virtues of free enterprise expounded from a man reputedly connected with his government's murderous death squads was too grotesque to escape journalists' attention.

But buzzwords ordinarily slip by, noticed only when they are scouted in the odd assortment of contexts where they appear. These contexts are themselves an identifying clue to their presence. Advertisements are promising ground. There the buzzword stands out because it is strategically placed to lure us to diverse, often incongruous products and services. Thus *efficiency* appears in ads for computer software and for courses in Indian mysticism. An IBM (International Business Machines) ad for a word-processing program heralds "a good way to introduce the whole family to the speed and efficiency of word processing." At the same time, the advertisement for the guru, Maharishi Mahesh Yogi, promises that students enrolling in his course can attain "nature's perfect balance" and "supreme efficiency."[5] The umbrella of "efficiency" in these two ads is amusing, then disconcerting. If large, diverse groups can be baited with that one verbal hook, there is reason to believe that an unexamined value is at work in American life.

Newspapers heighten the suspicion. Even reputable journalists are susceptible to the buzzword. On a single day in 1984, "efficiency" appeared, without definition, in three out of four *New York Times* editorials. The *Times* editorial page criticized AT & T's "failure to organize itself for efficient service," then quoted a doctor's statement that heroin is "the most efficient drug for controlling pain in extremely ill patients," finally turning to business subjects to state that corporate "mergers by themselves don't make companies less efficient."[6] Whether the term means cost-effective, productive, or something else, the editorial writer does not say. Implicitly, "efficiency" is a trait or goal so desirable (and, by implication, so well understood) that it needs no explanation, no definition.

It gets none when it is applied to personal behavior and appearance. *The New Yorker* magazine reports that San Francisco mayor Diane Feinstein "looks efficient," while a college president remarks that her children do their chores "with the same degree of efficiency or inefficiency as they always have." A management consultant describes herself as an "extremely efficient worker . . . focused and organized," while an aspirant housekeeper describes herself in a want ad as "clean, efficient, responsible."[7] No word of explanation is offered. Presumably, everyone—big-city mayor, businessperson, adolescent, or housekeeper—is complimented if dubbed efficient.

And why not?—for at the other extreme lies the obvious contrary, waste. It is the contemporary antithesis of efficiency, and a buzzword as well. Emotionally "waste" is the demon that threatens well-being and even portends destruction. Covertly, the word takes on demonic proportions in the pages of the very newspapers and magazines that extol the virtues of efficiency. The *Boston Globe* quotes a speaker: "Government [in the Reagan administration] has become a symbol of inefficiency, waste, and foolishness." A columnist warns that if Congress continues its customary ways on public works projects, there will be "delays, inefficiency, and waste." In its editorial pages, the *Globe* presents a "Glossary" feature on "Waste," tracing its Middle English origins and negative contemporary usage in connection with radioactivity and toxicity. A presidential committee headed by businessman J. Peter Grace publishes a book-length survey on government cost control, with the martial title, *War on Waste* (1984).[8] Evidently, "waste" is the enemy whose defeat will result in a peacetime era of "efficiency."

With efficiency and waste locked in combat, why should the terms themselves cry out for scrutiny? On what basis can they be called buzzwords and be shown to be harmful? Why, in fact, should speakers and writers even take the trouble to define them? *Waste,* by popular consensus (and dictionary definition), refers to useless expenditure or consumption—and *efficiency* refers to effectiveness and competence. Surely the literate public understands this. So why should information come clogged and stalled with seemingly unnecessary definitions that only serve to belabor the obvious?

Why?—quite simply because there are unstated, coded values that underlie the buzzwords. These values, unexamined, cause harm because they diminish imaginative and intellectual initiative and because, on a subconscious level of thought, they indict those excluded from them. To get at those values, to understand their power, we need to ask where these terms come from in our cultural experience. We need to take a backward glance at the past uses of the terms *waste* and *efficiency*, because these terms are a legacy from early twentieth-century political-social movements that touched individuals and families at every level of American life. It is ironic, in fact, that two terms once vital to national life should come back with a vengeance to become buzzwords of the 1980s.

In two important ways, the early 1900s were similar to our own era. First, the high cost of living was a pressing, urgent issue, especially for the middle class. "We cannot much longer endure the continual growth in the cost of the common necessities of life," said one writer.[9] Prominent economists blamed numerous sources, from tariffs to trusts to profligate housewives and "middlemen." However the economy was jiggered, prices did not budge downward. Perhaps equally distressing, America of the early twentieth century entered an age of limits. Just as the Arab oil embargo of 1972 signaled that Western powers like the United States could no longer exploit the natural resources of the less-industrialized nations in a freewheeling way, so the turn of the twentieth century brought Americans to the harsh realization that they had literally run out of continental frontier space.

One earlier twentieth-century figure who recognized the implications of the closed frontier was the historian Frederick Jackson Turner, who confronted America's change from a pioneering-agrarian population to a corporate-industrial culture and from spatial boundlessness to bordered limits. In the essays and addresses he prepared over some twenty-five years (1893–1918), Turner showed why a certain segment of the nation should become preoccupied with the contraries, waste and efficiency. The new consciousness of closed national borders and thus of finite resources prompted Turner, and numerous others, to recognize efficiency as the new mandate for American civilization and wastefulness as a threat to its survival.

Turner launched his momentous frontier thesis in an address entitled "The Significance of the Frontier," delivered at the Chicago World's Fair of 1893 before an academic audience. The power of the address came from its ominous implications, for Turner opened his talk with a pronouncement on the closing of the very frontier he believed had given shape to the American mind. "There can hardly be said to be a frontier line" anymore, said the superintendent of the United States Census for 1890. Quoting him, Turner circled back into the American past, concluding his talk with an elegaic statement: "Four centuries from the discovery of America, the frontier has gone, and with its going has closed the first period of American history." As Turner recognized, the age of unbounded movement through unbounded space had ended. For the first time, America entered the age of limits.

In essays and addresses over the next twenty-five years, Turner tried to confront the implications of his findings. In 1914, twenty-one years after he first advanced his frontier thesis, the Harvard professor delivered the commencement address, "The West and American Ideals," at the University of Washington. He told the graduates that America now looked in shock at a changed world. He said that the nation's problem was not how to "cut and burn away" the dense forest, but how to conserve and wisely use the remaining timber, and how to put arid desert soil under agricultural production by means of the new scientific farming.

Turner's statement is remarkable for its presumption of finite resources that must be husbanded with utmost care. The wilderness was gone, free land a thing of the past. Scarcity loomed ("population is increasing faster than the food supply"). The new age of limited space and limited resources required, first, a consciousness of changed conditions, and the development of new attitudes appropriate to a postpioneering era. These attitudes must translate into concerted efforts to realize new, higher levels of utility from existing finite resources. In sum, the "shock [of] a changed world" mandated a new American value—efficiency. In an age perceived to be one of finite resources, efficiency is requisite to survival. Those who behave in the old ways, freely exploiting the environment, jeopardize American civilization. There is just one word for them—they are *wasteful*.

From this new vantage point, Turner looked once again at his Westering pioneers to pronounce them a wasteful lot, for the new realities of closed borders and limited resources altered his value judgement of the pioneers' actions. The new consciousness and the value—efficiency—that expresses it made the pioneers look destructive and wasteful in hindsight: "Fired with the ideal of subduing the wilderness, the destroying pioneer fought his way across the continent, masterful and wasteful."

The historian forgave them their ignorance but warned that the same mistake cannot be made in modern times. The need is imperative. "When we lost our free lands and our isolation from the Old World," Turner wrote of America at the close of World War I, "we lost our immunity from the results of mistakes, of waste, of inefficiency."[10]

Turner's was just one voice in a new public discussion about the meaning of waste and efficiency in early twentieth-century American life. A second important spokesman was the Scandanavian-American economist and cultural critic Thorstein Veblen, who was said to enter the new century like a sonorous, tolling bell. In style and substance this was true, for Veblen soon became one of America's most talked-about critics of culture, even if his difficult, sonorous prose made him a figure more discussed than read. His one commercially successful book, *The Theory of the Leisure Class* (1899) was a scathing indictment of waste measured against a utilitarian standard of value.

Veblen saw waste in every quarter of America, from its food to its fashion. He was troubled to see public esteem accorded to the leisure class of persons and property that were distant from productive, useful employment. Veblen's standard is functional. Waste, Veblen cautions his reader, denotes an expenditure that fails to serve human life or human well-being on the whole. Veblen's examples under this functional heading include "carpets and tapestries, silver table service, waiters' services, silk hats, starched linen, many articles of dress," including corsets and seasonal fashion and frippery.

Such waste, in Veblen's terms, signals the failure to meet the functional criteria of the "economic conscience." Every expenditure must be subjected to one test: Whether it serves "directly to enhance human life on the whole." This criterion compels Veblen to designate "waste" in endless categories, from livery to lap dogs, from ladies' hair to gentlemen's race horses. He felt American culture had become barbaric, perverted by a prevailing pecuniary standard of value. In his judgment, that standard even debased the concept of "cheapness," so that goods produced at low cost become despicable, no matter how serviceable and ameliorative they are for the populace at large.[11]

The historian Turner and the economist Veblen were just two participants in a full public discussion on the meaning and implications of waste and efficiency in early twentieth-century American life. A wide-ranging discussion was conducted in newspapers, in magazines, and in public forums. Its participants ranged from presidents to housewives, all of whom exploited distinct meanings of the terms. *Waste,* when paired with *efficiency,* implied all things retrograde and in the worst sense primitive. The word became a negative test of cultural status for all Americans.

And *waste,* like *efficiency,* clustered into certain well-defined meanings. The first is Turner's, expressing anxiety over the possible exhaustion of finite resources. The historian found an echo in the popular economics writer, Stuart Chase, in his book, *The Tragedy of Waste* (1927). "When we review the methods by which the pioneer lays waste our unreplaceable national resources," says Chase, "it seems as though we touch bottom indeed—a race of weevils consuming its substance." President Theodore Roosevelt was also anxious about the diminishment or consumption of the nation's raw materials. He warned: "We have passed the time when we will tolerate the man whose only idea is to skin the country and move on." And the conservationist Gifford Pinchot similarly condemned the "drain upon our non-renewable coal." Not surprisingly, World War I sharpened sensitivities to the exhaustion of material. "The world will be much poorer after the war," one writer said. "The [general] store will be less. Waste will be more quickly felt." Such statements refer, of course, to the diminishment or depletion of resources.[12]

There is another definition of *waste* that took a prominent place in the discussion: "*to fail to take advantage of.*" In this meaning, "waste" becomes the unrecognized opportunity, the missed chance for some order of gain. In this sense the word *waste* becomes one of alert expectation, not of dire threat. If a provident America could reject its squandering ways, couldn't it also seize the previously unnoticed opportunity and take advantage of it?

Many thought the nation could do just that. Understandably, their voices tended to concentrate on matters of business or economic life. The table of contents of Henry J. Spooner's *Wealth from Waste* (1918) is a panoply of opportunities available in the name of waste. The author, an Englishman, dedicated his book to the American efficiency engineers, Frank and Lillian Gilbreath, and proceeded to locate waste in every conceivable aspect of Western culture, from food adulteration to underutilized land to the "waste of more or less trifling things," such as candles, soap, and cigar ash. One section of Spooner's book, entitled "The Romance of Waste," celebrates the alchemy by which refuse and residues are turned into fabrics, oils, and numerous useful products.[13]

Such opportunity was widely discussed in business, manufacturing, and economics texts. (A glance at the *Periodical Guide to Literature* through the 1910s and 1920s shows the extraordinary extent to which "the romance of waste" preoccupied industrialists and manufacturers who were intent upon the potential for reclamation and by-product processes.) One landmark study, *Waste in Industry* (1921) compiled by a committee of engineers, issued a spate of recommendations for the building trades and for certain manufacture. The committee was convened by Herbert Hoover, then president of the Federated American Engineering Societies. It located four areas of industrial waste, significantly listing its recommendations under the heading "Opportunities and Responsibilities."[14] A reader of the report sees at once that to undertake the divers responsibilities is to seize the overlooked opportunities hidden under the rubric of "waste." The analytical report is really a summons to action. Waste becomes the opportunity for a new abundance.

But the term was as frequently used according to a different definition—one very close to Veblen's. The idea of squandering or of useless expenditure (of money and goods, of time and effort) figured in divers discussions. The department store merchant Edward Filene proclaimed that business graft wasted consumer dollars: "In a word, high prices are caused by waste." Melville C. Dewey, inventor of the library classification system named for him, pronounced himself "an uncompromising foe to every kind of waste and lost motion." As a proponent of the simplified spelling movement (in which Theodore Roosevelt took part), Dewey remarked that "one seventh of all English writing is made up of unnecessary letters; therefore one tree of every seven made into pulp wood is wasted."[15] Dewey may sound cranky, but it is important to notice that newspapers presented thoughtful discussions on the subject of waste-as-squandering in the mid-1920s. The Pittsburgh *Times* and *Gazette*, the New York *Times, Herald Tribune,* and *World,* the Providence *News,* the Schenectady *Union Star,* even the small Katonah (New York) *Villager*—all devoted considerable space to the subject of wastefulness in American life.[16] These newspapers, unlike their 1980s counterparts, were not satisfied to use the term without discussing its meaning and its values.

The young Walter Lippmann, at that time a promising jounalist, provided a most succinct survey of the new awareness, and defiance, of waste-as-squandering:

> It's a movement to end waste in the world. It includes almost anything, from
> forestry to housekeeping, from brick-laying to personal hygiene. There are more

and more people in the world who hate waste and can't rest until they end it. The idea of doing a job in double time; the spectacle of people foozling and fuddling without plan, without standards; the whole idea of wasted labor and wasted material is a horror to them.[17]

There is a good reason why Lippmann and the others, denouncing waste, should gravitate to the definition of squandering or of useless expenditure or consumption. The meaning itself provides a certain basis for pragmatic action beneficial to all Americans. For, in their view, improvident acts or habits can be changed, rectified. The squanderer can reform. Redemption is yet possible, if behavior undergoes a change. As Rudolf Cronau asked rhetorically in his book, *Our Wasteful Nation* (1908): "What must we do to be saved from a dismal future? First of all, we ought to stop our insane riot of destruction and wasteful extravagance."[18] His tone is both admonitory and hortatory. He employed waste-as-squandering as an activist definition that appealed to the potential for changed patterns of behavior at every level of Americal life.

It is worth noticing that the public discussion of wastefulness and efficiency in the earlier twentieth century included the voices of poets and novelists. Writers from Ezra Pound to Henry James, from Upton Sinclair to William Carlos Williams denounced waste by name, believing it inimical to the life of the imagination and of the society as a whole. Robert Herrick even named a novel for it. His *Waste* (1924) was a blanket denunciation of corruption in government, business, family, and personal life in this century. It is evident that the prominent twentieth-century poet T.S. Eliot had a good deal of company when he identified the modern world as a *Waste Land* (1922), a spiritually arid realm without emotional or intellectual vitality. Unlike Eliot, the other writers believed, or at least hoped, that waste could be eradicated for the benefit of society as a whole. The cultural critic Lewis Mumford, for instance, rejected inefficient environmental planning and architecture: "Once we assimilate the notion that soil and site have uses quite apart from sale, we shall not continue to barbarize and waste them."[19] "*Once we assimilate the notion*"—the phrase conveys both skepticism and yet confidence in future action.

Everyone who denounced waste had in mind its affirmative contrary, efficiency. The term was positive, upbeat, even idealistic. Efficiency was a goal, an aspiration, a standard. But it was subject to wide-ranging debate and discussion in American culture early in the century. "Efficiency" was an integral part of the Progressive political movement, which sought to revitalize American democracy by making it more participatory, less partisan. The efficiency movement, as it is called by historians of the period, included the thought of Louis D. Brandeis and of Walter Lippmann, even as it prompted such cultural baguettes as the composer Scott Joplin's "Efficiency Rag." Like waste, efficiency was closely scrutinized for meaning and for its sociopolitical implications. In addition, it had a central figure, Frederick Winslow Taylor, with whom the term was identified.

Many speakers and writers addressed the issue, but Taylor is credited with founding the movement.

Taylor, the son of a family with Quaker and Puritan New England roots, grew up in Philadelphia as a reportedly likable, rigid, intense, and dutiful boy. He was interested in medicine and engineering but was expected to follow his father into the practice of law. Problems with headaches and eyesight curtailed his academic work at the end of prep school and, following a few months' rest at the family's Philadelphia home, young Fred began work as an apprentice pattern-maker in the factory of a family friend. He flourished and, following the apprenticeship, went to work at the Midvale Steel Company as a journeyman machinist. Within six years he was chief engineer, soon devising a high-speed method for cutting steel. Taylor completed a home-study course in mathematics and physics to complete degree requirements in mechanical engineering. Within a few years he resigned from Midvale, became a self-employed consulting engineer for manufacturers and businessmen, and ultimately went on to become president of the American Society of Mechanical Engineers.

Taylor's influence was felt beyond the factory floor, though it started with his interest in the problems of mechanical efficiency and in the skills necessary to solve those problems. As an engineer, he understood the term *efficiency* to mean the ratio of work done or energy developed by a machine or engine according to the energy supplied to it. This was an application of the laws of thermodynamics to machinery, and it was ordinarily expressed in a percentage. Taylor saw, however, that the input–output ratio could also be applied to workers and their activities and finally to society at large. Though humanists tend to find Taylor's application machinelike and thus dehumanizing, it must be recognized that his system was intended to increase production and bring about new levels of abundance throughout American society.

Taylor's genius lay in the ability to separate seemingly simple tasks into their smallest components, to analyze each for excess or extraneous motion, then to reform them so precisely and economically that they wasted no mechanical motion of the worker's body or of his tools. Taylor claimed that he performed tens of thousands of experiments to ascertain the optimal level of factory-worker efficiency, and in the opening decades of this century he envisioned his methods extending "to the management of our homes, the management of our farms, . . . of our churches, our philanthropic institutions, our universities, and our governmental departments.[20] Thus, the efficiency movement began with conditions in the factory itself but ultimately broadened to include every quarter of American life.

Taylor had grounds for his prophesy, for his method had succeeded in the Bethlehem Steel Company in the late 1890s. There he applied his stopwatch studies to coal shoveling, changing workers' shovels and manipulating their motions. His effort resulted in a 50 percent company cost reduction and a 60 percent rise in workers' wages. After some three years of experiments, the work performed by 600 men was now accomplished by 140 (though Taylor made no guesses about the fate of the 460 displaced workers; presumably they found employment—or charity—elsewhere).

Taylor's work came to public attention in the years 1910 to 1912. In fact, the efficiency movement was launched in the American press through the Eastern Rate Case, which made his name synonymous with efficiency. Briefly, Eastern railroads sought a rate increase from the Interstate Commerce Commission to pay for promised wage hikes to workers. The shippers, however, filed suit to block the increase. They hired Louis Brandeis to represent them, and he won the case with testimony from Taylor's new apostles, who argued that the railroads could be run much more efficiently—that they could be saving one million dollars per day.

"A million dollars a day!" became the rallying cry of the new Efficiency Movement formed in the wake of the court case, and it was taken up by a public anxious about the stubborn persistence of an inflationary economy. Books and articles on efficiency soon appeared in abundance; efficiency societies were formed all across the United States. Herbert Croly, the founding editor of *New Republic* magazine, made efficiency a central part of his book, *The Promise of American Life,* and Lippmann incorporated it in his concept of governmental and societal "mastery." Its advocates ranged from the writer Charlotte Perkins Gilman to the muckraking journalist Ida Tarbell, who had written the definitive expose of the Standard Oil trust. Informally, the philosopher William James was designated as the humanistic father of the movement because of his essay, "The Energies of Men," which said: "Compared with what we ought to be we are only half awake. . . .We are making use of only a small part of our possible mental and physical resources."[21]

The ensuing public discussion of efficiency brought several definitions into application in American life. Competency in performance was an important one, as was the definition long applied to the word *economy*—namely, prudent planning so as to avoid unnecessary waste or expense in the disposition of resources.

These meanings of efficiency attached to individuals and groups, as the historian Samuel Haber has splendidly documented in his *Efficiency and Uplift.* On a personal level, it denoted attributes of effectiveness and implied hard work, application to tasks, competence. Though masculine in association, its spread into household affairs showed how much "efficiency" cut across gender lines. *Ladies Home Journal* was beseiged with requests for additional information when it published a series on efficiency in the home, and *Good Housekeeping* offered its readers a pamphlet on arranging work and appliances to achieve "The Household Efficient."[22]

But efficiency also had important political overtones and social implications in the Progressive era. To figures like Brandeis, it signified a certain professionalism and suggested social policy soon to be formulated according to facts gathered systematically by experts with whose judgment the public would presumably concur. Thus it signified, from the outlook of those like the editor-author Croly, the end of tyrannical "bosses" and the inauguration of the age of enlightened leaders. Political reformers like Theodore Tilden saw its nonpartisanship as the opportunity for a more equitable democracy in America. For the social application of efficiency implied, at least in theory, social harmony under the leadership of the "competent."[23]

Given such hope placed in the power of efficiency, it may begin to seem as if *efficiency* was a catchall term in the early twentieth century, virtually a buzzword in its own time. To some extent that is true, for it was applied everywhere, from Sunday schools to cigarette lighters. The term appeared in advertisements for dishwashers and touring cars (just as *waste* was an advertising copywriters' favorite for hot water heaters, ironing machines, and prefabricated houses).[24]

There was, however, an element of caution in the hopeful exuberance over efficiency. In an ineffable way, the term implied success, and some doubted that everyone could achieve it even under the most auspicious circumstances. Some speakers therefore worried about the place of those who could not qualify as "successful" in a culture predicated upon efficiency. These voices, moreover, expressed uneasiness about America's embrace of an ideal based so solidly upon a machine-business-industrial model, even if Benjamin Franklin's maxim, "Waste not, want not," gave it the blessing of nostalgia. They feared that goals of efficiency excluded other important aspects of human life.

These concerned voices joined in debate. "It is high time we were considering what is meant by efficiency, and just what the pursuit of it involves," wrote a contributer to *Century* magazine in 1915. He complained, "The world has become a factory," and argued that modern Americans were losing a sense of the importance of "space in which to wander, to run, to lie down, [losing] that leisure to absorb the meaning of the whole, which is the divine heritage." A writer in the *Atlantic* concurred. "The efficiency of the future," he said, must "permit recreation and mental and moral development." Paraphrasing Scripture, he said that the results of efficiency would be reached only when "the cities shall be full of happy people working in the mills thereof."[25]

At least two writers chose the short story as the form in which to suggest that efficiency, in and of itself, was a dehumanizing goal. In "Efficiency," the socialist journalist Ernest Poole presented an aging business executive who, having sacrificed his youth and midlife for his business, insists that his junior partner take his wife abroad for travel, recreation, and renewed companionship. The partners' factory throbs with "such efficiency as is found in no other country on earth," yet so absorbs these men that they become deadened to their closest family members. Jogged into a realization of what has happened to him, the senior man works to save his junior partner's humanity before he, too, forfeits his life in the name of business-industrial efficiency.[26]

The fictional critique of efficiency was not confined to the business setting. "The Efficient Wife," a short story appearing in *Woman's Home Companion* in

1923, featured a heroine who makes a muddle of housekeeping and resists her efficient neighbor's view that the kitchen is a laboratory and cooking a series of chemical experiments. This young housewife is admirable for her empathy for others' troubles, and readers were invited to concur with her husband, who "wouldn't change her for the most efficient graduate of a domestic science course."[27]

A most searching critique of the American value of efficiency came from Laura H. Wild, a professor in a small Ohio college in the 1910s. Her work appeared in the journal *Education* in 1911–12. She began with a mechanical definition:

> Men are demanding that their engines shall do the most work in the least time with the least waste. This is called efficiency and is viewed very largely from a utilitarian standpoint as we think becomes a practical people.

Wild identified the very words that, applied to people, denoted efficiency in the early—and later—twentieth century: "capable, competent, responsible." And she clearly saw that those excluded would be called "incapable, incompetent, unstable, unsteady, wavering, drifting, aimless, and indifferent." She notes how the stragglers in the social order are considered to be irritants and a constant drag upon society.

Then Wild's essay turned to the example of children, perhaps her own but plausibly those of any of her readers: "My child? Shall he be a straggler?" She calls the thought abhorrent and, anxious, warns the boy that the admirable people are those "with a purpose, an aim in life, men of grip." She is proudest of her daughter when the girl is called "capable."

Yet anxiety remains. If the child proves to be a straggler, boy or girl, "shall I blame him? Shall I say of course it was his fault? There are a lot of hard luck folk in this world," Mrs. Wild concludes, "and they sing the song of the unsuccessful—a pathetic song but true." She puts the question: if her child is among the unsuccessful, will she blame him or herself or the schools or the economic system?" In large part, she has already provided the answer, having noticed how workers are "thrown away as soon as useless, or producing less than the next man asking for the job."[28]

Laura Wild could not, finally, sustain her critique. She sideslipped into sentimental nostrums and urged that efficiency be grounded in "elemental enthusiasms" instead of mechanism. But she, together with others, located the crux of the issue and brought it to light, unlike those who once again use *waste* and *efficiency* in public discussion of the 1980s, when the terms are with us once again, stripped of interpretation in this later part of the twentieth century. In an era of sophisticated electronic media, a full public examination of waste and efficiency in American culture eludes us. Our press and airwaves resound with the bare words only.

And they are buzzwords, reverberating with values unexamined even by those who would try to examine the human costs of adherence to them. At a 1984 conference, "Home, School, and Workplace," Eliza Collins, senior editor at the *Harvard Business Review,* discussed the business ideology that she believes, makes it difficult to be a working parent. The employing organization, she explained, is seen "as a huge impersonal machine wholly without emotional response and devoted solely to efficiency and making profits." At the same time, employees are considered to be an entity apart, "basically lazy and inefficient and in need of coercion and control."[29] The critique of mechanistic efficiency hums beneath the surface of Collin's remark, and yet she is also angry at the supposition that employees are "inefficient" that is, unsuccessful—society's "stragglers" in Laura Wild's term. Collins had good reason for her tone of anger, for to be a person without efficiency in America of the 1980s is to be a loser, a failure. That is the hidden, subliminal message of the buzzword. In Collins's context, it implies that the 1980s working parent is at fault whenever difficulties arise from the strain of balancing lives at home and at work. If problems arise, personal "inefficiency" must be the cause. By this logic, those who suffer must really be to blame. They have failed to measure up to the standard of success.

This implied meaning of efficiency-as-success has new Darwinian overtones in the buzzwords of the 1980s. "Efficiency" suggests the presence of a great divide between winners and losers, between the capable and the shiftless. Thus, a young Kansas farmer portrays his less-prosperous neighbors as lazy: "They all try to outdo each other with sob stories . . .[over] coffee at the Jewell Cafe" all morning, unwilling to "go through the pain," the "hard work." Successful in *his* farming operation, he says, "We have some poor managers in farming today, and now it's thinning-out time. We're getting rid of the poor managers and the inefficient ones." He adds that the early 1980s is a "survival-of-the-fittest period in farming."[30] Though based in agriculture, his statement could have come from someone in any occupation. As one of the "fittest," he can pronounce himself on the side of the efficient and imply that the world is well rid of all others.

In fairness, not everyone in the 1980s uses the buzzword *efficient* in such egoistic triumph. An annual university report prepared by Derek Bok, president of Harvard University, provides a useful example of an alternative. Before the university's Board of Overseers, he attacked what he called the "grossly inequitable and inefficient" American legal system. Bok noticed the disparity between a "nation which prides itself on efficiency and justice" and a legal system that in fact "cannot manage to protect the rights of most of its citizens." In juxtaposing efficiency and citizens' rights, Bok reverted to the democratic mandate of the Efficiency Movement of the 1910s and 1920s. He reminded his audience that efficiency and democratic ideals ought not to be at odds. He deplored the "grossly inequitable and inefficient" legal system, which excludes those without money and serves others so ravenous for success that they "ignore the interests of others in the struggle to succeed."[31] Bok is one who has heard the buzzword, deciphered its meaning, and held it up for scrutiny. He provides a lesson to us all.

Will we learn it? Or, to turn the question around, what if we do not? The issue gains special urgency in times of tight budgeting for health care, for human assistance, for education. In a time when individuals and groups are judged in the name of efficiency, those on the edge are in peril—those without money, without good health, without the advantages of birth, breeding, and education. Not many citizens are more than a step or two from that edge. Sickness strikes, good people lose jobs, bodies are impaired. All of us will grow old. Before we do, it is to our mutual benefit to listen to these words we use so freely. They may suit our momentary convenience, but if we are not careful, they will victimize the hapless and brutalize those of us who speak them.

# 3

# Visualizing Stereotypes: Updating Walter Lippmann

*Bernard Rubin*

> There comes a time . . . when the blind spots come from the edge of vision into the center. Then unless there are critics who have the courage to sound an alarm and leaders capable of understanding the change, and a people tolerant by habit, the stereotype, instead of economizing effort, and focusing energy . . . may frustrate effort and waste men's energy by blinding them.
>
> Walter Lippmann

## Lippmann the Perceiver

Walter Lippmann published his seminal study, *Public Opinion,* in 1922.[1] The book directed students interested or involved in the then-novel field of social psychology toward concentration on scientifically based studies of public opinion. Reporters, managers, and publishers instrumental in the dominant worlds of print media were also intrigued by his considerations of mass communication, which joined journalism, political science, and psychology to their concerns about government and mass movements. Scholars and practical workday journalists began to perceive forces and manifestations through Lippman's interpretations. The book must be understood as a comprehensive analysis of societal changes and resultant effects upon democratic theories.

As introduction to the original edition, Lippmann quoted from Plato's *Republic* (Jowett translation). The passages he chose dealt with human beings who have been imprisoned in a den since childhood, chained to "prevent them from turning their heads." There is a fire "blazing" behind them. A low wall is between the prisoners and the fire. Dancing before their eyes are the reflections in shadow form of their own bodies or of men or "figures" of men and animals, "made of wood and stone and various materials," who pass the wall. Observing the scene, detached from the physical circumstances, are two analysts of the situation.

The first observer comments, "This is a strange image, and they are strange prisoners." In reply, the second observer concludes, "Like ourselves, and they see

*Public Opinion* (New York: Harcourt, Brace, 1922), pp. 111–112

only their own shadows, or the shadows of one another, which the fire throws on the opposite wall of the cave. . . . And if they were able to talk with one another, would they not suppose they were naming what was actually before them?"[2]

Lippmann intentionally directed his readers to how "The Pictures In Our Heads" (the title of his first chapter) are formed. He saw humanity as Plato saw those prisoners: "It is the insertion between man and his environment of a pseudo-environment."[3]

There we have the essential clue to his visionary appreciations of public opinion. The mass media portray what cannot be observed directly. The individual can see immediately ahead or to the side for a short distance but depends upon refracted evidence for understanding about the wider world. As a consequence, reality for most people on most subjects is filtered through the media of communication, which are contemporary mankind's substitution for Plato's fire-shadow play. Lippmann can then boldly jump to the conclusion that serves as a foundation for much of his work. Experts—be they interpreters, translators, reviewers, or any of the myriad technicians, scientists, managers, administrators, or governors so prevalent in a global environment turning more and more toward centralized industrial-technological-scientific dependence—will paint the pictures. What they see, or think they see, will loom large for everyone else. "A report," said Lippmann, "is the joint product of the knower and known, in which the role of the observer is always selective and usually creative."[3]

To get any message over, whatever the subject, Lippmann needed to find how the channels of communication work between creative sender and mass audience receivers. At that point, he depended on his intuition and common sense, mixed with wide-ranging sociological observation and reading. The young prognosticator took his limited experience and leaned on the interpretations of many others. Where he struck out on his own was in the area of then-prevailing democratic theory, which was accepted as axiomatic by philosophers who wanted to see America's citizenry as rationalistic. To borrow from a current phrasing, "One Person, One Independent Thinking Activist" could have been their slogan.

Lippmann did not accept rational, intellectual, participating human beings as the norm. He concluded that social psychology was a better source of truth about people than political philosophy. In his view, it was necessary to inject a strong dose of realism into the discussion of mass communication processes if Plato and Freud were to mix with Bell, Marconi, Pulitzer, and William Randolph Hearst, as well as with Theodore Roosevelt and Woodrow Wilson.

What Lippmann opined about drama—be it political, or of the legitimate stage, or from the silent movies circa 1922—is indicative of how he saw public receptivity vis-à-vis stereotypes:

> What will be accepted as true, as realistic, as good, as evil, as desirable, is not eternally fixed. These are fixed by stereotypes, acquired from earlier experiences and carried over into judgment of later ones. And, therefore, if the financial

investment in each film and in popular magazines were not so exorbitant as to require instant and widespread popularity, men of spirit and imagination would be able to use the screen and the periodical, as one might dream of their being used, to enlarge and to refine, to verify and criticize the repertory of images with which our imaginations work. But given the present costs, the men who make moving pictures, like the church and the court painters of other ages, must adhere to the stereotypes that they find, or pay the price of frustrating expectation. The stereotypes can be altered, but not in time to guarantee success when the film is released six months from now.[4]

We note several basic foundations for Lippmann's concentration on stereotypes. First, he was intellectually unimpressed with the rhetoric that held that mass society, even in his democracy, was inevitably becoming more reasonable or more committed to intellectualism. Therefore, he, as an elitist, did not think it illogical for democracy to grow in accord with the talents of elites in every important artistic, political, and social area. Members of elites make the complexities of society understandable for the masses.

He saw practical reasons for formula message-sending about groups and about types of individuals, based on his concepts of stereotypes. For one thing, Lippmann did not believe that intricate, detailed information about a person or a group would normally be of interest to the consumers of information in a mass media environment: "Only gross differences of size or color are perceived by an outsider in a flock of sheep, each of which is perfectly individualized to the shepherd."[5]

Stereotyped information intrigued Lippmann, in part because he was pessimistic about possibilities for tearing down barriers for the "pioneering artist" who has "reverence for his material. Whatever the plane he chooses, on that plane he remains." Great art produced by persons of genius would not attract the masses as much as art labeled and packaged to please the majority of the citizenry. The "pioneering artist," he declared, deals with the "inwardness of an event," which he follows "to its conclusion regardless of the pain it causes. He will not tag his fantasy to help anyone, or cry peace where there is no peace." By contrast, "big audiences . . . insist that a work of art shall be a vehicle with a step where they can climb aboard, and that they shall ride, not according to the contours of the country, but to a land where for an hour there are no clocks to punch and no dishes to wash."[6]

One is reminded of contrasts within "pioneering artist" groups that tend to certify Lippmann's arguments. To illustrate, there is a vast gap in the literacy interests of such contemporaries of literature as C.P. Snow and J.B. Priestley. Snow was concerned with individuals who instrumentally move or govern society. Even the romantic actors in his novels are inwardly motivated by ideals tempered by power and authority. Snow's preoccupations tended toward the portraiture of aristocrats and those who have decisive places in politics, business and industry, or government. In contrast, Priestley's novels almost exclusively concentrate on ordinary people. His literary techniques surround lower middle-class adventures in which nothing crucially dramatic or of wide importance to the world happens. Lippmann was much closer to Snow than to Priestley. He was able to assume a posture of detachment from the madding crowd so that he could carefully record its ways.

Why, then, do we accord him such honor as interpreter of how the mass media work? There are several good reasons for respecting his judgment, especially because he sensed *certain* rules of public opinion as influenced by the mass media, at the time when the United States was still drifting between nineteenth-century agrarian-biased idealism and twentieth-century technological realism. Lippman appreciated that one distinction between his times and what had preceded them was that ignorance about most out-of-sight events had been the rule for most people. In post–World War I America, there was ample evidence that most people, via the media, *could* learn about anything, anytime.

It is said that the bicycle—though seemingly on the verge of a technological breakthrough until the middle 1880s—was held up by the absence of the technology required to produce high-grade tensile steel for the frame, gears, and wheels. When that steel was available, the tinkerers and inventors hastened to perfect the simplest form of human-powered vehicle ever devised.

So it was with Lippmann and his contemporaries. Agitated into creativity about public opinion analysis by their realization that everybody was now in the daily audience for news, views, ideas, and data, they raced to update theories in accord with practicalities and probabilities.

Lippmann was stereotyped early in his career as a *pundit!* For news analysts and editorial writers, he set a standard that they followed. His influence, as a mature journalist, over the directions taken by editorial policy managers and by nationally reputed journalists was enormous. Even as a neophyte reporter-critic, Lippmann's perspicacity commanded attention.

Beginning with his first book, *A Preface to Politics* (1913),[7] which introduced the American intelligentsia to the elegance of mind refined by his studies at Harvard University, he grappled with decisive issues. Among other things, he called for reliance on a managerial class of experts, in the context of his doubts about the validity of majority votes as important when crucial decisions necessary for the growth of a technological society had to be made.

Respectful readers of *A Preface to Politics* ranged from Lincoln Steffens, with whom he discussed the contents, to Ernest Jones, who in a review in the English Freudian journal *Image* "recommended" this first book "most heartily as an impressive attempt to apply modern psychological knowledge and insight to the problems of sociology and political science."[8]

In 1923, Edward L. Bernays, eminent pioneer of the modern public relations profession, gave his respects to Lippmann's concepts of stereotyping in his *Crystallizing Public Opinion:* "Psychological habits, or as Mr. Lippmann calls them 'stereotypes', are shorthand by which human effort is minimized."[9]

By 1928, in a landmark reader in public opinion, Professor W. Brooke Graves accorded Lippmann the honor of excerpting from *Public Opinion* on the subject of stereotypes in the second article in the 1281-page volume. The first article was taken from *Public Opinion in Peace and War* (1923)[10] by President Abbott Lawrence Lowell of Harvard University. In Graves's first page of introduction, he writes that many will agree that the concept of the stereotype was "the greatest contribution to our thinking in the social sciences that has been made during the past generation."[11]

It must have been exhilarating for Lippmann, who graduated from Harvard University in 1910—in a class that included T.S. Eliot, Robert Benchley, Heywood Broun, Conrad Aiken, John Reed, Stuart Chase, Francis Biddle, and Samuel Eliot Morison—to have been acclaimed for his "recent notable book," *Public Opinion*, by Lowell in his 1923 volume. Lowell saw stereotypes as a "general formula . . . But all such formulas are merely approximations, not safely applicable beyond the limits within which they are fairly accurate."[12]

What are the limits beyond which stereotypes are not accurate? To apply the classic Lippmann formula to the visual media—the electronic and motion pictures of our day—we must review some key points he and his critics raised over the years:

> Just as the most poisonous form of disorder is the mob incited from high places, the most immoral act the immorality of a government, so the most destructive form of untruth is sophistry and propaganda by those whose profession it is to report the news.[13]

> From our recent experience it is clear that traditional liberties of speech and opinion rest on no solid foundation. At a time when the world needs above all other things the activity of generous imaginations and the creative leadership of planning and inventive minds, our thinking is shriveled with panic. Time and energy that should go to building and restoring are instead consumed in warding off the pin-pricks of prejudice and fighting a guerilla war against misunderstanding and intolerance.[14]

One of the limits to be set on those dealing in stereotypes is that all should avoid propagandizing or otherwise manipulating the news so as to consciously distort known truths that the public should receive. Personal pleasure or bias must not be fed into the stereotype formula. A second limit is that communicators should avoid descent, in and through their work, into the depths of emotional bitterness toward persons or groups, where so much public hope for the future depends on goodwill and sincerity.

A third limit to be placed on stereotypes by communicators applied to Lippmann personally. For all his intellectual genius, he was stunted in some ways. He, too, had what he called blind spots: "That spot covers up some fact, which if it were taken into account, would check the vital movement that the stereotype provokes."[15] As will be noted later in this chapter, Lippmann preferred his vision of society, which sometimes obscured his own origins, the downtrodden, or even the penultimate horrors meted out routinely by oppressors to those they catch and clutch to death.

The stereotyping limit that Lippmann failed to impose upon himself at times is to avoid missing a story or dealing with a situation because of refusal to adjust to reality. Personal selfish interest cannot be allowed to squelch public responsibility. The stereotype should not please the communicator if it is an affront to decency and honesty.

Harry S. Ashmore, the distinguished journalist and editor who faced reality squarely many times when both truth and courage were in short supply around him, hit upon one essence of Lippmann's character. Ashmore, writing at a time when Lippmann was in full professional stride in the late 1950s, notes what appears to explain virtues but also explains defects:

> His style is that of a man who operates at considerable remove from those who occupy the center of the stage of history. Thus, he appears as an informed observer without personal commitment to any individual, or even to any fixed point of view, and is absolved of the suspicion that he might use his considerable powers to reward a friend or punish an enemy. The impression, whether it is accurate or not, is that in his long passage through high places he has remained singularly free of the human obligations that accrete to lesser men and sometimes blur their view.[16]

The stereotyped view should not be created by communicators whose sight is so clear on some subjects that they are blind on others.

## Applying Lippmann Today

One can applaud a clarion call from Pope John Paul to "good Christians" in the context of one of his pilgrimages around the world without requiring proof that the masses of people observed in the television scenes live up to his high standards. "Born-again" Christians are, it seems, forever explaining to the rest of us how one arrives at such a state of grace. Stereotypes are not substitutes for identifications or definitive characterizations.

It is easier to package the "You've come a long way baby" *new woman* in a cigarette advertisement than it is to depict the so-called *liberated woman* in a documentary film. Stereotyping works best when moral, social, economic, political, and philosophical issues are not central to the communication process. That is not to say that profound issues and values are not easily conveyed by stereotypes, but that only fools or very wise individuals would *rely* on stereotyping as a prime means of conveying important ideas. More accidents are possible when one uses stereotypes as substitutes for deeper, explanatory methods of communication than are appreciated. Try, for example, to typify all middle-class blacks in one short-burst word or pictorial effort (painting, photograph, and so forth.) If you don't succeed, try to stereotype all poor native Americans, all Moonies, all of the steel industry's unemployed, or all of the students of theology at the Harvard Divinity School.

Nevertheless, stereotyping influences more people daily for short-and long-run effects than any of us would like to admit. The highest appeals for inspired activity and the crudest calls for mean work are framed in stereotypical language that describes *them* or *us*. Racists find stereotyping most useful for packaging lies, slanders, deceits, and innuendoes as they go about the business of tearing at groups they would destroy. At the other end of the social scale are honest do-gooders who disseminate stereotypical messges with patient anticipation of a commonwealth devoted to personal and intergroup harmony. They paint the pictures they would like to see.

In *Public Opinion,* Lippmann transferred the word *stereotype* from its usage in the printing industry (molded type plates used to produce exact copies from the originals) and signaled its utility whenever people want to catalogue, categorize, or capsulate ideas or situations so that others may make easy references for easy recognitions.[17] He made us realize that "what matters is the character of the stereotypes and the gullibility with which we employ them." Let us refer to several of his illustrations:

> He is an intellectual. He is a plutocrat. He is a foreigner. He is a "South European". He is from Back Bay. He is a Harvard Man. . . . How different from the statement: he is a Yale Man. He is a regular fellow. He is a West Pointer. He is a Greenwich Villager. . . . He is an intellectual banker. He is from Main Street.[18]

In 1922, Lippmann did not realize how unsavory all of the *he* this and *he* that would come to be for all humanists anxious to live in a world of opportunity and respect regardless of sex. He was enough of a savant, though, to warn us that there was a direct connection between "blind spots" and stereotypes: "Uncritically held, the stereotype not only censors out much that needs to be taken into account, but when the day of reckoning comes, and the stereotype is shattered, likely as not that which it did take wisely into account is ship-wrecked with it." Lippmann had his own blind spots. One story that he did not deal with sufficiently was the destruction that overcame European Jewry subjected to Nazi designs.

Indeed, one of the conspicuous lessons about stereotyping to be learned from this expert, whose influence with editorial writers and columnists exceeded that of his contemporaries in journalism, is how devastating bias can be. For reasons having to do mainly with his own psychological needs and fears, Lippmann wanted, as a young man and as an older man, to be with what he perceived to be the American majority. He molded himself into a lead-type slug and wrote WASP. Uncomfortable with his German Jewish background, he cast a suspicious eye on the hordes of poor Jewish immigrants emigrating to the United States from eastern and southern Europe. To a large degree, their looks, ways, and religious customs offended him. Not only was he perplexed to find out that they were out of step with the prevailing Anglo-Saxon heritage and drives (how could it have been otherwise?), but he was determined to be the advice giver, showing them the way to an enlightened status.

The fascinating aspect of this Lippmann fixation was how dogged he was in its defense and how he elaborated on the theme through the years, even refusing to deal personally with the holocaust. We are indebted to Ronald Steel, his biographer, for the incisive *Walter Lippmann and the American Century*, which reveals a brilliant person with a few prominent mental warts. We might bear in mind that Lippmann was more and more pessimistic, as the years went by, about the virtues of public opinion as determined by the masses of citizens.

To return to stereotyping by Lippmann, in 1922, the same year that his *Public Opinion* appeared, Lippmann wrote (I choose one of his less blatant comments to reveal the mental approach):

> I worry about Broadway on a Sunday afternoon, where everything that is feverish and unventilated in the congestion of a city rises up as a warning that you cannot build up a decent civilization among people who, when they are at last, after centuries of denial, free to go to the land and cleanse their bodies, now huddle together in a steam-heated slum.[19]

Eleven years later, he explained, with the disinterest of the truly dispassionate, that repression of the Jews, "by satisfying the lust of the Nazis who feel they must conquer somebody and the cupidity of those Nazis who want jobs, is a kind of lightning rod which protects Europe." To be fair, Lippmann admitted that there was "ruthless injustice . . . meted out to the German Jews," but one had to look at the whole picture, and, downplaying the "animal passions of a great revolution," hear "the authentic voice of a genuinely civilized people."[20] After World War II, Lippmann never wrote about the death camps, though the full story of the holocaust was revealed by legions of his fellow journalists.

I have dwelled on Lippmann for what seems a good reason. There is a lesson in the fact that he made stereotyping so clear to all the students of public opinion from 1922 to today, yet failed to appreciate how deeply intellectual prejudice could serve as well as naked emotionalism for the molding of distorted pictures of persons and groups. One is forced to ask to what extent bad stereotyping can be traced to sheer snobbery or stupid bypassing of the real issues of press coverage of the poor, the distressed, and the downtrodden by the superficially *educated* who have trained themselves to avoid reality.

So far, I have emphasized the descriptive powers of stereotypes, concentrating on psychological backgrounds to what is communicated. There is another aspect that receives less attention but is equally important. Much stereotyping evolves from what is *not* communicated. Much stereotyping results from what is omitted in the mass media.

Recently, I had need to pore through the past three years of issues of *Newsweek* magazine, looking for topics to assign for student research. I wanted to make sure that the list I drew up for term paper work for a class in public affairs and communications did not depend upon my memory alone, so I did some content analysis of important news magazines. It became clear as I examined the stories of *Newsweek*, issue by issue, that there was extremely limited coverage of Asians, blacks, native Americans, Hispanics, and students included in a number of examples I wanted to track.

To be sure, there were feature stories whenever some news event was linked to a group member, but there was little else. *Newsweek*, I knew, has had its troubles with coverage of women's affairs. Several years ago, the magazine management was revealed, in a lawsuit brought by its women employees, as somewhat insensitive even to such matters as the equality of its editorial personnel. Spurred by the judiciary, the owners took corrective action. I also knew that coverage of minorities by the bulk of the American electronic and print press was not satisfactory to liberal critics. However, I learned more from turning pages of *Newsweek*.[21] I learned that actions do not necessarily lead to *reactions* and thereby complete the processes of relationships. Given *what I didn't see* in the pages of that magazine about the day-by-day, week-by-week, year-by-year lives of minorities in this country, I concluded that there must be a profound public reaction to the absence of reporting. I surmised that stereotypical images must be created when clients of the mass media have to fill in their own shorthand pictures of peoples who remain shadows or blurs in the press. Using the common illustration about the perception of content—"Is the glass half-full or half-empty?"—it is evident that when we deal with news, the context any of the media provide us with determines how we view the world. The empty portion of the news "glass" would actually be fillable if there were proper interest in subjects usually ignored or bypassed.

Nationally glorified politicians, manipulators of giant businesses and industries, international terrorists, and theatrical personalities are usually found in the filled part of *Newsweek* or the *Boston Globe* or the ABC, CBS, and NBC networks' evening news programs. They typify what is considered newsworthy. In a sense, the mass media are organizational stereotypes because they so seldom stray from what was made clearer before. On the other hand, the masses of ordinary citizens are usually out of view or, if analyzed, made more shadowy by media reliance upon stereotypical coverage.

When utilized fairly, the stereotypical imageries of groups depicted in the mass media have certain virtues. However, there is widespread concern among the groups depicted about the casual manner in which they are designated or categorized. The Irish-Americans must have had enough of rote comments about the "fighting Irish." "Stolid Swedes," "clannish Italians," "stupid Poles," "business-oriented Jews," "musically gifted blacks," "cruel Indians," "greasy Hispanics," "puritanical Yankees," and "cunning Asians" should all be consigned to historical treatments about prejudice. If there be truth to such stereotype casting, as is alleged by some scholars even today, those who use it should be forced to provide evidence in the context of each of their reports.[22]

The persistence of stereotyping can have a discouraging effect upon young people and may account for lack of progress in certain areas. Mr. Romatowski, who had served on the Yonkers, New York, Municipal Housing Authority for fifteen years as of early 1979, spoke to the issue in trying to account for the reason why leadership skills he considered abundant in Polish-American organizations hadn't led to much evident leadership on the wider political scene:

> We just don't get anywhere in politics. I could understand it with the first generation. They weren't educated. But I can't understand it with the second generation. Some of it probably stems from the old stereotypes, which are just now breaking down.[23]

Television is a prime mover of stereotypes. My colleague, Dr. Earle Barcus, conducted a content analysis for Action for Children's Television. He studied thirty-eight hours of children's programs shown in Boston during January 1981:

> Of the 1145 TV characters that appeared . . . only 42 were black and 47 belonged to other minority groups. . . . 3.7 percent of the characters were black; 3.1 percent were Hispanic, and 0.8 percent were Asian.

As for females, Barcus said that "only 16 percent of all major characters in the program sample were female."[24]

I did a small computer run on minorities and stereotyping to get samples of how the wind was blowing during the last two years. Here are some examples, beginning with a hopeful current:

> U.S. textbook publishers have made major changes in elementary school presentations because of highly vocal pressures brought by women's groups and minorities in past two decades. Illustrations now tend to show boys and girls in equal numbers and integration between white and black children. Racial stereotypes have been largely eliminated, along with sex-biased language and passive feminine symbols.[25]

Officials of Venereal Disease National Hotline challenges stereotype of venereal disease victims as young, poor and non-white. Reports only 18% of callers are under 20 years old, while about 83% are white and over 50% earn more than $15,000 annually.[26]

Report by University of Pennsylvania's Annenberg School of Communications found that commercial television may be blocking public understanding and support of science. Survey of large samples of U.S. viewers finds that scientists are portrayed as older, less romantically involved, more dangerous, more doomed to failure, less sociable, less attractive and shorter than other television characters. Finds science to be held in lower esteem by women, low income groups, nonwhites and less educated viewers.[27]

Magda Abu Fadil asserts only U.S. minority that remains butt of ethnic jokes, slurs and outright prejudice is Arab community in U.S. Asserts most other minorities have organizations for objecting to offensive material.[28]

Residents of Portstewart (Northern Ireland) explain how country's political and religious troubles have impacted their lives. Say there are few adult men or women in the country who are not conditioned, upon meeting a stranger, to automatically mark him as either Protestant or Catholic, through clues of name, occupation or accent.[29]

Stereotyping leads are sometimes slyly hidden in the context of an otherwise innocuous story; just enough is provided to make a point, whether that point is justified or not. Editors should hesitate to censor bias out of such a story, but they could justifiably ask for more data so that the author could decide if he meant what he said. The *Boston Globe* ran a story by one of its staff members about a fine new author who sold her first novel on her first submission to a publisher. Susan Monsky so impressed the firm of Houghton Mifflin with sixty completed pages that they accepted the book *Midnight Suppers.* Carol Stocker's Living Pages feature, almost one-half page in length, was something of a tribute to the new author. At the risk of being picky with a few lines taken from context, I take those few gratuitous lines out for your review: "Monsky tells the story in a soft-spoken Southern accent which doesn't quite seem to go with her Semitic features and intellectual-looking wire-rimmed glasses."[30] She grew up in Montgomery, Alabama. As for the Semitic features, one has the feeling in reading the piece in the *Globe* that Lippmann's advice for Jews to lay low in this society until they were indistinguishable from the folks he admired still festers. I pick on what seems to be a small business of stereotyping *because it is so small.* Hidden away in an otherwise laudable account is the hint that Jews are really different.

Today, imagery through stereotypes of groups tends to harm more than help those groups. Too many issues of the most vexing and pressing sort have to be determined on an individualistic basis. Simplistic assignments of outlook on the extremely sensitive subject of abortion, for example, may be made by reference to a religious group's declared stand. As a consequence, Catholics should be easy targets for identifications about outlooks and decisions. One could stereotypify any individual who was a devout Catholic and who responded to Church teachings piously and automatically. Most Orthodox Jews would presumably be susceptible to such identification, as would a great number of Protestants. The problem comes because we are such a concentric and democratic society. Individuals differ on even so basic a subject as the rights and duties of human beings, even when they attend the same church on holy days and share the same religious traditions. One must be careful to delve deeply into the subject before mixing people into the same public opinion batter. One believer may be totally against abortion; another may see it as an escape route of moral worth under certain conditions; still another may be at odds with the basic clerical stand for personal or humanistic or social or economic reasons.

With abortion the given subject, it soon becomes clear to the researcher that public opinions that can be allied sweep across faiths and vary according to time, place, condition, who, what, when, how, and where.

The "*Moral Majority*" has certainly taken its bruises from the mass media, which persist in depicting its leaders and members as all cut from the same tree. It is so easy to use stereotyping when reporters can, in words and pictures, show fundamentalists whose origins and outlooks owe so much to the so-called Bible Belt. Any reflective review reveals far more complexity. Reporters find themselves dealing with, among other things; a basic branch of the generally conservative social movement in the country; a series of responses (under one banner) to the increased permissiveness in the presentations of the mass media—both print and electronic; comparatively recent developments affecting the nature of public and private education in the nation; an alliance of religious and civil associations calling for enhancement of what they consider to be traditional values; one series of responses to the overurbanization of our society; and an important alliance trying to shape foreign policy. It is far too easy to encapsulate the Moral Majority movement of similar but diverse groups in terms of stereotyped pictures. And the media take the easy way too often. Let them show the "old boys" and the demagoguery as it exists, but they should also report the Moral Majority as a complex mosaic of persons, groups, interests, and views. A stereotypical picture into which the Moral Majority may fit as a whole may prevail, but that picture should be the sum of its parts, not just a corner of a bigger scene that is out of focus.

Now that I have made it clear that the Moral Majority is too complex to be digested in mere outline, may I remind you that I have not attempted organization evaluation for your review. Should you ask me to begin such a project, I warn you that if I came up with stereotypes from my research, they would be numerous and clear pictures. My stereotypes would, in the words of television, be a storyboard etched fine with much detail.

Can a stereotype be detailed? How else are we to conclude other than to plump for detail when looking into human rights; the nuclear freeze; the middle class; the labor movement; Japanese employment, managerial, and technological prowess; the contestants in the Middle East crises; child abuse; clerics in politics; obscurity in the media; oligarchies and peasants in Latin America; or feminism as a movement and as a cultural phenomenon?

The mass media are hungry to find ways around research—in short, to get as much out of as little research as possible. Ms. Marva Collins, a black women teacher who lives in Chicago, initiated her own experiment in teaching about six years ago, founding a private school in her home. The students were primarily black youngsters. At the Westside Preparatory School, she and her staff attempted to improve academic skills, building lesson plans on methods designed to increase the motivation and inspiration of students, many of whom had been considered uneducable. The CBS series "60 Minutes" showed her and her students "poring over Shakespeare, Tolstoy and Plato." As is not unusual whenever fame can dissolve into notoriety, some controversy resulted from the publicity. In "dozens of articles in national publications," Ms. Collins has been labeled a "superteacher" and a "miracle worker."

Whatever the final judgments on her Westfield Preparatory School, she has complained, "I've never said I'm a superteacher, a miracle worker, all the names they gave me. It's unfair to expect me to live up to it. I'm just a teacher."[31]

Another complaint about stereotyping through word pictures was published in a 1982 "My Turn" essay in *Newsweek* by a former professor at Hofstra Law School who moved to the Amanda Cooperative Village in 1980. Sheila Rush describes the Village as a spiritual community located in Southern California where she went for spiritual inspiration and growth. It is a work-study community, which Rush notes

> is organized as a village, with an elected government, open decision-making forums. . . . There are both private and community-owned housing and businesses, a farm, a dairy, a market, schools, a meditation retreat and a temple used for spiritual observances. . . . People come and go as they please . . . three rules: no drugs, no liquor, no dogs. We have a spiritual director whose influence is undeniable, yet no greater than that of the founder of any organization whose wisdom and compassion have been confirmed by experience.

What bothers Ms. Rush is that reporters can visit and see whatever they want with "few if any restrictions . . . on whom they can talk to, what they can quote" write about a community she doesn't know. "They call it a 'cult'. . . . At best we are a 'commune'. . . . Our spiritual director is said to be a virtual dictator." She concludes:

History reveals that public acceptance of new religious groups takes time. In the meantime, I hope and, yes, pray that offending members of the press become more aware of their biases and of all their possible consequences.[32]

Ms. Rush has a point. When we think back to the Jonestown tragedy—one that was not grasped in its essentials by the press, the State of California, and the U.S. government in time to save the lives of hundreds of people—we ought to expect that charges be verified, that press designations be confirmed, that sloppy stereotypes be avoided.

In 1971 Pope Paul VI approved "Communio et Progressio," a document dealing with modern mass communications media. Basically, the pastoral instruction, according to the editors of *America,* "demonstrated an awareness that the rapid development of communications technology had resulted in a real shift in consciousness, from a Gutenberg era dominated by print to a video age where image, symbol and more immediate impressions formed a new human language." The educational and social opportunities before the media gave rise to a certain optimistic tone in the instruction. A decade later, the editors of *America* cite evidence of the "cultural erosion" that the media can promote. One illustration points up how Western life has been often stereotyped: "Observers working in economically developing nations point out that mass media invariably present images of modern urban life and an affluent, Western style of living that young people in rural areas find unsettling."[33]

In my own numerous trips to the Third World in Asia and Africa, I find indisputable evidence to support the foregoing contentions.

The *Minneapolis Star* announced a policy in late 1980 to keep injurious stereotypes and labels from its news pages. Commendations for the new policy came swiftly from the Jewish Community Relations Council and the Anti-Defamation League of Minnesota and the Dakotas. The director of the Council wrote Stephen Isaacs supporting the "laudatory aim, not easily accomplished considering the cultural stereotypes which have become part of our folklore and thus embedded in the mental images so many people hold of other groups."

Isaacs wrote that the newspaper strives to maintain news columns that are free of inadvertent slurs—whether based on race, color, nationality, locale, religion, marital or parental status, physical and/or mental status, sex, sexual preference or age. . . .

The policy statement calls for alertness to "unwitting complicity" in what amounts to reinforcing roles or labels tending to sustain stereotypes that may be offensive, whether blatantly or subtly.

Writers and editors are reminded that they should be sensitive to unintended but invidious dual standards sometimes applied to men and women in newspaper descriptions. Isaacs gave readers an example of citing family status when women make news, but using professional status when men do.

The *Star*, the report says, should avoid mentions of race unless that mention is specifically germane to the point of an article and should not routinely use shorthand descriptions of juries unless race or sex is used to make a point in the article.[34]

We all have a great stake in media stereotyping, and we are reminded frequently of the moral, philosophical, political, and social consequences. I was very much disturbed and continue to be so by the plights of Haitian refugees who somehow made it to our shores—usually to the closest points they could reach in Florida. Within sight of some of the luxury hotels of Miami, women, men, and children drowned when vastly overcrowded boats, held together by bits and pieces of wire or wood or cord, disintegrated. Others came to this haven after drifting without food or water for many days. Fleeing from political tyranny, from the poverty of the poorest country in the hemisphere, and toward the hope that the United States still represents around the world, they sought sanctuary. They were met by a hostile federal administration, which declared that they were not necessarily political refugees but were economic refugees. As economic refugees, they were likely to be sent home. Some who made it to small Caribbean islands of other sovereign governments were sent back against their will.

Why were the Haitians not treated like the vast majority of the Cuban refugees? Was it because they were categorized as undesirable blacks who spoke patois French and who fled with little other than their lives? Was it because they were stereotyped as peasants—black, untutored, unskilled peasants who could not contribute to any grand political debates framed by East-West politics? Was it because we Americans have made a stereotype out of the word *refugee*? What was good enough for one type of refugee should be equally good for other types of refugees. We will have to come to grips with such issues.

Our middle-class aspirations—which I am devoted to—do not blind my eyes or close my heart to what is going on in the world. Those who fled from "Baby Doc" Duvalier and his henchmen—who take whatever water there is from the rock of economic despair that is Haiti—deserved better than they got. It took too long for John Q. Public to sense the issues, even though he has at his command the best and most democratic communications system in the world.

What is at the root of such confusion and misapplications of traditional policies toward refugees? I believe we are trained by television news to watch the pictures so closely that we are almost unmindful of the captions, so to speak. We have been trained to observe interesting scenes without having our blood go hot or cold. Those interesting scenes have sometimes been horrible, but we sense them as part of the horror of the theater or of the films of which we are such devoted fans. The smell of disaster, the sense of danger, the genuine anger at what is being done to our brothers and sisters steams out of our minds like vapors from the tea kettle just removed from the fire. A few moments and all is cold; the emotional taste of whatever contents remain is gone. We observe the scenes of the tragedies in the news like robot televiewers responding by command to electronic signals. It is not too harsh to say that so much of what we see is falsely classified as entertainment. We have gone too far in merging fictional adventure with realism. El Salvador, Guatemala, Nicaraugua, and Haiti are all observable through the filter that too many of us intellectual, middle-class types find useful to keep pain and anguish out of our minds. There are no left-right politics in what I am saying. Let arch ideologues deal with such. The Soviets screen Afghanistan from their people with controls over the media and idiotic word games. These enemies, according to the leftist totalitarians trading in disinformation, are "bandits" and those are "running dogs" and those are "lackies of imperialism." When it comes to stereotyping, the antidemocratic forces in the world, from Nazis to Communists, make us look like babes.

It is equally hard for us to see the real problems of the unemployed, because there is so much juggling of pet stereotyping phrases, such as "the media society," "the service society," the "automated economy." For two years, we have dealt better with the price of gold than with the travesty inherent in offering butter and cheese to our poor when our granaries and storehouses overflow. Too much of what we see are partial stereotyped pictures with vital segments ripped away because of our blind spots.

I refuse to believe that, as citizens of a community cherishing the ideal of equity, we cannot make stereotypes work more for us than against us.

One key to progress would be to recognize that we are often servants to the masters of advertising. Those masters have trained us to respond like Pavlov's dog to stimuli. "Buy this" or "want that" is what it is all about. Let us mix in the advertising more of the "know this," or "understand that," or "feel this," and "see that," with the eyes, the brain, and the heart working in conjunction with one another. At the very least, it is high time to take the first steps toward a reevaluation of stereotypes. Above all, it is appropriate that study commence on the uses of stereotypes for social purposes.

## Scratches on the Screens

The most grave charge leveled at the managers of the motion picture and film industries is that they have consistently been guilty of depicting powerless or downtrodden or struggling groups erroneously. Most public imagery of such groups has depended upon stereotyping, and that stereotyping has provoked bit-, terness and suspicion and hatred.

Consistency is no virtue when social harmony is regularly thwarted by creative people. While much of the problem has been documented, there is not enough appreciation of how much carryover of bad habits is to be noted in recent and current work.

Racism has been and is promoted or prompted through film and television imagery. The approximately 12 percent of the population of the United States that is black has endured much vilification on the screen from the first days of the movie industry. Conversely, most of the issues and circumstances faced every day by blacks are absent from motion pictures or television schedules. The "Buckwheats" of the *Our Gang* comedies have remained more fixed in the screened constellations than have the "Roots"-type attempts of television to depict black history and circumstances. There are few parts for black actors that command attention from vast audiences. Television's "The Jeffersons" or "Benson" deserve comedic plaudits at the same time that they deserve adverse criticism as reductions of the experiences of millions of people to the slapstick vaudeville level.

In a recent issue of the British journal *Screen*, Robert Stam and Louise Spence stress stereotyping by commission and omission through the years.[35] Examples: *King of Jazz* (1930) "paid tribute to the origins of jazz . . . completely bypassing both Africa and Afro-Americans." And where, they ask, were blacks in Hitchcock's 1957 drama, done in "documentary-like" style, *The Wrong Man?* "The subways and even the prisons" in the New York City of that film are "totally devoid of blacks."

*Shaft* (1971), in their view, merely plays a substitution game to cater to egos of a black male audience. The black here is simply a substitute for whites in similar films. They critique television's "Mod Squad," which has persisted into the 1980s through reruns. Placing black characters as law enforcers creates positive images that have less than substantial reinforcements for ordinary blacks every day.

"Roots," the television series that commanded more mass attention to black origins than any previous television effort, is, for Stam and Spence, exploitive imagery. One may argue with their conclusion, but would the counter argument be influenced by the desire not to cast a bad reflection on a production that rose so far above others? Students of stereotypes are sometimes so anxious to fight denigration of individuals and groups that they have a kind of blind spot on the subject of positive-tending stereotyping works. Stam and Spence label "Roots" a cooptive version of Afro-American history. . . . a film which cast blacks as just another immigrant group making its way toward freedom and prosperity in democratic America." It is hard for this observer to be as harsh, knowing that history is more saga telling than the professional historian will admit. Each generation reframes the old sagas to suit its purposes. Was "Roots" positive cooption? Should it have concentrated on realistic stereotypes that hard evidence would show more accurate? To illustrate, "Roots" is built on the nuclear family concept ("retrospectively projected onto Kunta's life in Africa"[36]). How would another creative producer have handled the problems that are posed? We are reminded: "Questions of image scale and duration . . . are intricately related to the respect afforded a character and the potential for audience sympathy, understanding and identification."[37] Mass communicators are obliged to reach beyond evidence of stereotyped products of the media, to understand the central issue of their complicity.

Because symbolism is so vital to human beings, the symbols transferred by television and films may be more important than any review of specific story themes or general contents. This point is repeatedly made by theoretical analysts concentrating on the mass media. Perhaps it is useful that an appreciation or interpretation of the usage of the word *theoretical* be given here, slanted to the author's perspective. The theoretician depends upon specific knowledge, but has the determination to struggle beyond what is commonly termed data to a conclusion that makes sense of all the evidence at his disposal. That evidence consists of hard data and circumstantial material that helps reveal some underlying truth.

It is easy to be trapped into prolonged citation of specific data from television and film worlds without asking what is basically happening. We are closer to posing the question after applying some theoretical conclusions drawn by careful scholars.

In *Road of Propaganda: The Semantics of Biased Communication*, Karin Dovring, the Swedish journalist and mass communication scholar, reminds us of the pertinence of identity relationships between slogans and key symbols:

> The more identification symbols are used, and the more these are already well known to the public, the faster the slogan, supposed to comprehend the public demand, becomes a key symbol itself. It penetrates the areas of interests and demands and rises to the level of identification with the established community myth. As a part of the ideology it can even be used for attention-calling since its communication is already accomplished.[38]

One perceives that real progress against deleterious stereotyping will not be made until we mass communicators understand that most symbolic identification of groups represents community consensus at any given time. Democracy is inevitably tied up with consensus achievement by politicians and by mass media influentials. It must be true that so much protest against unfair stereotyping has led to such puny industry efforts to combat such denigration, because many leaders of the communications world are among the least anxious to go ahead of the social status quo. Controversial mass media products are avoided unless categorized as necessary showpieces in an almost totally bland schedule of presentations.

Social uplifting of groups has always been marginally interesting to television and motion picture moguls, so long as audiences don't complain that they are instigators of radical change. Most moguls prefer to live within the precincts of the society they accept as conventional.

Artists, investigative reporters, political activists, social worker reformers, and the like, on the other hand, complain that for all the innovative films and television programs of any calendar year, worthwhile because of contents that combat antidemocratic stereotyping and that fight against the blind spots in our social and political life, the tendencies and the effects of the total effort are predominantly negative. Surveyed in that light, the battle against unfair stereotyping doesn't seem to be going too well.

Lippmann himself is at the heart of the dilemma. Critics of the media were mesmerized by his rendition of stereotype theory when he first evolved his arguments. What most analysts have failed to recognize is how dated some elements of Lippmann's approach are. Throughout his career, he was an essentially nineteenth-century analyst (both as a novice reporter and as the sagacious old pundit interviewed on television at length each year by Eric Severeid). He looked at the world through the printed word and was hopeful that "experts" would learn enough from each other, largely through printed reports, to lead the world.

In nineteenth-century style, Lippmann counted heavily on leaders influencing events. Despite the fundamental and dramatic shifts in his lifetime, Lippman believed that intelligent leaders would prevail over the forces of irrationality, brutism, and banal evil. Perhaps that is why he ignored (or preferred to consign to an inner recess of his subconscious) the Nazi-perpetuated genocide!

This man of print grappled with one issue of television—its limited offerings—but never saw deeply into the problem. In the worlds of the printed word through which he traveled intellectually, one could always count on some forum for any subject. A book, or an article in a learned journal, or a newspaper report, or a critique in an obscure intellectually oriented magazine could always be found to delve into the subject or segment of a subject in which he was interested. In a sense, Lippmann could popularize stereotypes and thrive on the ways his peers considered the dangers, because he was inwardly sure that the intellectual shorthand stereotypes represented would always be followed up with more complete, fair, and representative portraits.

He did not entertain the thought that stereotypes could be dead ends. Even though, at times, Lippmann manufactured dead-ended imageries of groups, he felt intellectually secure that some other expert would convert his dead ends into open intellectual highways if the facts warranted.

When Lippmann surveyed television, he saw the fact of its comparatively few channels stifling public interests. In 1951, commenting on the televised Kefauver inquiry on interstate crime, he observed:

> With television, an event is broadcast or it is ignored: either it is in enormous headlines or it is nowhere at all. This power to choose what the great mass of

the people shall see . . . is altogether too great to be left to the judgment of a few television companies and to private arrangements made by committees and commercial sponsors."[39]

Television, for Lippmann, was far too limited an instrument to carry on intellectual progress in the fashion of the print media.

If leaders of television are so slavishly devoted to the status quo, as a general rule, and if Lippmann was both innovative and somewhat antiquarian when it came to reliance on the powers of ideas transported through print, how has television handled the problem of stereotypes? The answer is deceptively simple. *Television has carried on the tradition of the forerunning motion picture industry and has concentrated primarily on evocations that have an instant visual impact.*

Portrayals of three-dimensional quality only serve as highlights superimposed on a darker area. Lippmann never fully accepted that true literacy might be gained through pictorial communication, via the film or television industries. Leaders of those industries have been subdued by peer judgements that communication of nuances surrounding individuals or groups is always difficult and often dangerous. A creed has grown up around the motion that only *artists* can conjure up full-fledged depictions of individuals or society that emphasize more than surface values. Those managers have seen themselves as manufacturers of ready-made, one-size-fits-most-customers mental clothing. Most are as antiquarian and print-oriented as Lippmann was. He wanted mankind led by experts; most television and film industry managers don't really want to lead at all and prefer to separate art from the everyday commerce they engage in.

For every television product that shows a person or group as a psychological, sociological, economic, or philosophical whole, there are scores that rely on cosmetic cartoon characterizations. Until we all admit that we haven't achieved more than Lippmann—indeed, much less, since he showed us the basic geography of the stereotype—we will go on lamenting reliance on superficiality in mass communication. Stereotyping contrary to democratic goals of fairness will prevail so long as we agree with Lippmann that television is inherently second-rate in comparison with print. That just isn't so!

With all deference to the beauty and powers of the print media, we are on the verge of a new era of mass communications. In a few short years, video cassettes have become like library books in the Third World, not only for the dominant classes, but also for those whose literacy is more visual than print-oriented. What most people of the world learn of happenings, art, politics, science, and so on, will soon depend upon some version of motion pictures, transmitted by television. The average product that is prepared for television audiences will have to rise above the trite and superficial, or we shall continue to pay for ignorance and disinformation, facing up to the costs of suspicion and bitterness.

In technologically advanced regions, the challenge is no less profound. If television's products continue to take advantage of gullibility, false notions, and prejudices via one-dimensional depictions, the effects upon the body civil and politic will not benefit our democratic goals. One must be pessimistic if depictions of the poor, the rich, blacks, children, Orientals, the aged, religious groups, and so forth, continue along present lines.

The complaints are so routine, and come from so many segments of society that one wonders if they can be met with complacency by leaders of the industry. Today's leaders of conventional television must be wondering if a new kind of television revolution impends because of the pressures from technological changes and public demands.

Because it is clear that television will become more personally valuable to individuals as a means for virtually limitless accessing of information from recordings or from numerous cable, satellite, or conventionally broadcast channels at home and abroad, one is tempted to conclude that we could be offered fairer pictures of each other. The predominance of unfairly drawn stereotypes could diminish in proportion to the variety of sources to be drawn from. Just as stereotypes are more easily handled in print simply because there are so many descriptive choices for the curious about any group or person, so they could be more manageable for television's consumers. Those consumers will be less subject to propaganda that goes counter to their own inclinations.

Lippmann's basic theory of stereotypes is correct, but he erred as driven by his own ego. The coming age of individualistic electronic communication, to follow what we now signify as television, will allow most perceptive persons to have the same opportunity to be right or wrong. Providers of programming aimed at millions of people at a single showing will have to be more mindful of the competitive situation. If the consumer doesn't like this news or that news, there will be other choices a-plenty. If the creator of a product wants an audience in the new age of electronic communication, he will have to act more like an author or publisher in the book or magazine businesses of today. Acceptance of products will be selective and personal to a degree not yet reached.

Until the golden day of predominantly three-dimensional television dawns, we will have to contend with growing dissatisfaction among the industry's consumers. Complaints about unfair stereotyping are ever louder and more numerous and emanate from virtually all organized groups. Taken together, they constitute an indictment against the mass media on the charge that stereotyped *shorthand* communication generally runs counter to the objectives of true education. Instead of being molded from a sweepingly descriptive composite of the pictured individual or group, the message goes beyond distortion to lies.

One fascinating aspect is the range of those demanding redress. Some of the most powerful economic elements in the country share in the plaintiff's indictment. To illustrate, the Mobil Oil Corporation, through its advocacy advertisements (primarily placed in print organs), has for some time hit upon those influential television news presentations and entertainment offerings that, it claims, simplify issues and events and personalities to the point of disinformation. Three of the myths Mobil's public affairs department would have us beware of are "1. The myth of the villainous businessman"; "2. The myth of the informed public", and "3. The myth of the crusading reporter":

> A 1980 study by the non-profit, research-oriented Media Institute . . . found that "two out of three businessmen on television are portrayed as foolish, greedy or criminal; almost half of all work activities performed by businessmen involves illegal acts; and . . . television almost never portrays business as a socially useful or economically productive activity."
>
> TV's myth of the villainous businessman could . . . in the long run, undermine the public trust in the basic exchange relationships that form the underpinnings of our free enterprise system.[40]

In "2. The myth of the informed public", the Mobil conclusion is that, on television, "anyone whose role is directed toward profit-making is a 'bad guy'— just as he is in a TV adventure show." Mobil declares that theme is a "basic scenario for television newscasts on economic issues," featuring "the following mythic cast of characters":

> *Liberal politician:* Defender of consumer interests and environmental protection.
>
> *Conservative politician:* In the pocket of big business.
>
> *Social activist:* A "public interest" representative. Has unruly hair and wears folksy clothes.
>
> *Business executive:* Motivated by greed for more profits, unwilling to put the country's good ahead of his company's.[41]

Finally:

> Among the upcoming journalists, members of the "TV generation", only one-quarter of the Columbia School of Journalism students interviewed [by Professors Stanley Rothman of Smith College and Robert and Linda Lichter of George Washington University] . . . believe that the private enterprise system is fair and almost 40% advocate public ownership of corporations.[42]

Lippmann would have understood the Mobil complaints, but he probably would have interpreted those complaints in the light of television realities. Aren't myths and stereotypes created, in part, to overcome the difficulties of trying to reach masses with intellectual arguments or analyses? While Mobil objects to one set of myths, that corporation doesn't try to grasp the reality that it may be demanding a more accomodative set of myths and is not as concerned with presenting objective reality to the general public. In regard to the conflicts of opinions and the data that shape opinions, Lippmann observed:

> The mind . . . was evolved as an instrument of defense and for the mastery of specific difficulties: only in the latest period of human development have men thought of trying to comprehend a whole situation in all of its manifold complexity. . . . In actual affairs they have to select isolated phenomena, since they have only limited energy and a short time in which to observe and understand: out of the infinite intricacy of the real world, the intelligence must cut patterns abstract, isolated and artificially simplified. Only about these partial views can men think. Only in their light can men act.[43]

Lippmann contemplated "partial views" from this perspective in 1937, but his remarks are directly linked to his elitist comprehensions of public opinion in 1922. By 1955, he had refined the problem, tracing another aspect of "the democratic malady" in his segment of *Essays in the Public Philosophy* entitled "The Decline of the West." As against the experts he advocated so faithfully, he saw democratic politicians paying a price for success. Being "insecure and intimidated men," with "exceptions so rare that they are regarded as miracles or freaks of nature," the "decisive consideration is not whether the proposition is good but whether it is popular." The "men under them who report and collect the news come to realize in their turn that it is safer to be wrong before it has become fashionable to be right."[44]

We have to ask ourselves whether complaints against stereotyping can be met by honest television entrepreneurs. Or is Lippmann correct, and must we reluctantly conclude that the stereotypes manufactured are not used by accident but deliberately, primarily by television creators and managers who are another breed of politicians? If they were to come down hard for television products based upon reason, truth, impartiality of researchers, and a profound search for fairness, would they not defy the realities of a *mass media?* Would they not have to reassess the entire scope and meaning given to the word *entertainment* and strive for programming that both attracts and educates? Would they not have to finally deal with Lippmann's conclusions that mass man can only grasp a little at a time, while they are faithful to the goal of raising or at least sustaining rational exchanges between individuals and groups? Would they not have to contend with the substantial problem that, if Lippmann is right, the politicians have so framed the setting for discourse to their publics that crude popularity has become the be-all and the end-all of society? To really mount a creative counterattack against unfair stereotyping through good works, they would have to be prepared to stand by works that were *both fair to the subjects and unpopular.* The unpopularity would stem from public resistance to images that were clear and contrary to accepted distortions.

Women, ethnic groups, the elderly, the physically or mentally handicapped, and other categories of people would be reflected by new, cleaned mirrors. To clean those mirrors, television leaders should recognize that their problems are in part distinct from those common in the motion picture or print media industries. The reasons are simple. First, the film industry's products are typically independent treatments of subject matter, no matter how much any film or genre is a copy of another. Television, on the other hand, has from its beginnings relied upon formats to the degree that, at any one period, the public receives substantially the same range of products from all commercial networks. Even when public television introduced novel ideas such as the miniseries to develop new audiences, the concepts too often degenerated into formulas. Once the concept was understood by commercial network leaders and galvanized by the popularity of new programs, the formula was adopted and made up into a popular brew.

Action for Children's Television, an organization headquartered in Newton, Massachusetts, gives us insights into ordinary daily fare uncovered by researchers recently:

> Only 3% of all characters are in the 65-and-over group; a disproportionate number of these are male. . . . Men outnumber women 3 to 1 . . . TV women are more passive and less achievement oriented than men. . . . the proportional representation of minorities in TV comedies and dramas has actually declined over the last decade. . . . In 1981 it was reported in a study dealing with commercial television specifically aimed at children that out of a total of 1145 characters in the programs studied only 22% were female . . .; only 3.7% of all characters were black . . .; of all characters with speaking parts, 57.5% were white and 33.8% were animals, robots or other non-humans.[45]

Documentation on inaccurate stereotyping is extensive, and much of it is in book-length research devoted to impacts on specific groups. Among the impressive works are Ralph E. Friar and Natasha A. Friar, *The Only Good Indian: The Hollywood Gospel* (1972)[46]; William B. Helmreich, *The Things They Say Behind Your Back* (1982)[47]; and Leonard C. Archer, *Black Images in the American Theatre* (1973).[48]

Lippmann's suspicions about aspects of democracy in this country and the intellectual force of public opinion under democratic systems of government anywhere are substantiated. Archer documents the persistence of antisocial stereotyping of blacks in television shows that attracted huge television audiences. "Amos 'n' Andy," the carryover from the original radio format, was strenuously denounced by leaders of the National Association for the Advancement of Colored People. Writing in 1951, Walter White, NAACP executive secretary, was most direct: "If the television industry and advertisers who are eager to sell their goods and services in a $5,000,000 Negro market had previously presented Negro characters as 'normal human beings' and as an integral part of the American scene, a series like Amos 'n' Andy and Beulah could be taken in stride." After thundering against television's then-habitual depictions of blacks (doctors—charlatans and thieves; women—cackling hens and tempestuous shrews; all Negroes—allergic to toil) White declared: "Unhappy the system of segregation in the United States that permits far too many Americans no opportunities to know Negroes except through the medium of television."[49]

We have come a long way in twentieth-century time and circumstance since "Amos 'n' Andy." Today's television viewers with long memories or access to reruns might recall "Sanford and Son," "Good Times," and "That's My Mama," a trio of series that carried on the racist tradition against which Walter White struggled. They might also remember the episodes in the "Roots" saga and such programs as "The Autobiography of Miss Jane Pittman" as more elevating and impressive efforts to get at the inner dignity and backgrounds of blacks. The two latter programs depended upon stereotyping in part to further the story lines, but the stereotyping was designed to increase the knowledge and strengthen the humane inclinations of audiences.

Less easy to categorize is the currently running series "The Jeffersons." Slick, produced by people who know every entertainment trick attractive to mass television audiences, and well acted, this series projects beyond the common experiences of most blacks in the United States, portraying financially successful blacks and reverse-discriminatory sentiments in conflict with socially good relationships between friends black and white. According to William A. Henry III, the Pulitzer prize-winning television critic, the programs reinforce "what television has already taught Americans, and what they yearn to believe: that a social revolution has been won." The main character, George Jefferson, is a reverse Archie Bunker:

> He is too mean spirited and too much a bragging buffoon to be admired for his character. . . . His business acumen is so little in view that his wealth seems merely a stroke of luck. . . . he seems uninterested in the plight of less lucky blacks. He does not live in the ghetto, he spends little time there, he devotes scant energy to black causes . . . he behaves like a nouveau-gauche white. . . . He is not an inspiring role model to black youth.[50]

The native American has been as maligned by motion pictures as much as any group, and television picked up on the approaches and themes that had prevailed in the film industry since the earliest silent movies. In television's early years, as many old films as could be acquired cheaply from the Hollywood studios found their way onto the black-and-white TV screens. They are still a television staple, with little counterstereotyping work challenging the imageries of the "red man," the "savage," the "scalp-hunter." The native American, oppressed in real life, was not often depicted with dignity or understanding but was usually the foil to the courageous settlers or cavalry soldiers in the frontier west. Virtually no understanding of native tribal ways or cultures was or is communicated. If the roles were good, whites usually played Indian parts in such films. The end result of decades of stereotypical indoctrination was massive public indifference to native Americans, supported by massive public ignorance. The classic portrayals of the brutal savages in the westerns constitute a great bulwark for racism in this country.[51]

Television's own products have not often been celebrated for accuracy or sympathy for the native American. In "The Lone Ranger," transferred from radio to television, his companion Tonto was one of the small screen's noble Indians who appear from time to time as exceptions to prove the rule about stereotyping. Typical of television stereotyping was the "Wagon Train" series. In many episodes, Indians were shown as drunken, cowardly outlaws. Another series, "Riverboat," is said to have depicted the "Indians as inhuman fiends." In the series "Wanted—Dead or Alive," "a typical program showed Apaches massacring a group of whites in the desert." Series such as "Laramie" and "Overland Trail" are similarly criticized.

When television replays Hollywood's Indian epics, it acts as an agent for bigotry in the opinion of many native Americans. The following comments from young Indians polled in 1971 about particular films were published in the "Akwesasne Notes" by The White Roots of Peace, Mohawk Nation:

> *Soldier Blue* (1970)—The only good part . . . was the massacre of the Indians by the Cavalry. That saved it because it showed the truth. The rest was junk. . . . *The Stalking Moon* (1967)—The Indian was shown as a totally primitive animal who'd kill anything. . . . *Little Big Man* (1970)—Chief Dan George was great and Dustin Hoffman was bad. But the picture actually showed some things realistically. . . . *A Man Called Horse* (1970)—Same old savage stereotype. White actors playing cigar store Indians.[52]

After tracing the histories and analyzing the contents of prominent stereotypes (examples: Jews—"the Jewish mother," "shrewd businessmen"; Italians—"belong to the Mafia," "talk with their hands"; blacks—"violent criminals," "great rhythm"; Japanese—"sneaky," "women servile and obedient"; Poles—"dumb," "racists and bigots"; WASPs—"hardworking industrious, and thrifty," "cold and insensitive"), William B. Helmreich concludes that we should not assume antistereotyping positions that deny elements of truth in the shorthand descriptions:

> It turns out that approximately one-third of the stereotypes can be said to have a good deal of truth to them. . . . Bigots will not, however, find much support for their prejudices from the relatively high number of valid stereotypes . . . because most of the stereotypes for which support can be found are positive or flattering to the group involved, whereas those that seem highly inaccurate tend by and large to be negative.[53]

Television's leaders will find little comfort from Helmreich's conclusion, because the industry does too little to counter the inaccurate stereotypes. In 1979, the U.S. Commission on Civil Rights, in its study *Window Dressing on the Set: An Update,* reported:

> Television drama continues in its failure to reflect the gender and racial-ethnic composition of the American population. . . . Minority males are disproportionately seen in comic roles. . . . Minorities, regardless of sex, are disproportionately cast in teenage roles; in contrast white male characters are disproportionately cast in adult roles. . . . Minorities, regardless of sex, are less frequently portrayed in an identifiable occupation than majority characters.[54]

Discrimination against women by televison was rampant. As of 1979, sex stereotyping presenting a composite picture of women counter to real life was the norm. According to Louis Nunez, the Commission's acting staff director, the distortions were legion:

> We found 40 per cent of female characters on TV in the 21 to 30-year-old bracket, while only 20 per cent of the male characters were in that bracket. . . . Female minority characters have no identifiable job 46 per cent of the time. . . . Forty per cent [of white female characters] have no identifiable occupation. . . . To the extent that television serves as a creator or reinforcer of beliefs about the kinds of occupations that are appropriate for people, we thus found it plays a negative role in regard to women.[55]

In November 1982, further negative news about women's roles in television news organizations appeared. The absence of female anchors on any of the major networks (except for week-end roles) was noted. In a study funded by Gannett, Knight-Ridder, and the American Association of University Women, Jean Gaddy Wilson, the project director, reported that, in addition to the implications of the shortage of women as network anchors:

> In the local markets, the news team is usually led by a man, with a woman in a deferring role; on the corporate level very few women rise above middle management. . . . General managers and news directors, producers and directors are usually male. Promotion directors, community affairs directors are usually women.[56]

In the summer of 1983, Christine Craft, a former co-anchor on the nightly news on KMBC-TV in Kansas City, Missouri, was awarded $500,000 in a suit she brought alleging that she had been demoted because she was "too old, unattractive and not deferential enough to men." The facts are that Ms. Craft is in her mid-thirties and is as acceptable in appearance as anyone could wish. Her victory, though not final, should be celebrated by all reporters, regardless of gender.[57]

Sexism on television, abetted by reliance on stereotype portrayals, is still pervasive. Television advertising plays a major role in promoting sexist imagery. Successive studies since the 1950s have reached similar conclusions, asserting that the data show that women as sex objects highlight the selling pitches for numerous products. Again, women are infrequently portrayed in professional roles. The National Advertising Review Board report of 1975 provided numerous illustrations of the sexist theme. The National Airlines "Fly me" campaign was perhaps no worse than the Continental Airlines "We really move our tail for you" advertising.

Sex-biased advertising takes many forms. A 1978 study analyzing 367 television commercials and concentrating on product representatives found that "81 per cent of the women were portrayed with domestic products, while 19 per cent of the women and 64 per cent of the men were portrayed with non-domestic products."[58]

Effects on children of television's stereotypes have also been explored frequently. One 1979 study found that "adolescent girls exposed to a heavy dose of beauty commercials were more likely than a control group of girls not exposed to the commercials to believe that being beautiful is an important characteristic and is necessary to attract men." Another study relates the benefit of counter-stereotyping against the type of propaganda just described. A 1975 investigation "revealed that children who were shown a commercial featuring a female judge were more likely than a no-exposure control group to rate the profession as an appropriate one for females."[59]

## Better Stereotyping?

Throughout his professional life, Walter Lippmann provoked his colleagues in the worlds of journalism, politics, and scholarship, trying to make them see beyond headlines to where issues precipitate events and to how sentiments and emotions run a constant race with facts. Those who tangle with dilemmas of juggling what we now like to term *data* with less solid circumstantial evidence never had a better wordsmith to describe connections between ideas grasped and those just beyond clear comprehension. One of his major achievements was to champion reason in an illogical framework of human relationships. He preferred the sane, thoughtful comprehension of a problem to the quick and easy pronouncements that too often pass for solutions.

Snared by his own adherence to the elitist-based intellectual potentialities of humankind, he sometimes had difficulty dealing head-on with perversion and cruelty. Lippmann wanted his colleagues to truly assume the mantles of leadership he himself felt comfortable with.

Even in explaining how stereotypes work, he tried to resolve the issues of how the press ought to deal with such shorthand fairly. To understand Lippmann, one ought to accept the fact that his own passages into unfair stereotyping came about because he had too little tolerance for cultural diversity and was too ready to believe that tyrants could be weakened by truths revealed about their viciousness.

Nearing the zenith of his career as television was emerging from its electronic womb, Lippmann was accepted by news and public affairs managers of the networks as a model pundit. Right from its beginnings, television was best at presenting broad outlines of social, political, and economic happenings. Lippmann, as always, was ready and eager to summarize after tending to the tasks of research on his own. His first appearance on television (later to become an annual ritual) took place in early July of 1960, when he was interviewed at length on CBS-TV. *Television: The Management Magazine of Broadcast Advertising* treated the interview in the prominent article "Television and Politics" in its July 1960 issue as something of an event of tremendous consequence. Opposite the first page of text was a full-page photograph of the great man facing his interviewer, seated in a lawn chair in the verdant surround of his garden. The videotape camera is pointed squarely at him.

> At left is Walter Lippmann. He has never been a political candidate. He has been on television only once. But in this one telecast may well lie the key to television's true strength and significance in politics. To most observers, political function reached its zenith in the recent nominating conventions. Millions upon millions of people were able to watch prospective candidates for the nation's highest office in action. . . .The basic question is, what can television contribute, by way of information and opinion, to the electorate's political enlightenment? In this direction, one of the most important breakthroughs was the recent telecast with Walter Lippman. . . . Here a significantly large audience, again numbering many millions, had the opportunity of sitting down, watching and listening to the sage comments of one of the most respected observers on the political scene. Controversial but enlightening, and of immediate political pertinence, were Lippmann's discussions of the role of the Presidency, of the qualifications for leadership, of recent history.[60]

Television's capacities to deal with stereotypes in a socially progressive manner have not grown much since Lippmann passed the torch of criticism to others, despite the medium's tremendous potentials. News programs have become so important that, since the mid-1950s, more people rely on television for the news than on print media. Documentaries on television, although always a scarce commodity, have also done much to add to the luster of the small screen. Election reports, beginning with the opening nominating highlights at the start of each electoral season, have won high praise for immediacy and liveliness. For all such achievements, the medium does its best work on its own terms.

Usually, subtleties are lost because of the concentration on showmanship. The historical backgrounds to important stories are routinely sacrificed altogether or reduced to gross summarizations. Analysis, always difficult to depict pictorially, is never a preoccupation of television's public affairs people. Stereotypes were and remain a mainstay.

We all try to answer important questions about stereotypes with which Lippmann struggled as well. Why, for example, are stereotypes so enduring, especially in their perverse forms? Why are stereotypes so impervious to personal experience and hard facts? How can television and the other mass media budge them with democratically affirmative work?

Is Jacques Ellul correct when, in his provocative analysis of the roles of propaganda, he concludes, "propaganda is principally interested in shaping action and behavior, and with little thought"?[61] Is television so dominated by the advertising fraternity and its influences that it has become more interested in getting commercial propaganda over than it is in provoking any other consumer reactions?

Are we soon to enter a period of better stereotyping because of the new devices of this electronic age? Will diversity of opinion and of message, fostered by cable transmission, satellites, home player-recorders, and so forth, introduce more media fairness, or will technical novelties increase in number as the levels of true intellectual stimulation plateau or fall?

According to one estimate, the average American watches television for 1,300 hours a year.[62] Many of our less socially beneficial stereotypes, in basic formats, predated Lippman's earliest inquiries and are still with us now. Television is the greatest instrument for the transmission of quick and impressive information that the world has seen. Can we light up the blind spots behind its most visible stereotypes?

# 4

# "Killed by Idle Gossip": The Psychology of Small Talk

*Ralph L. Rosnow*
*Marianthi Georgoudi*

Almost everyone seems to know what everyone else means by "gossip," save the researchers who have confronted it as a technical concept. Is it news or isn't it? Is it malicious or nonmalicious? Is it fact or fancy? Is it harmful or harmless? The sociologist Albert Blumenthal once noted the ambiguities inherent in the definitions of *gossip* used by social scientists. Blumenthal confessed his misgivings for having elevated such a nebulous term to a prominent place in his own writings.[1] Fifty years later, the situation has not changed much, except that now no researchers admit to feeling embarrassed at using *gossip* to indicate a technical term.

One intriguing characteristic of gossip on which most researchers would probably agree is its "contextualist" nature; that is, the meaning of gossip is to a high degree a property of the context in which it is situated.[2] In a sense, too (and we will come back to this point), gossiping is primarily characterized by a particular attitude of exchange of information. Whether such an exchange involves nomads sitting around campfires trading news about local practices of animal husbandry,[3] lawyers or physicians putting a newcomer in his place by hinting in a technical argument at some personal fact about someone prominent in their profession,[4] or street urchins conversing in the "he-said-she-said" argot of the urban ghetto,[5] gossip is situated interpersonally and cannot be conceived apart from the relational context in which it arises. Indeed, the very notion of what is gossip and nongossip depends on where, when, and before whom the exchange was made. Ulf Hannerz remarks: "The same information may be gossip or nongossip depending on who gives it to whom; the communication that Mrs. A's child is illegitimate is not gossip if it is occurring between two social workers acting in that capacity while it is gossip if Mrs. A's neighbors talk about it."[6]

This chapter explores the psychology of this genre of communication (or meta-communication) defined as "small talk" and "idle talk" (terms that capture the seemingly superfluous nature of gossip), with emphasis on the contextualist point of view. The nature of gossip, which treads a thin line between impression and reality, is that it does not occur in a social vacuum. Instead, it starts like any information framed to give meaning to some observation or experience. Thus, the knowledge communicated or received can create a reality all its own. We begin by giving a conceptual definition of gossip and also note some of the properties that distinguish it from another ubiquitous form of communication, rumor. Next we turn to examples that illustrate its wealth of general functions in the marketplace of social exchange. Gossip can titillate the imagination, comfort or excite, manipulate or maintain the status quo. We then discuss the preconditions of gossip—that is, the contexts in which it will be most likely to arise and flourish. Gossip can also ostensibly do harm, and in the final section we consider its presumably negative consequences. In an extreme case, it was reported that a young woman was driven to suicide by the vicious sniping of old crones. On examining the circumstances of her death, the coroner's jury brought in the verdict "killed by idle gossip."[7]

## What is Gossip?

One researcher called gossip "the elusive butterfly";[8] another called it "intellectual chewing gum."[9] Whatever terms investigators have used to describe gossip, clearly it is a slippery subject. Sometimes its identity is concealed under an assumed name, like "shop talk" and "shooting the breeze" (the masculine euphemisms for gossip). Nevertheless, one common property of gossip is its derogatory connotation. The Victorian novelist George Eliot observed: "Gossip is a sort of smoke that comes from the dirty tobacco-pipes of those who diffuse it; it proves nothing but the bad taste of the smoker."[10]

Whatever people may believe to be true about its pragmatic value, gossip has been regarded scornfully for ages. Around 700 B.C., Hesiod castigated it as "mischievous . . . grievous to bear." Maimonides, almost 2,000 years later, warned against gossip's captivating way of slipping into subjects expressly forbidden by the Talmud. Even today, it is hard to find a culture in which gossip and scandal do not go hand in hand.[11] For example, *kakase* is the Fijian word most readily translated as "gossip" in our own pejorative sense of an undesirable, sometimes malicious activity engaged in by persons with nothing better to do than pass along unsubstantiated news about others.[12] The Filipino word *tsismosa*, from the Spanish *chisme* (for "gossip"), is a demeaning term for a busybody whose meddlesome gossip pries into the affairs of others.[13]

When carried to extremes, gossiping is considered more than merely a breach of etiquette. Among the West African Ashanti, malicious tale-bearing was punished by cutting off the offender's lips.[14] The Seminole Indians of the American Southeast have long regarded "talking bad about anyone" in the same category as lying and stealing, sins of commission that are believed to diminish the perpetrator's chances of ever reaching "Big Ghost City" in the spirit afterlife.[15] In our own American society, there are laws to protect individuals from the villainous barbs of defamatory gossip.[16] The "right to be left alone" is also widely regarded as a fundamental or human right; there are major international codes that specify protection against attacks on an individual's honor and reputation (such as the European Convention on Human Rights, promulgated by the Council of Europe in 1950).[17]

It is interesting that the English word *gossip* did not always have a derogatory connotation. Alexander Rysman has traced the origin of the word to "God sib," for the relation a family would have with someone they chose as a godparent for one of their children. [18] In the same way that the *d* in "God's spell" was dropped to form *gospel*, so is *gossip* the diminutive of "God sib." By the Elizabethan period, the word *gossip* was used to denote an individual relationship, typically masculine, suggesting a "tippling companion." Another meaning referred to the idea of women running around tattling at a birth—men were not allowed to attend birth. In later years, as the sexist stereotype took hold, gossip came to be considered the peculiar weakness of women. To call a man a gossip was to suggest a rare character defect. Leo Rosten, the writer, mentions that the Yiddish word for a gossipy woman, *yenta*, also manages to become a stronger sexist slur when used to describe a man.[19]

Is there any evidence that women do gossip more often than men? An exploratory study by Jack Levin and Arnold Arluke recently addressed this question in the context of the gossip of college students.[20] Levin and Arluke collected data at Northeastern University by having observers overhear conversations in the student lounge. The researchers found that women did in fact devote a slightly larger proportion of their conversations to gossiping about third parties than did men. Lest we prematurely accept the stereotype of the "gossipy woman," it should also be noted that Levin and Arluke found that male and female gossip was indistinguishable with respect to positive or negative tenor. Men and women were equally positive and negative in the prevailing tone of their small talk. The women students, though, were more likely to gossip about close friends and family members than were the male students. The men were more likely to talk about celebrity figures and campus acquaintances. Popular stereotypes notwithstanding, these sex differences, the researchers concluded, seem to reflect traditional sex-role divisions and suggest a complex picture of both the quantity and quality of male and female gossip.

To go back to the idea of gossip as constituted by an attitude and mode of exchange, three characteristics in particular define an item of information as gossip. First, the remarks always have a moral or normative orientation—that is, an evaluative tone (either positive or negative) that may be explicitly or implicitly attached to the personal or intimate event or action being discussed. For example, American presidential campaigns, from nomination to election, are notorious for being composed in reality of two campaigns: the one open to the public in speeches, debates, media advertisements; and the other a whispering campaign of morally or normatively oriented small talk.[21] There are countless examples going all the way back to the beginning of campign politics in this country. Thomas Jefferson was whispered to have been the father of several black children and to have debauched a white Southern belle while on a visit to her father. On Garfield's assassination, Chester A. Arthur, then vice-president, was whispered to have been carrying out illicit relations in the White House with a prominent Washington socialite. When such stories get into the news media—as in the 1972 presidential campaign, when Jack Anderson repeated a false story (for which he later made a full apology and retraction) about the alleged inebriety of the Democratic vice-presidential nominee—they have been termed "factoids" by the writer Norman Mailer (that is, unfounded gossip that appears in the press and is repeated afterward as fact).[22] Thus, one fundamental characteristic of gossip is not whether the information is fact or fancy—it can be either—but that what is being discussed, while it may seem trivial, begs to be taken seriously because it deals profoundly with moral or normative quality or character.[23]

A second defining characteristic of gossip is that style of presentation becomes very important, and the significance of what is said is subordinated to the manner in which utterances are made.[24] What is being said must be "packaged" to appear as "idle talk," even if the ulterior motives or purposes of such an exchange are quite profound. Edwin Almirol, in his study of gossip and the pursuit of reputation in a Filipino community in central California, observed that the "art" of gossiping might begin with a show of disinterest or even a vague contempt for it. If the person showed interest in knowing things about other people, the person would be immediately branded a *tsismosa* and as a consequence not get any information.[25] The notion of idleness here is thus used to denote a characteristic of the process or the activity (the "art" of gossiping), rather than the purposes of the exchange. This is a fundamental characteristic from the contextualist point of view, since it emphasizes that it is the manner of exchange that will distinguish an item of news as gossip (not the subject under discussion or what exactly is being said). For example, discussing the divorce situation of a friend with a therapist would not be regarded as gossip, because both the style and context of discussion do not constitute "idle talk." The exchange is focused on the particular issue, which is deemed important for the purposes of the interactants. At a party or in a cafe, however, the participants are not trying to sustain a focused interaction on a particular issue. If the same topic is brought up, it is done so in an "idle" fashion, characterized by a kind of "belle indifference." If the setting changes and the ambience loses its quality of idleness, then we would say that these people were not gossiping, or at least not *just* gossiping.

A third defining characteristic of gossip concerns the content of the information exchanged or received vis-à-vis the context of the discussion; it may be thought of as the "legitimacy" factor. What counts is not simply that the information is of a personal or intimate nature—many rumors also focus on personal affairs—but that the news is "nonessential" in the context of the exchange. Take, for instance, a faculty committee that is discussing the academic credentials of a potential new faculty member. We could say that these people are literally "talking behind the candidate's back" (since the target individual is absent), but we could hardly call this gossiping. What if the discussion, however, drifted to this candidate's marital situation or culinary preferences or political affiliation? We would probably consider this information as going beyond the "legitimate" boundaries of the question at hand, which is whether the person merits appointment as a faculty member. When the information seems superfluous (in the sense of being unnecessary or excessive), we think of it as constituting gossip—that is, as going beyond the requisite context of the exchange.[26] Thus, gossip only indirectly sustains the ongoing exchange, since people seldom enter a situation intentionally to gossip. They enter the situation for some other reason, and the relationship will not be broken off if the exchange "accidentally" goes beyond boundaries that have been informally set in the process of discourse or explicitly set beforehand.

In our discussion so far, we have also alluded to the idea that *gossip* is not simply a synonym for *rumor*. In some instances, to be sure, it is difficult to tell the two apart, but there are differences to be noted nonetheless. The sociologist O.E. Klapp summed up the differences as follows:

> Gossip is internal news and the small community or primary group is its locus, whereas rumor comes from the larger society, the world outside. Gossip is intimate and personal in focus, whereas rumor is more impersonal and tells of the doings of strangers. Gossip is chatty and conversational; there is a sense of relationship betweeen the talker and hearer which helps make the news interesting; whereas the interest of rumor arises from external urgency, the possible importance of remote events. In gossip there is a high consensus among the participants because they belong to the same community and know and have a lot in common, whereas there is lower consensus, greater heterogeneity of opinion and greater ignorance of actual events shared by the participants of rumor.[27]

## What Are The Functions Of Gossip?

Although gossip may appear superficially to be insignificant, its underlying value lies in its myriad functions in the marketplace of social exchange. In the following discussion, we will explore three general (not mutually exclusive) functions of gossip: to inform, to influence, and to entertain.

### To Inform

One major function of gossip is its news-bearing aspect. Gossip, as much as any information, because its structure and content are responsive to local tensions, can be a rich source of information about the community.[28] In some cases, children informally designated as "gossip gatherers," using their unassuming social role to gain entry to closed adult society. For example, John Szwed made a study of the patterns of drinking habits in a Roman Catholic parish in western Newfoundland and of how information flow in the parish was maintained by means of gossip. The children in this community were used by their parents as "informers" to ferret out information. Their "nonperson" status secured them freedom of access to private exchanges and also protected them from running the risk of critical sanctions for divulging this information.[29]

Of course, gossip is not the primary preserve of adults. By the age of three, children have been observed to exchange small talk about other children who are not present. The nature of children's gossip, it has been found, is remarkably similar to the gossip of adults.[30] However, one intriguing difference is that children also often gossip in front of the target person. Marjorie Harness Goodwin, in her study of the "he-said-she-said" gossip of black, working-class children from west Philadelphia, uncovered various instances in which the target child was present when the interaction transpired. She also reported specific instances in which the information exchanged was intended to shape or reinforce the structure of attitudes in accord with the news-bearing aspect of gossip. For example, she tells of several cases in which the target person was baldly and directly informed by the speaker of some offending action. The information content of such exchanges, which might be seen superficially as provoking a conflict, instead represented a way of avoiding possible conflict. The person who was speaking had been affronted in some way and, because this was public knowledge, was obliged to give the appearance of taking action in order to save face. It would be the failure to take action that could have escalated into conflict, so the information exchanged served the practical purpose of allowing the speaker to maintain a commitment that could be commented on by sympathetic onlookers to the dispute.[31]

Another intriguing illustration of the information function of small talk concerns its exploitation in the classroom. H.J.S. Taylor, a British educator, was concerned that pupils being taught English as a foreign language seemed perpetually bored. To counteract this, a flow of gossip was introduced to lubricate the formal classroom instruction ("Who's got any news?" or "What's the weather like today?" or "Any TV programme to discuss from last night, or tonight?"). The pupils were invited to express what was uppermost in their thoughts at a particular moment, thereby relaxing the lessons and introducing spontaneity into the English class. The information received or exchanged also served as an enculturating tool, since the children became immersed in the culture of the community in a way that could not be achieved simply by having them get a fair idea of English syntax. This use of gossip, Taylor asserts, made English a "living" language rather than a "dead" language of mechanical transformation and exercises, with little attention paid to actual social usage.[32]

*To Influence*

A second major function of gossip is to influence a situation by "pulling" or "pushing" attitudes and actions in a given direction. As we have already seen, the information and influence functions of gossip are difficult to separate. Consider the gossip columnist who provides readers with news about the behavior of prominent individuals. The news has a moral as well as a normative orientation, which may serve as an effective mechanism of socialization and social control.[33] It may be helpful to think of the influence function in terms of whether it refers to some accidental (or fortuitous) concomitant factor of the information function, as opposed to whether the gossip is intended solely or primarily to influence attitudes and behavior. For example, some anthropologists have interpreted Western gossip as the "civilized" alternative to witchcraft and sorcery in more "primitive" cultures. It is theorized that more primitive people stick pins into the effigies of an unliked object; whereas in Western culture, gossip is transacted in place of this mechanism of aggressive hostility and retaliation.[34] Here the influence function is easily separated from the information function, though we should reiterate that there are limits to how far a speaker can go. Previously, we noted that the Ashanti cut off the perpetrator's lips when his gossip exceeded the boundaries of propriety, and in our Western society there are laws prohibiting libel and slander.

The information function of gossip, apart from that of influence, can also be easily recognized in certain instances. To be able to gossip together, people first must know one another so as to establish mutual interests. Exchanging information with someone about others can be part of the process of getting to know that person well enough to gossip about more intimate matters.[35] Social psychologists liken this "social penetration process" to peeling away the skins of an onion.[36] The conversations move from less to more intimate exchanges until the exploration of mutual selves results in a commitment between the partners. It has been theorized that small talk also allows the interactants to obtain needed "comparison information" in an indirect and painless fashion.[37] That is, people pursue second-and-thirdhand information in order to make comparisons between themselves and others. Such comparisons allow individuals to evaluate their own achievements and abilities when no objective standards are readily available, while avoiding the possible embarrassment associated with the more direct acquisition of information. It has been postulated that a person will be more likely to gossip with peers than with inferiors or superiors for accurate self-appraisal if the person wishes to avoid direct comparison but wants to obtain the needed information.

However, to get back to the second major function of gossip, people not only want to learn what makes other people tick but also want to influence how they feel, perceive, and act. The social anthropologist Max Gluckman, in a classic article, described how the "rules of gossipship" are like a kind of gamesmanship in which the participants each try to win the game without actually cheating.[38] The struggle is fought with concealed malice, by subtle innuendo and pointed ambiguity. Among certain people of privilege, he noted, the rules of gossipship stipulate that the right to gossip marks off a particular group from other groups. To gossip about certain persons is a privilege that is extended to individuals only when they are accepted as members of a group or set. Thus, gossip can be a way of putting a newcomer in his place, showing him conclusively that he does not belong. It can also be a means of cementing a professional relationship by excluding the unitiated via some subtle manipulation of perceptions. Robert Wolff mentions how two philosophers, engaged in small talk, might demonstrate that someone else is simply a "fool":

> For example, a naive speaker asks one philosopher, in the presence of a second, whether Albert Schweitzer was a great thinker, "Oh yes," the first philosopher replies, "he was a thinker universally admired!" The naive speaker takes this as a simple yes, and concludes that Schweitzer was indeed a great philosopher. But the second philosopher understands the reply as an ironic remark, the real meaning of which is that although outsiders and the unitiated may think of Schweitzer as an intellectual heavyweight (hence a thinker "universally admired" by fools), insiders know him to have been a purveyor of fatuous bromides. The awareness on the part of the two philosophers of the misunderstanding by the naive first audience is a part of what is being asserted by the ironic remark. Contained within that awareness (we may assume) is a recollection on their part that they too once thought of Albert Schweitzer as a great philosopher, and an accompanying sense of the distance they have come, and the path they have had to travel, to arrive at their present true evaluation of his supposed wisdom.[39]

The effort to influence attitudes and perceptions through the medium of gossip is not always so subtle, of course. Benjamin Franklin, the "founding father," it seems, of just about everything in this country, was also a fearless gossip and the originator of the American gossip column. No great booster of equal rights, he chose a "female" pen name, "Silence Dogood," to scold and nag newspaper readers. One of his first targets when he moved from Boston to Philadelphia was the publisher of a rival newspaper, a person he castigated as being a bumbling fool who belonged in another line of work where stupidity would be no obstacle—such as philosophy or politics, Franklin noted. Modern gossip columnists are considerably more restrained, to be sure.[40] Nevertheless, many often seem to specialize in socialization and social control by highlighting with plaudits the behavior they admire and with barbs the behavior they frown on. An intriguing side effect is that they, in turn, may become fitting subjects of gossip. The Hollywood columnist Louella Parsons once commented: "I have been sniped at by experts. And why not? Almost everyone who has attained any kind of public stature in his or her profession can expect sometimes to see a reflection in a cracked mirror.[41]

## *To Entertain*

This brings us to a third major funcion of gossip, which is to entertain or amuse, to pass the time of day in an agreeable, diverting, amusing manner. Witness the recent gossip mania of the print and electronic media in the giddy name of "news" for voyeuristic readers and viewers, weary of the serious issues, whose natural reaction is to believe what they read or hear. Nearly every newspaper and local TV newscast has a "people in the news" section that tries to turn small talk into entertaining fact—without actually calling it by its more odious name, gossip.[42] If enough people are drawn in, the gossip can initiate a full-blown rumor with a life of its own, and that, in turn, may entail more gossip (people talking about the rumor!) Thus, gossip may be both a generative mechanism and the result of rumor—that is, both process and product.

An illustrative case that has been explored in some detail was the fantasy story that first circulated in 1969 concerning the Beatles' Paul McCartney. The story asserted that McCartney had been decapitated in a car accident after leaving his recording studio in London and had been replaced by a double. The Beatles' albums were purported to contain numerous "clues" to affirm the validity of this bizarre fiction. On the cover of *Abbey Road*, for example, John Lennon's being dressed in white was said to be a clue to the "fact" that he was representing a "minister." It was also said that Ringo Starr, dressed in black, represented an "undertaker"; George Harrison, in work clothes, was a "gravedigger"; and McCartney's "double" was barefoot to suggest the way "corpses" were buried. The Beatles were purported to be leaving a cemetery, and a Volkswagen Beetle parked by the side of the road carried the license plate "28 IF"—which was supposed to be a clue to how old McCartney would have been *if* he had lived. Other "clues" were contained in the lyrics of songs or buried in sound tracks and exhumed only after ponderous detective work by fans who threw themselves into this fantasy that swept across American adolescent society. When McCartney appeared in *Life* magazine to repudiate the reports of his demise, the cover (which showed a blowup of McCartney's torso) was interpreted as further evidence that it must be a look-alike, not the actual Paul McCartney. On the reverse of the cover was a car advertisement; when the page was held up to the light it revealed a "ghostly" car superimposed across McCartney's chest so that the top of his head was blocked out. This "news" became a basis of further innuendo and wild speculation.

The McCartney story is characteristic of the fun-and-games approach to gossip (and rumor) when it is offered forth as nothing more than entertainment. It also illustrates the tenacious quality of some reports, especially when there is fun in repeating and embellishing them in spite of the fact that everybody "knows" they are not true. Another interesting observation was made when exploratory research was conducted in an effort to track down those people who were spreading the story.[43] It was thought at the time that these active liaisons were bound to be sociable individuals, on the assumption that gossip (and rumor) requires a fertile breeding ground of friends and acquaintances in order to flourish. Surprisingly, those spreading the story reported that they dated and got together with friends less often than did "dead-enders" who heard the story but failed to repeat. No other personality or demographic differences were discovered, and therefore this one difference loomed large in the researchers' conclusions. The finding led them to speculate that gossiping may be a way of trying to gain esteem. Someone without many friends might worry about his or her self-esteem, and this person might pass on a juicy story in hope of building a new friendship. The recipient of the story bestows "status" on the teller merely by accepting the news. Consistent with this interpretation, there was apparently a point of diminishing return for the "status-seekers." Eventually, nothing new could be added to the tale, and any teller gained minimally and may even have lost status by continuing to be obsessed by the "mystery."

## What Are Gossip's Preconditions?

If gossip is characterized as superfluous information, why does it arise at all? And in what contexts is it most apt to originate? In a sense, we have touched on these questions already by showing that the "superfluousness" of gossip is more apparent than real. By being oriented to fulfilling definite social functions, gossip inevitably transmits, or becomes converted into, a social value that governs, manifests, or enhances the relationship between the participants.[44] In any reciprocal relationship, the gossipy subset of exchange will be inseparable from the relational context. One crucial precondition of gossip, then, is sociability. There must be a level of amiable familiarity between the participants, or a desire to establish such a level, which is directed toward promoting social interaction.[45] Gossip rarely occurs among strangers or among acquaintances whose relationship is based on maintaining a strict aloofness with one another. To gossip with another person may inevitably reveal an intimate detail about oneself, so it is not something to be undertaken lightly if the relationship is construed as unsociable. For example, Almirol observed that the social rules governing gossip stipulated that one never gossips with strangers. When people gossip, they must be sure where the loyalty of the other person lies, since gossip is very much a covert activity that depends on a sociable setting to be effective in checking violations of community values.[46]

Some situations are defined to be sociable so that gossiping may flourish. The office grapevine is such a situation, in that the predominant flow of "shop-talk" is usually restricted to subjects of social interest (who will likely get the next promotion, who recently had a baby, and so forth). Interestingly, it is found that only a few of the persons who know this information ever actually transmit it (around 10 percent).[47] Other situations may be specifically sanctioned to encourage widespread participation—for example, a social occasion like a party or a small drinking group. Robert Paine made a study of the endless camp conversations of reindeer herdsmen in Kautokeino, who were forever asking each other questions like, "How long has So-and-so been rich?" and "How long will he stay rich?"[48] For these people, gossiping about wealth was presumably a way of measuring one's success and gauging others as competitors in an essentially anarchic situation. Szwed, in a similar study conducted in a Roman Catholic parish in Newfoundland, observed that drinking groups established a framework of social relationships that naturally allowed for gossipy exchanges of information (due to the levity and to the depression of inhibitions associated with the situation).[49] "Talk show radio" is an example of how a situation may be specifically sanctioned as "sociable" in spite of the fact that one party to the interaction (the radio personality or "talk jockey") does not know the other party personally.[50] Here an effort is made to establish an ambience of informality (for example, by addressing one another by first names) to encourage a spirited exchange of small talk and self-disclosure.

No matter how oblique the references contained in such an exchange, they must remain clear to the parties involved. Hence, a second precondition of gossip is that the participants share a common frame of reference.[51] Members of communities and social groups, especially, value similarity of attitudes and beliefs, although not every member will agree with every other member on all issues. Nonetheless, presence in such a group tends to modify one's beliefs and feelings so that they are more consistent (or conforming) with those of other members. This results in a stock of knowledge that can serve as the backdrop against which gossip may develop and be shared in a meaningful way. The more exclusive the group, the greater, presumably, will be the amount of gossip in it.[52]

Social psychologists have made extensive studies of group membership, and their findings throw additional light on the effects of efforts to achieve conformity on individual perceptions. A classic study by Solomon Asch was designed to determine the effects of group membership on judgement. A subject arrived at the research lab along with several others who were actually confederates of the investigator. All subjects, once they were seated together at the same table, were told by the experimenter that they would be asked to make judgments about the lengths of several lines. Each subject was to judge which of three lines was closest in length to a standard line. The confederates always stated their judgments first, after which the subject gave his opinion. The confederates, acting in collusion with the experimenter, sometimes gave obviously incorrect judgments. One-third of the subjects, Asch found, gave the same opinion as the others in the experiment. Interviews with this group of subjects uncovered three distinct motives for yielding to the pressure exerted by the incorrect majority: unawareness of being incorrect; doubts about their own perceptions, along with lack of confidence; and a desire to appear the same as the majority.[53] From this study, we can see that conformity may come about for a variety of reasons. By analogy, the shared perceptions that are a precondition to give, accept, or return gossip may also materialize for a variety of reasons when group members try to establish a common frame of reference.

Although group members may intentionally try to achieve conformity, it can also come about through much more subtle processes. In a study by Muzafer Sherif, the effects of groups on individual perceptions were examined. Subjects observed a point of light in a pitch-dark room. Although the light was stationary, in the mind's eye it appeared to move under these conditions. Sherif had subjects report the distance the light "moved" while they were alone and also when they were in groups. He found that a subject's judgments of distance were influenced by the responses of others when the subject was placed in a group after making initial individual judgments. Judgments of group members tended to become more and more alike with each successive trial. Those who made their first judgments in groups tended to acquire a norm from the group, so that when they were tested individually, they reported the same distance of light movement as that reported by others who were also in the group.[54] We might suppose that strangers thrust together in a social milieu will have a tendency to modify their judgments toward a shared interpretive framework in the way that Sherif's research subjects modified their judgments toward the mean group judgment and retained this judgment when they were later tested individually.

A third precondition of gossip is that the situation presents at least superficially, a feeling of privacy or protection. Gossiping involves exchanging information about an individual or a group that the subjects may wish to keep as their own exclusive possession.[55] It could be embarrassing, even costly, to be caught red-handed dipping into that private pool of information. Privacy gives a place for emotional release without the feeling of being culpable or held liable for one's remarks.[56] This is not to say, however, that the situation is always perceived accurately or that one can have blind faith that there will be no breach of trust. For example, in 1975, Secretary of State Henry Kissinger's private remarks at a private dinner party were transmitted inadvertently to a lounge where journalists were waiting to record toasts exchanged by Kissinger and his hosts. A tape recording of his observations had him gossiping about a number of prominent political figures. When Kissinger's dinner-table gossip showed up in a front-page article in the *Washington Post,* he and his hosts were forced to issue a spate of apologies.[57]

The question of privacy is of particular concern in the helping professions, since illness subjects patients to a situation in which they may be obliged to disclose the most personal details about themselves. H.W.S. Francis reminds us that classical medical ethics present a very exacting standard, both outside and inside the profession.[58] The Hippocratic Oath states "And whatsoever I shall see or hear in the course of my profession, as well as outside my profession in my intercourse with men, if it be what should not be published abroad, I shall never divulge, holding such things to be holy secrets." Florence Nightingale expressed similar sentiments in counseling that a nurse "must be no gossip; no vain talker; she should never answer questions about her sick except to those who have a right to ask them."[59] The right to privacy is also implicit in all the various European and American ethical codes for psychological research and professional standards.[60] Nevertheless, difficult choices arise both in research and in clinical practice when the implications of what has been disclosed and the reluctance to divulge this privileged communication are in conflict.[61]

## Martyrs of Gossip?

Several writers have alluded to the regrettable consequences of gossip. Indeed, the title of this chapter baldly raises this issue. Almirol also mentions, for example, that one person in his study (who was presumably the target of gossip) attempted to commit suicide and that another person threatened with bodily harm those whom he believed had been gossiping about him.[62] Writing in *Munsey's Magazine* in 1912, Richard Le Gallienne stated the case for the "martyrs of gossip," who, he argued, are inevitably adjudged to be guilty no matter how ludicrous or disreputable the idle tales told:

> Too often has the sorry spectacle been seen of greatness and goodness going down before the poisonous tongues and the licking jaws. Even Caesar himself had to fall at last, his strong soul perhaps not sorry to escape through his dagger-wounds from so pitiable small a world; and the poison in the death-cup of Socrates was not so much the juice of the hemlock as the venom of the gossips of Athens. In later times, no service to his country, no greatness of character, can save the noble Raleigh from the tongues determined to bring him to the block; and when the haughty head of Marie Antoinette must bow at last upon the scaffold, the true guillotine was the guillotine of gossip. It was such lying tales as that of the diamond necklace that had brought her there. All Queen Elizabeth's popularity could not save her from the ribaldry of scandal, nor Shakespeare's genius protect his name from the foulest of stains. In our own time, the mere mention of the name of Dreyfus suffices to remind us of the terrible nets

woven by this dark spinner. Within the last year or two, have we not seen the loved king of a great nation driven to seek protection from the specter of innuendo in the courts of law? But gossip laughs at such tribunals. . . ."At least there must have been something in it" is always the last word on such debatable matters; and the curious thing is that, whenever a doubt of the truth is expressed, it is never the victim, but always the scandal, to which the benefit of the doubt is extended.[63]

Le Gallienne's florid prose notwithstanding, there have been media, literary, and social science allusions to cases in which the target of gossip was falsely accused and (presumably) suffered accordingly. Whether motivated by an intended or a subtle conformity to the group, the community, or the culture, the consequences of gossip often reflect the extent to which norms can be enforced on individuals who ostensibly threaten or violate them. In the case of a Middle Eastern couple, gossip about the wife's extramarital affairs may have grave consequences for the individuals involved, though the report of a similar incident in the upper classes of Western society may simply excite the imagination of even unsympathetic or antagonistic neighbors and friends. In the former case, the particular family or social class involved may literally excommunicate the target persons and even proceed to impose legal sanctions. Particular types of societies in different sociocultural and historical stages may not only determine the consequences of negative gossip but in fact provide the "victims." Closely knit communities in which normative rules are sustained, for example, by a female or male gerontocracy may target an outsider or a "deviant" insider, usually a younger person, as in the case of the young woman who was "killed by idle gossip."[64]

The malevolence of innocent indifference of the gossipers aside, small talk often proves instrumental to the maintenance of the very conditions that define its origins and render it a socially intelligible act. Though an interpersonal exchange of a strikingly ephemeral character, its capacity to discredit, isolate, or even prevent nonconventional behavior invests it with a social significance that stands in stark contrast to its apparent triviality. Yet what drove the young woman to suicide was not gossip per se, but the reception of the kind of information channeled through it by the particular community (a case of social ostracism in which the "executioner" was notably absent).

One may look at the information revealed in gossip, be it actual or fabricated, and recognize current concerns and perceptions of individuals, groups, or subcultures, Take, for example, the case of a candidate for political office and the gossip that may arise about his participation as a youth in a fraternity prank or about a rather unpleasant divorce procedure. The consequences effected by such gossip are distinctly relevant to set expectations about the type of social persona a politician "ought to" possess. In contrast to a private citizen for whom a traumatic and prolonged divorce procedure would stir sympathy and understanding and a college adventure would evoke tolerant amusement at a sign of youthful "creativity," such incidents may contribute to the formation of a public image that would focus on the candidate's lack of responsibility. Similarly, allegations of a candidate's brief association in early adulthood with a socialist organization or cause may, in the context of American politics, virtually eliminate the person's chances for election, though the same disclosure might scarcely raise an eyebrow in the context of European politics.

Despite the fact that gossip neither generates its own subject matter nor defines its target, it is a socially construed phenomenon. Its identity merges with the identities of those phenomena that appear as intrinsic aspects of the life of a culture and the structure of a society. Its transitory nature and its consequent elusiveness do not prevent its transformation into a means for the generation of concrete consequences for the individuals it affects. The dictionary defines gossip as "idle talk," but its idleness, in the contextualist sense, is only a reminder of the "tricks" that the social world affords for its observers.

# Part II
# Alerting Publics, Protecting Freedom

# 5

# Warning Visions: Films Concerning Social and Political Dangers Threatening Our Civilization

*Roger Manvell*

Film has gradually come to be recognized as the great innovatory art form of the twentieth century, especially as it has acquired range and maturity in its handling of the wider spectrum of human experience during the second half of the century. In fictional narration, it has taken a worthwhile place alongside the older arts of the drama and the novel. In the presentation of fact, seen in the genre known as documentary, film created an entirely new form of audiovisual mass communication, starting with the primitive newsreel, which visually recorded the more obvious events in the period of the silent film. With the coming of sound-on-film (around 1928), it gave us a means of building up a vast archive of history in both aural and visual terms, preserving aspects of the past in living, speaking form. Film was also widely international in origin; even the humblest Third World community could record some of its activities on film and take a place, however restricted, alongside the massive cinematic productivity of the more advanced nations—especially the United States—which was to become increasingly exhibited on the screens of other nations.

Although most fiction films are, perhaps, relatively frivolous and represent only passing entertainment, from the very start—in the work of such artists as D.W. Griffith (USA), Eisenstein and Pudovkin (USSR), and G.W. Pabst (Germany), among others—even the silent screen took on a dimension of serious social and psychological comment sufficient to show that a new art form was being developed. In addition, early in the 1920s, the American explorer Robert Flaherty among the Eskimos and South Sea islanders showed the service film could render to anthropology. In consequence, films began to take their place alongside literature and drama in the area of social analysis that warned society of the dangers with which it was allowing itself to be afflicted: increasingly mechanized warfare, unnecessarily violent revolution, encroachments on civil liberties by organized crime, vicious racialism, human oppression and genocide, unequal rights between the sexes, and many other broad problems that have disturbed the peaceful progress of our international societies in this century. More recently, the cinema has been in the forefront of the media in dealing with the gravest dangers that lie ahead if humankind ever embarks upon nuclear warfare.

In the latter half of the century, television—the close cousin to film as a means of mass communication—has enormously widened the audiovisual dissemination of fictional stories, projected both for entertainment and for expansion of human experience and comprehension, and factual material, displayed and interpreted through different forms of documentary. With television, a single work can be viewed in a 24-hour time span by millions of people in many nations, far exceeding the audience of cinema theaters. Without doubt, as a means of reaching the general public, the combined forces of cinema and television are without equal. Both are capable of displaying works in a form that is hypnotically effective.

In this chapter, I have attempted to show how, since the early years of film, the medium has been used by certain filmmakers to put on record their concern for the many dangers that threaten the well-being of our civilization. The films discussed here are films of warning about the dilemmas of our time, many of which are among the more significant to have emerged during the brief span of twentieth-century film history.

In a sense, all films of serious dramatic intention involve some measure of warning about the menacing ambiguities in human nature, about relationships fraught with danger, about the larger issues of predatory political activism, about the threat represented by the increase in violent crime, and about exposure to the devastations caused by war. But most of these films are dramatizations of things that have already happened, things with which we may already be familiar. *All Quiet on the Western Front* (USA, 1930), *Tell England* (Britain, 1931), and *West Front 1918* (Germany, 1930) all exposed the dangers and horrors of war, but they were about a war already long concluded, and they were more than a decade after the event. In other words, the warning was generic; the films were about war in general and were occasioned by the bitter aftertaste of an experience recollected with pain. Similarly *The Lost Weekend* (USA, 1945) and *The Man with the Golden Arm* (USA, 1955) warned about the dangers of alcoholism or drug addiction. They were significant because they represented pioneer work in the serious treatment of their subject in what is, after all, a medium normally regarded by the public as entertainment and so tends to avoid subjects likely to cause mass audiences exceptional distress or embarrassment.

Our concern here is with that much rarer event, the release of a film that dares to warn the public about a major threat that may lie ahead. Such films are of necessity comparatively rare, if for no other reason than that most people do not normally consider such warnings the kind of entertainment for which they are prepared to line up at the box office. There is a far stronger demand for films that look back over unpleasant experiences that are sufficiently distant to become exhilarating in retrospect.[1] The comparatively late appearance of films reconstructing and interpreting the direly unpopular war in Vietnam—notably, *Apoc-*

*alypse Now* (USA, 1979) and *The Deer Hunter* (USA, 1978)—is a case in point.

A list of the great international events of our century would include the following:

World War I

The disintegration of the imperial powers' imperial holdings, and the troubles stemming therefrom.

The rise of the communist powers: (1) USSR, (2) China, (3) elsewhere.

The rise of fascism: (1) Japan, (2) Italy, (3) Germany, (4) Spain.

WorldWar II

The Korean and Vietnamese campaigns.

Upheavals in Latin America

Two films—one made in the 1920s, the other in the 1930s—attempted to look into the future and warn of social upheavals to come: Fritz Lang's *Metropolis* (Germany, 1927), the most expensive film to be produced in that country during the silent film period; and the much more significant and extraordinary film, *Things to Come* (Britain, 1936), the joint venture of Sir Alexander Korda, H.G. Wells, and the director William Cameron Menzies, a specialist in film design and spectacle. *Metropolis* survives in the history of cinema mainly as Lang's most ambitious silent film, with remarkable cinematography and spectacular, stylized urban settings inspired by Lang's excitement when he saw Manhattan on his first visit to America. Although his fantasy-vision of the future obviously has to be taken symbolically, it involved a concept of the ultimate confrontation of capital and labor. I have written previously of *Metropolis* as

> a film which not only projected large-scale vistas of a luxurious city of skyscrapers above ground, with their overhead roads, but a vast underground city housing the slave-workers and the Moloch-like factories which devoured their labour. In addition, there were symbolic fantasy-sets—the dream image of Moloch itself into whose devouring body the processions of automata-workers march . . . and the robot image of Maria, the saintly leader of the workers, manufactured in the strange laboratory of the mad inventor, Rotwang, the tool of the dictator, in order that her evil image may supplant that of the saint . . . . [A] naive conclusion is reached in which the workers' representative shakes hands with the dictator, symbolizing thereby the union of brain and labour through the supremacy of the heart. Naturally, *Metropolis* was to become one of Hitler's favourite films, with its illusion of the ultimate benevolence of the master-race. H.G. Wells when he saw the film regarded it as ludicrous and sentimental.[2]

H.G. Wells became increasingly pessimistic about the future of society during the 1930s, seeing his long-held vision of a utopian world society sustained by a benevolent elite of inventive scientists becoming increasingly impossible of realization. My closest friend of the period was one of Wells's sons-in-law, and I remember only too vividly hearing Wells express his extreme pessimism on the eve of the world war he had dreaded but had forecast in his script for *Things to Come*.[3] He foresaw devastation on a scale parallel to that forecast now for nuclear war. The film, one of the largest and most expensive in Korda's mercurial career as producer, warned that in a world of imperfect democracies and imperialistic dictatorships, modern, mechanized warfare could well mean the destruction of civilization. After the mass bombing raids that destroy the symbolic city of Everytown, the world is reduced to ruins in a universal Armageddon. Humankind reverts to barbarism and—once the world is reconstructed along lines that appear, visually at least, not all that different from the inhuman, abstract structures of *Metropolis*—a new, scientifically informed generation emerges that seeks inspiration and exultation in a "new world of conquest among the atoms and the stars," as Wells put it. Throughout the successive episodes, the forces of progress and reaction confront each other in perpetual struggle to gain control. Wells, however, was bitterly disappointed with the film in its final form, admitting that, from his elevated standpoint, it was "a mess of a film." As Norman and Jeanne Mackenzie noted in their biography of H.G. Wells, *The Time Traveller,* Wells "had hoped to use the film as an object lesson on the dangers of war and the need for scientific planning to create a new world of peace and leisure. But it became a crude morality play, in which Wells appeared to be trying to frighten the wits out of the public and then offering them an inhuman future dominated by autocratic technicians."[4] Although audiences were inevitably alarmed by the spectacular portrayal of mass bombing from giant aircraft, the film tended to influence public opinion in the direction of pacificism and the appeasement of Hitler, rather than establishing the firm need to prevent all future commitment to war, as Wells had intended. Wells may have been justified in his sneering comments on *Metropolis,* but the film with which his name was inevitably associated was in its own way just as melodramatic, relying like its predecessor on impressive visuals but reflecting in a crude, simplistic form of action the ethical issues involved in the techniques of modern warfare. The key characters became mere mouthpieces for Wells's hypotheses. For Korda, the film was "a document for peace," but it failed to make a profit at the box office.[5]

World War II began in Europe with Hitler's invasion of Poland in September 1939. America became involved after the raid on Pearl Harbor, creating a state of war between the United States and Japan that led, in turn, to the mutual declaration of war between America and Germany; all of this occurred in December 1941. The only feature filmmaker in Europe who gave serious, direct warning of the war to come and the ill-prepared state of the nations to face it was Jean Renoir of France—first with *La Vie est à Nous* (1937), a propaganda film directly related to the Franch Communist party that gave open warning of the threat posed by Hitler and Mussolini, and second, more indirectly, with *La Règle du Jeu* (1939), a dark tragicomedy exposing the moral weakness rife among the French aristocracy and landed gentry, the very people of the Right who, in Renoir's view, would be most suspect of collaboration if Nazi Germany ever attacked France. The film was made during the uneasy period following the Munich agreement betraying Czechoslovakia to Hitler. It was released only weeks before the declaration of war and attracted continuous censor trouble until it was finally banned as too demoralizing to be screened and a likely cause of social disorder. Renoir himself regarded it as having a relationship to his own epoch similar to that of Beaumarchais's *The Marriage of Figaro*, staged on the eve of the French Revolution.[6] As for America, the cinema there, as in Britain was held to be a place of entertainment for people representing all political persuasions, not a place for the presentation of polemical subjects likely to cause a disturbance. The German and Italian embassies were on the watch for any films that overtly attacked their leaders or their fascist governments and were ready to protest and have offending films withdrawn. A number of these films were to be made in America, however, once the war had begun in Europe.

The two and a quarter years that separated the Anglo-French entry into the war (early September 1939) and direct American involvement (December 11, 1941) presented an entirely new situation. Just as Britain and France were predominantly pacifist during the period, Hitler and Mussolini were building up their war machine, and Franco was providing the dictators with a "war game" in Spain, so America had remained predominantly isolationist as far as Europe was concerned. But the actual declaration of war, followed in 1940 by Hitler's successive invasions into the democracies of Western Europe, created a massive theater of war and occupation that was impossible for filmmakers to ignore. They disguised their coverage by making films of espionage, ostensibly from a neutral standpoint but increasingly hostile in tone to the dictators. Whether the resultant films can be regarded as films of warning in these circumstances—that is, films released prior to the events they present or expose—becomes a matter of opinion. America was not involved in the war but stood increasingly on the brink of involvement, though it took action by Japan to tip the scales. During this interim period, and even before it, several outstanding films appeared that, in one way or another, stood as films of warning for the still-neutral United States; the key titles were *Blockade* (William Dieterle, 1938), *Espionage Agent* (Lloyd Bacon, Spring 1939), and *Confessions of a Nazi Spy* (Anatole Litvak, prewar 1939).

As early as 1938, Walter Wanger was responsible as producer for *Blockade*. Dieterle, the director, had come as a refugee from Germany. The film was scripted by John Howard Lawson, later to be one of the "Hollywood Ten," and the star was Henry Fonda. *Blockade* was an espionage melodrama set in a blockaded port during the Spanish Civil War, and it revealed a bias toward the government side in the conflict. At one point, Fonda says, "Where is the conscience of the world that it allows the killing and maiming of civilians to go on?" Warners produced two films the following year, before the outbreak of war in Europe—*Espionage Agent* and *Confessions of a Nazi Spy*—both of which were melodramatic in style. The first concerns an American consular representative who finds that his new bride has acted as a spy for the German Secret Service; he resigns his post, and the couple then return to Europe to expose the network of Nazi agents working within the United States. *Confessions of a Nazi Spy* (with Edward G. Robinson and Franz Lederer) was openly anti-Nazi and boldly treated the nationwide activities of the pro-Nazi German-American Bund in the States. Warners was threatened by the Bund with a $5 million libel suit, and the film undoubtedly came as a shock to the American public on the eve of the outbreak of war in Europe. By 1940–1941, the number of films dealing openly with the effects of fascism and violent anti-Semitism in Europe markedly increased, including Hitchcock's *Foreign Correspondent*, Frank Borzage's version of the novel by Phyllis Bottome, *The Mortal Storm*, Chaplin's *The Great Dictator* (with its burlesque satire of Hitler and Mussolini)—all released in 1940—and Fritz Lang's *Man Hunt* (1941), which involved a fictional attempt on Hitler's life. In *The Great Dictator*, Chaplin, throwing fictional verisimilitude to the winds, made an open, if naive, plea at the end of the film to Hitler's armies: "Soldiers! Don't give yourselves to these brutes—who despise you—enslave you. Let us fight for a new world—a decent world." These were all, in their way, films of warning about the political situation in a Europe already at war. They were addressed to an America whose back was still more than half-turned to these events, despite the overt sympathy of President Roosevelt and the aid he was giving to Britain, which had to face the Axis alone in Europe for some eighteen months after the fall of France in the summer of 1940.[7]

Hitchcock's wartime film, *Lifeboat* (1944), could also be considered a film of warning. Whereas many films turned the Nazis into characters of burlesque (as in Ernst Lubitsch's 1942 film, *To Be or Not To Be*, set in newly occupied Poland) or of outright melodrama, Hitchcock (still a British national) portrayed the confrontations that occur in a lifeboat containing survivors from a ship torpedoed in mid-Atlantic by a German submarine. Among the men and women in the lifeboat is an additional survivor who turns out to be the commander of the submarine. He has lost his vessel and is subsequently picked up from the water by the people who were his victims but who do not realize who he is. As I have written of this film elsewhere:

> The group includes a Negro, a woman journalist, a near-communist stoker, and a near-fascist millionaire businessman. Part of the contemporary criticism of the film was that the treacherous Nazi was by far the most resourceful person in the boat. The film, photographed largely in close-shot, was meant to prove that the Nazis were not film villains, but real people, efficient and difficult to beat. It was, said Hitchcock to Truffaut, "a microcosm of war. . . . We wanted to show that

at that moment there were two world forces confronting each other . . . and while the democracies were completely disorganized, all the Germans were clearly headed in the same direction. So here was a statement telling the democracies to put aside their differencies temporarily and to gather forces to concentrate on the common enemy, whose strength was precisely derived from a spirit of unity and of determination."[8]

In Britain, once war was being waged, films of definite warning became immediately concerned with the potential dangers to security posed by idle gossip. Of these—most in the form of brief, official shorts shown in the theaters[9]—the principal feature film was Thorold Dickinson's excellently made *Next of Kin* (1942, starring Jack Hawkins) produced by Ealing Studios in direct association with the War Office, which contributed about a third of its modest costs. It was described at the time as a "propaganda documentary in dramatic form" and the Armed Services assisted in its production. It involved the tragic outcome of a commando raid on the coast of German-occupied France, the details of which were pieced together by two highly trained enemy agents (both British) from odds and ends of careless talk. At the end of the film, one spy is caught, but the other is left to continue his nefarious work. The film was directed with great authenticity, and many of those taking part were officers and men on active service. More remarkable was another Ealing film, scripted by Graham Greene and directed by Alberto Cavalcanti,[10] *Went the Day Well?* (1942). Parallel in some respects to Renoir's *The Rules of the Game*, this film dared, in this midwar year, to suggest that members of an extreme right-wing group among the upper-class elite would be prepared to welcome into a quiet English village a contingent of German commandos disguised in British army uniforms. For a while, the village becomes German-occupied territory until it is eventually relieved by legitimate British forces. The film was unfortunately uneven in direction—Cavalcanti's experience lying chiefly in documentaries; nevertheless, no other film, wartime or postwar, would so directly suggest that the British squirearchy could foster traitors and collaborators of the kind already active in France. It was a grim warning, and the film had no success at the wartime box office.

It is worth noting the interesting position of Soviet-German relations and their effect on the film of warning. Sergei Eisenstein, Russia's outstanding filmmaker, emerged from comparative disfavor in the eyes of the Stalinist regime to make an anti-German historical film, *Alexander Nevsky* (1938), which emphasized the German threat to Russia in the form of a historic parallel—the invasion of Russian territory by the Teutonic knights in the thirteenth century, an invasion repelled by Prince Alexander, a national hero. Eisenstein used a mix of mass spectacle and grotesque comedy to portray the grimly helmeted knights at war. The film was immediately suppressed, however, when the German-Soviet pact was suddenly and unexpectedly negotiated with the height of cynical expediency in August 1939, so safeguarding Hitler's invasion of Poland and allowing Stalin his share of the future prize. When Hitler invaded Russia in 1941, the film was hurriedly taken off the shelf to reassert its warning of the ancient German threat to the Russians. Another film of warning—this time of Nazi Germany's persecution of the Jews—was also released in 1938: *Professor Mamlock* (directors, Adolf Minkin and G. Rappoport). It was to be shown in both the United States and Britain before the outbreak of war. Rappoport was a refugee from Nazism, seeking asylum in the Soviet Union, just as Lang had done in America. During the war itself, the Soviet Union was to make many films of warning, reconstructing events taking place in German-occupied territory in such a way as to maximize resistance to the Nazi invasion in the great areas still free of the German presence. One of the most admirable was *The Rainbow* (1944), Mark Donskoi's film about an occupied Ukrainian small town, complete with its Russian collaborators working with the small, degenerate German unit in charge of the community, who are valiantly opposed by the women, children and old men left as victims to the oppressors.

Among the immediate postwar films in America that sounded a note of warning on grave social issues were Chaplin's *Monsieur Verdoux* (1947) and Robert Rossen's *All the King's Men* (1949), the latter based on the novel about right-wing political corruption in the South by Robert Penn Warren. The book was, in turn, based on the political exploitation exercised by Louisiana's former governer, Huey Long, who in effect established a state dictatorship at the time of the Wall Street crash and the succeeding economic depression that lasted until his assassination in Baton Rouge in 1935. The novel and the film were timely warnings that even in modern, democratic America, a fascistic regime (so recently defeated in Europe and Japan) could only too easily slide into power in a single state in the Union unless prevented through the efforts of citizens of perception and goodwill. The message of *Monsieur Verdoux* was more veiled; gestated since 1944 and finally made in 1946, it exposed Chaplin's view of the cynicism of the cutthroat competition encouraged by the more extreme forms of capitalism and warned against the erosion this could represent in democratic freedom. The film had initial trouble with censorship (all fully recorded in Chaplin's autobiography) and met with a generally unfavorable reception from press and public. In my biography of Chaplin, I wrote of this film:

> The true Verdoux, a simple, humane, sensitive man in accord with the Chaplin tradition, has been soured by society; his secure job gone, he takes to crime, living on the black market of his wits, murdering eccentric old ladies after giving them a few moments of unexpected happiness when they think they have found a new "husband." But he kills with the same ruthless efficiency with which a soldier is trained to kill in battle. He has been dehumanized by the cruelty which he has found active in contemporary competitive society, alike in war as in peace. When he loses through some catastrophe the family he loves, and for

whom he labors, the final bitterness enters his soul; he allows himself to be arrested and tried for murder. After the death sentence is passed, he says, "I shall see you all very soon," implying that society in destroying him is in the process of destroying itself. He tells the press, when a reporter seeks an interview with him in his cell, that "crime does not pay in a small way," that robbery and murder are the natural expression of "these criminal times. . . . One murder makes a villain, a million a hero."

In spite of its reception, Chaplin wrote of the film in his autobiography, "I believe *Monsieur Verdoux* is the cleverest and most brilliant film I have yet made."[11] Nevertheless, the film told against Chaplin when the crunch came, and he was, as a British national, refused reentry to the United States in 1952. These were the bitter years of the successive investigations of Hollywood by the House Committee on Un-American Activities.[12]

They were also the years that saw the rapid rise of the cold war. As with its earlier treatment of Nazism, Hollywood at first failed to give the particular issue of communism a serious evaluation. Films such as *The Iron Curtain* (1948), *I Married a Communist* (1949), *The Red Menace* (1949), and *The Red Danube* (1949) came in quick succession. There were also *Big Jim McLain* (1952), in which John Wayne as a government agent breaks a communist spy ring in Hawaii, and *Blood Alley* (1955), in which Wayne escapes to Hong Kong from communist pursuers. Made in a more downbeat documentary style was *I Was a Communist for the FBI* (1951), but the film that attempted to deal seriously with the particular menace of brainwashing was John Frankenheimer's *The Manchurian Candidate* (1962, with Frank Sinatra, Laurence Harvey and Angela Lansbury). In Britain, George Orwell's fable, *Animal Farm* (published in book form in 1945 and directed by John Halas in 1955 as the first full-length animated cartoon with a wholly serious theme), showed how a police state originated in the kingdom of the animals after gaining their freedom from the petty tyranny of farmer Jones. Orwell's *1984* (published in 1949 and filmed, somewhat indifferently, in 1956) looked into the future to the founding of an irrevocable dictatorship in which the media are fully exploited to suppress all human freedom of thought and action, including the curtailment of language itself through the gradual erosion of all words except those acceptable to or established by authority in the official idiom of Newspeak. In *1984*, the press was wholly controlled by the authorities—even past issues of the state press being "doctored" to keep past "history" in line with present ideology.

The deep-seated antipathy of the more responsible public for the cynical exploitation of human misbehavior characteristic of the worst kind of popular journalism and catered to by its hired servant, the muck-raking journalist, has led many films involving journalists to act like a warning against placing a blind trust in the press. While *All the President's Men* (USA, 1976, directed by Alan J. Pakula) has more recently done much to redress the balance in favor of the responsible journalist—for in this film another kind of warning was manifest, with journalists performing their proper function as the watchdogs for justice and insistence on the freedom of the press to expose wrongdoing in all places, high or low—many films about the press and other popular media have represented them as being served too often by unscrupulous men and women out to get their story, with tragic consequences for the ethics of sound journalism. This was the tenor of the most famous and recurrent of all films on the yellow press—*The Front Page* (USA, 1931, directed by Lewis Milestone, later remade as *His Girl Friday* in 1940 by Howard Hawks and, with its original title restored, remade for a third time in 1974 by Billy Wilder, a former journalist himself when working in pre-Nazi Germany). *The Front Page* had originated as a stage play by Ben Hecht and Charles MacArthur. The ruthless exploitation of people's misfortunes and personal tragedies for the sake of getting an exciting "human" story and so increasing press circulations or viewer ratings lies at the root of such films as *Five Star Final* (USA, 1931, directed by Mervyn Leroy), *Nothing Sacred* (USA, 1937, directed by William Wellman), *The Sweet Smell of Success* (USA, 1957, directed by the British filmmaker Alexander MacKendrick), *Inherit the Wind* (USA, 1960, directed by Stanley Kramer), and *Ace in the Hole (The Big Carnival,* (USA, 1961, directed by Billy Wilder). One of the best-known of all films, Orson Welles's *Citizen Kane* (USA, 1941) inevitably warned against the misuse of the power of the press by a megalomaniac publisher.[13] Of films that exposed similar vices in the other media, the more important are *A Face in the Crowd* (USA, 1957, directed by Elia Kazan), *Medium Cool* (USA, 1969, directed by Haskell Wexler) and *Network* (USA, 1976, directed by Sidney Lumet)—all warning us of the dangers facing sponsored television when unscrupulous men take control of programs, either as financial sponsors or as ambitious directors or star personalities.

More recently, Volker Schlondörff's *Circle of Deceit* (West Germany/France, 1981), which was shot in Lebanon, concerns a correspondent facing the ethics of his profession and personal involvement in factions and causes he is covering. Peter Weir's *The Year of Living Dangerously* (Australia, 1982) concerns an Australian television correspondent who becomes involved with politics in Indonesia. Roger Spottiswoode's *Under Fire* (USA, 1983), set in Nicaragua and shot in Mexico, shows what can happen when a press photographer—who claims initially, "I don't take sides, I take pictures"—allows himself to get caught up in the political events he is sent to cover abroad, conspiring with a particular faction to which he had become sympathetic, to the point of using his camera to photograph the corpse of a revolutionary leader in such a way as to support the contention that he is still alive. The film becomes a complex study in media ethics and the relationship between media representatives and political activists and presents a loaded warning to the public about the temptations and betrayals to which media representatives away from home, in areas of danger and stress, can become subject.[14]

In 1972, the young, Moscow-born film journalist and critic Jeanne Vronskaya, who left Russia to live in London in 1969, published *Young Soviet Filmmakers* (London: Allen and Unwin), her account of the work of important artists in Soviet cinema whose work had either been suppressed or prevented by the authorities from being shown abroad. The reason for the suppression is frequently that, in some way or other, however indirectly, these films are films of warning that express views unacceptable to the political censors. For example, the book features, among others of importance, the work of Andrei Tarkovsky and that of the woman director Larissa Shepitko. Tarkovsky's magnificent film, *Andrei Rublev* (1966; released 1971) portrays the struggle of a great innovative artist, a monk of the fifteenth century, to realize his vision against the overriding dogma of his time. Larissa Shepitko's *You and I* (1971) showed with unusual realism the life and attitude of youth in Siberia. The authorities naturally do not favor films that seem in any way to protest about social conditions or about the freedom of the artist's expression of such matters, though both of these productions were eventually available in the West. Such films are, by their very existence, films of warning, though the protest is often veiled in the form of reconstructed history or stylized fable. For example, in Czechoslovakia during the 1960s, before the Soviet intervention finally came in 1968, films were produced such as Ján Kádar and Elmar Klos's *The Shop on the Main Street* (1964), which gave rise to objection because it depicted anti-Semitism and, worse still, collaboration with the Nazis in a small town in Slovakia during the German occupation. No German protagonists are to be seen in the film; all the actions against the Jews in the town are taken by Slovak collaborators, the local fascist controllers. In Pavel Jurváček and Jan Schmidt's *Joseph Killian* (1964), a hallucinatory technique is used to reveal the insecurity of a young man at odds with society. Jan Nemec's *The Party and the Guests* (1966) became a Kafka-like fable about the dangers of nonconformism—a political allegory that ends in apparent despair. It seemed like a prophecy of 1968.[15]

A decade later, Poland's Andrzej Wajda, one of the world's most distinguished filmmakers and a supporter of the Solidarity movement, directed a succession of films—*Man of Marble* (1976), *Rough Treatment* (1978), *Man of Iron* (1981), and *Danton* (France/Poland, 1982)—all of which comment on the social scene in Poland and sound the note of warning. The first film exposes the propaganda methods used in the past (the 1950s) and the effects that these methods and the political system as a whole have on the characters of men and women working in the media. It is a film of great humanity as well as profound characterization. *Rough Treatment* is perhaps somewhat tangential to the basic theme of the series. It concerns the breakup in the private life of a successful Polish foreign correspondent on his return home from an assignment and, as a background vein running through the film, the unexplained erosion of his professional career—leading up to his unexplained death at the end. Is this an accident? Quite probably, but who knows? The film is termed by John Pym, the reviewer in the British Film Institute's *Monthly Film Bulletin* who covers most of Wajda's films of this period, an "oblique moral tale," a study in deceit and misunderstanding. *Men of Iron,* since its background is the strike in 1980 of shipyard workers in Gdansk, is near-contemporary, though the past colors the actions of the present, and key characters involved in *Man of Marble* recur in this, its successor. The young, independent-minded woman filmmaker, Agnieszka, for example, is now the wife of the strike leader, Tomczyk. The film, called "a masterpiece" by John Pym, treats in depth the problems of personal as well as political responsibility, the trials of being constantly subjected to dangerous pressures, and the personal stress that results from undefined threats that, often as not, are invisible, nonovert. Wajda, Poland's pride as a filmmaker—with the highest international reputation, going back to the 1950s—is also under constant stress as a survivor in these most difficult times. Even in *Danton,* adapted from a Polish play of the 1930s and made in France as a Franco-Polish coproduction, there is the inevitable suggestion of contemporary parallels in the confrontation between a very humanized Danton and an inflexible Robespierre, once friends and corevolutionaries, and in Danton's closed trial and subsequent execution at Robespierre's hands when he becomes the advocate of tolerance and so Robespierre's primary political opponent. Wajda's films of the past decade have become films of warning about what it is like for an intensely committed humanist to function from within an inflexibly committed socialist country.[16]

Films of warning in the postwar era have centered on the problems of nuclear energy (its expanding development, its potential dangers industrially) and on the proliferation of nuclear weapons under the competitive pressures of the so-called cold war. The Damocles's sword of the nuclear bomb and missile has been suspended over the heads of us all for more than a generation—a full forty years—but the more exact nature of its menace (in terms of its ever-increasing destructive capacity and the threat it poses in terms of widespread radiation aftereffects) has been properly realized only by those who have taken the trouble to acquire specialized knowledge (nuclear scientists, politicians, militarists, medical specialists, the better-informed antinuclear demonstrators, and the better-informed public). For the general public, even when adequate knowledge is available in official and other publications, the nuclear menace remains a vague concept, an ill-defined threat that has somehow managed to remain dormant through four decades of uneasy international relations, like some vast volcano on the verge of eruption.

The films, both fictional and documentary, that have been produced on the subject—primarily in America, Britain, and Japan—are either films that dramatize the vaguer aspects of public concern about the aftereffects of nuclear bombardment or documentaries that try to present whatever statistics are available and use them for propaganda against the *presence* of the bombs and missiles that are poised for defense and attack, let alone their eventual use. The considerable footage shot by the Japanese official units in Hiroshima and Nagasaki a few days after their destruction by atom bombs was for the most part withheld by the American authorities from public viewing for reasons of security, though this ban was removed around 1968 and prints were made available for use both in Japan and elsewhere. Some footage shot during the Bikini tests of 1946, when further atom bombs were set off in the Pacific, has also been made available and has become familiar in documentaries. This archival material has been used and reused in films, both factual and fictional, ever since. Everything that goes beyond these film records of 1945–1946 (together with a very few selected shots from recordings of later tests of far more powerful explosions) is, for the filmmakers, the work of hypothesis and imagination. The special-effects departments in the studios take over to formulate images of the unimaginable.

The watershed in this series of films, fiction and documentary alike, became Peter Watkins's *The War Game* (Britain, 1965)—the film celebrated for the furor it caused at the highest levels of the BBC, its sponsor when Watkins was a member of the BBC's staff. A total ban on its television transmission at home and abroad was imposed then and has obtained ever since.[17] The controversy *The War Game* aroused made its director's reputation, already well established initially by his film, *Culloden* (1964), which the BBC did show. Watkins, having left the BBC, then went on to make other controversial films—notably, *Privilege* (Britain, 1967), *Gladiators/The Peace Game* (Sweden, 1969), and *Punishment Park* (USA, 1971), a study in repression of dissidents in the United States during an unspecified future period. *The War Game* had won him an Oscar as the best documentary of 1966.

Prior to *The War Game*, the list of prominent films dealing with the subject is very varied, and the films themselves are mostly orthodox in conception. The best and most interesting include *The Beginning* (USA, 1947, directed by Norman Taurog), the first feature-length film on the subject—a dramatized documentary with an attempt at scientific exposition of events leading up to the development of the first atom bomb and its launching on Hiroshima; *Seven Days to Noon* (Britain, 1950, directed by John Boulting), in which the conscience of a professor involved in atomic research drives him insane, so that he threatens to detonate an atom bomb in central London unless all further work on nuclear research is brought to a halt; *Five* (USA, 1951, directed by Arch Oboler), the work of an independent filmmaker about the misbehavior of the five sole survivors of radiation spread around the world after a nuclear war—leaving in the end only a young man and woman to reestablish the human race; *Split Second* (USA, 1953, directed by Dick Powell), which involves escaped convicts and their victims hiding in a ghost town at the time of an atom bomb test; *The World, the Flesh and the Devil* (USA, 1959, directed by Ranald MacDougall), in which another fairy story is told about a young black man and white woman left to restart humanity after yet another nuclear holocaust, until a further white survivor intervenes to give the film a racial twist; *On the Beach* (USA, 1959, directed by

Stanley Kramer, based on Nevil Shute's fine novel of the same title), which was centered in Australia, the last surviving territory on earth, with only a short period of immunity from universal radiation after a massive nuclear war; and *Panic in Year Zero* (USA, 1962, directed by Ray Milland), which exploits violence after the inevitable holocaust—Milland's family having to defend itself ruthlessly against ruthless aggressors, every man for himself, until rescued by a surviving contingent of the U.S. Army. After these came two important films that ran neck-and-neck for release—*Fail-Safe* (USA, 1964, directed by Sidney Lumet) and *Dr. Strangelove* (Britain, 1964, directed by Stanley Kubrick)—both of which involved the premise that a U.S. plane has been sent out with a mission to drop a nuclear bomb on the USSR and the consequent dilemma in which the American president and the Soviet authorities are placed in their common desire to stop the international holocaust this will cause. The great difference between these two outstanding films is that in the serious drama, *Fail Safe,* disaster is averted (there is a fine performance by Henry Fonda as the president in this film), whereas in the grimly satirical comedy, *Dr. Strangelove,* the film ends as the holocaust begins. Japan, it should be noted, also made two films early on about the Hiroshima attack itself—the somewhat sentimental *Children of Hiroshima* (1953, directed by Kaneto Shindo) and a second, more savage and anti-American film called simply *Hiroshima* (1953, directed by Hideo Sekigawa), a film backed by the Japan Teachers Union. In 1955, Akira Kurosawa made *I Live in Fear,* a film about a wealthy industrialist who is driven to a state of collapse through fear of an immediate nuclear holocaust he believes is on its way, but who is finally declared insane through the pressures exerted by his family. "Your worry is the worry of all Japanese," declares a member of the family court to which the case has been submitted.

All these films can be divided into two distinct approaches to the subject: those that attempt to show the events leading up to a nuclear war (or its last-minute avoidance), including the actual atomic attack on Hiroshima, and those that attempt to portray the sufferings of survivors, hypothetically reconstructing what conditions would be like. All are films of warning, the Japanese films in particular demonstrating—sentimentally and not without some self-pity in *Children of Hiroshima* and angrily in *Hiroshima*—what it was actually like that once.

It is curious that *The War Game,* made on an extremely small BBC overhead budget of some £10,000 and some twenty years out of date in its basic statistics, has a much more authentic impact, even today, than its $4 million successor, *The Day After* (USA, 1983, directed by Nicholas Meyer), which, dressed by the presence of star performers such as Jason Robards and a spectacular display of special effects, somehow has the softened impact of a soap opera. Watkins' short film, playing less than an hour and shot deliberately in grainy black-and-white, almost like some desperate recording of a real disaster made for television with hand-held cameras, is far more moving, primarily because his helpers on screen are members of the ordinary public, including police and fire fighters, imagining the holocaust happening in their own community when a one-megaton hydrogen bomb has been exploded over an airbase in Kent, some six miles away from the town, which is shown to be an evacuation area from London. Somehow, Watkins managed to make these very ordinary, decent, and impressive people experience the event as if it were actually happening to them. It was shot on location in two Kentish towns, Rochester and Chatham, close to London.

Watkins had made a deeply disquieting film; and after prolonged discussion, the BBC authorities decided it was far too disquieting to inject into people's homes, even late at night. But mixed in with this particular alarm was most probably a desire to keep the BBC clear from the controversial Campaign for Nuclear Disarmament (CND), which by 1965 had been established for some eight years and was responsible for mass rallies protesting against nuclear weapons. The movement was, for the government and the armed services alike, a bête noire. The BBC has always denied that it yielded to official, governmental, or ministerial pressure in reaching this decision. Eventually, in 1982 (seventeen years later), it put on its own program, "Q.E.D.—a Guide to Armageddon," an attempt to reconstruct what would happen if London suffered a nuclear attack. Watkins has been described as saying the program was "bland" and antiseptic, with the result that it would encourage people to turn a blind eye to the inadequacies of civil defense should nuclear war ever be sprung upon them. Nevertheless, Watkins was never a prominent political figure, nor did he belong to the CND movement. Above all, he wanted people to *know* what the bomb and its use entailed. Now, in the 1980s, Watkins wants to make an entirely new, up-to-date, and more ambitious full-length film, but so far he has failed to secure the necessary backing.

The BBC did, however, permit the theatrical exhibition of *The War Game*—hence its Oscar award. It ran in a specialized theater in London for six months and has been distributed in many countries. It still has an extensive nontheatrical release, but it has never been seen on television anywhere; it is only shown to paying or private audiences at universities and the like, audiences who see it (the BBC maintains) by active choice, but nevertheless in far fewer numbers than those that television could reach at home and abroad.[18]

If *The War Game* is the perfect example of the film with every intention to warn from the as-near-as possible standpoint, factually speaking, Kubrick's *Dr. Strangelove* (its full, ironic title is *Dr. Strangelove, or How I Learned to Stop Worrying and Love the Bomb*) presents its warning from the standpoint of grim satire. It is a hilarious film, boldly conceived, and it was released at the very height of tension over the multinational spread of nuclear weapons in the 1960s. Satire is the barbed sword of comedy, with laughter as a weapon of aggression. Every key character is a loaded one, with a strong sexual undertone to both themes and names (Jack D. Ripper, Mandrake, Buck Turgidson, "King" Kong, Kissoff, de Sadesky, Bat Guano, Strangelove). When the climax comes as a result of the dementia of a single commanding general, and a unit is sent out with the mission to drop a nuclear bomb on a predetermined target in the Soviet Union, the single key plane is under the command of "King" Kong, a moronic man from America's deep south. The commanding general, Buck Turgidson, is a manic, "commie"-fixated lunatic who cannot keep his mind on the essential technicalities of nuclear attack, which he seems scarcely to understand. He joins the president (Peter Seller's Muffley) in the Pentagon war room and is cornered for his advice about what to do in this dire emergency. The only near-sane man—Peter Sellers in his second role as Ripper's aide, a Royal Air Force captain with an attentuated, upper-class English accent—takes what action he can from a position of little power. The president is a well-meaning man, but he is at a loss to know how to cope with the team of madmen with which he is surrounded or with Dimitri Kissoff, the Soviet premier with whom he tries to make rational contact over the "hot line" so that they may jointly remedy Ripper's paranoiac error, at the cost, if necessary, of American airmen's lives. Kissoff, however, is drunk. At all costs, Russia's unstoppable "Doomsday machine," automated to destroy the civilized world in the event of a nuclear attack, must not be activated. When it seems that nothing can be done to stop the single plane, under the control of "King" Kong, carrying the ultimate bomb to its target, Dr. Strangelove (Peter Sellers in his third role—the mad Nazi scientist who has been taken over by the Americans to be the president's nuclear adviser) suggests that the pick of these commanding figures, with a panel of desirable women, segregate themselves beneath the earth to propagate the *herrenvolk* of the future. With the satiric venom of a Swift, Kubrick, in his most ruthless film, warns us of the network of dangers we are setting up for ourselves in the nuclear arms race, making it seem something of a miracle that we have survived these twenty years since *Dr. Strangelove* was made. In the film, chaos is come again when Kong, riding astride the bomb as if it were a bucking bronco, plunges to his doom, and the doom of civilization, while Vera Lynn's honied voice intones the British Forces' tranquilizing song of World War II—"We'll meet again. Don't know where, Don't know when . . ."[19]

Since *The War Game* and *Dr. Strangelove*, there have been other films on the joint subject of nuclear energy and the nuclear bomb and their threat to human civilization. Among them have been *The Bedford Incident* (USA, 1965, directed by James B. Harris), centered on a warship carrying nuclear missiles; *Twilight's Last Gleaming* (USA/West Germany, 1977, directed by Robert Aldrich), a film that caused much controversy, in which an American army general holds the U.S. president for ransom on a site for nuclear missiles;[20] *The China Syndrome* (USA, 1979, directed by James Bridges) and *Silkwood* (USA, 1983, directed by Mike Nichols), both concerned with the hazard represented by the nuclear plants to their workers and to the public in the areas where the plants are situated; *Testament* (USA, 1983, directed by Lynne Littman), set in a remote Californian community that survives after America as a whole is devastated, though it is doomed to suffer extinction through radiation; and John Badham's *War Games*

(USA, 1983), in which a computer-addicted schoolboy manages to infiltrate accidentally into a secret military electronic exercise. Like *Silkwood* based on an actual event, *In the King of Prussia* (USA, 1982, directed by Emile de Antonio) reenacted a trial in Pennsylvania of a group of Catholic demonstrators who invaded a General Electric plant—called the King of Prussia—to damage nuclear missiles in the process of manufacture. The original members of the group appeared as themselves in this film.

In 1983 came the spectacular ABC television film, "The Day After," viewed on a single night in the United States by some hundred million people. What the film made only too clear was the utter helplessness of ordinary individuals as they view the takeoff of cruise missiles and realize that this can only mean that similar weapons must be on their way against their own home territory—in this case a rural area close to the nearest prime target, Kansas City. Although the film argued no specific case, government representatives in both the United States and Britain (where it was televised in December 1983) feared that it might play into the hands of the antinuclear movement—the same fear that affected Watkins's *The War Game*. It proved to be, however, solely a film of warning, not of debate.

Recently, there has also been a flow of feature-length and short feature-length documentaries emphasizing the menace of the U.S. and Soviet buildup of an ever-increasing stockpile of competitive nuclear weapons, to say nothing of the United States setting up missile bases in Britain and Western Europe. Some of these films deal specifically with medical hazards—for example, *Eight Minutes to Midnight* (USA, 1981), featuring the left-wing opponent of nuclear arms, Dr. Helen Caldicott; and *Race to Oblivion* (USA, 1982), narrated by Burt Lancaster and Shigeko Sasamori, a survivor from Hiroshima, which also presents medical comments by Dr. Caldicott and John Kenneth Galbraith. In *War without Winners* (USA, 1979), well-known public figures show that there can be no winners of a nuclear war. *America—from Hitler to MX* (USA, 1982) alleges the complicity of multinational corporations in the proliferation of nuclear weapons over the past forty years, and *Dark Circle* (USA, 1982) features the personal stories of those involved in making, testing, and selling the bomb.

Britain's contribution to this more recent output of films, produced mainly for television, includes the short feature-length production, *Carry Greenham Home* (1983), made by two students of the National Film and Television School. It is a record-documentary about the band of women who, over a period of several months, established a peace camp near Greenham Common in opposition to the base set up there for cruise missiles.[21]

In all these productions, it is often difficult, as I said at the beginning, to separate the serious films exposing current political problems and confrontations from the films of outright warning. The films of Constantin Costa-Gavras (Greek-born, now French), for example, are in effect dramas or even melodramas set in various storm centers of the world: *Z* (1969), an attack on the junta government in his native Greece for the assassination of the liberal Lambrakis; *The*

*Confession* (1970), dealing with a communist-led witch-hunt in Czechoslovakia; *State of Siege* (1972), set in Uruguay torn by guerilla activity; and *Missing* (1982) dramatizing the case of the missing reporter, Charles Horman, in Chile in the 1970s. The last two films pose the problems of U.S. involvement in South American affairs. Another example is the recent film that is so popular in the United States—*El Norte* (USA, 1983, directed by Gregory Nava)—which exposes the pressures that drive people living south of the United States to become illegal immigrants into the United States. It could be said that all these films warn their audiences of the social consequences of the ills they expose—as, indeed, do all films dealing with social and psychological malaise. In a world as troubled as that we now live in, exposure and warning are inextricably commingled.

# 6

# George Orwell's *1984* and the Freedom of the Media

*Roger Manvell*

In the peak of domes in the Byzantine churches of Sicily, there is set in mosaic the all-seeing eye of God. Wherever you move in these centers of Christian worship, this relentless eye appears to follow you. "Big Father" is watching you. In Orwell's *1984* (published some thirty-five years ago, a year before his death in 1950), it is the eye of Big Brother that watches, peering down from the vantage point of billboards. "It was one of those pictures," writes Orwell, "which are so contrived that the eyes follow you about when you move."[1] In every living-room, the ever-observing, ever-listening, as well as ever-communicating tele-screen exercises the control of the Thought-Police over the individual in commu-nized Britain:

> An oblong metal plaque like a dulled mirror. . . . The instrument (the telescreen, it was called) could be dimmed, but there was no way of shutting it off com-pletely. . . . Any sound that Winston made, above the level of a very low whis-per, would be picked up by it; moreover, so long as he remained within the field of vision which the metal plaque commanded, he could be seen as well as heard.[2]

We have managed to reach 1985 without, it would seem, the presence of Thought-Police, but in almost all homes the television screen is there, and in a growing number of homes computers are appearing as well. What do they signify?

*1984* had had its predecessors. In 1924, the Russian Eugene Zamiatin had published *We*, the diary of an individualist trapped in an unfree society of the far distant future. Living quarters there have glass walls; basic hunger has been over-come through the development of petroleum food; sex and love, representing a bastion of individuality and freedom, are in the process of being overcome. In-deed, "the way to rid man of criminality is to rid him of freedom."[3] Society—the United State, as it is called— is totally controlled by a Board of Guardians. Hap-piness is envisaged as existing in a state of perfect mechanization, and a univer-sally listening membrane ear watches for any sign of individualized defection, which is cured at once by means of a laserlike form of lobotomy administered by an official Well-doer. Zamiatin was exiled by Stalin in 1931 and died in Paris in 1937.

Aldous Huxley published *Brave New World* in 1932, seventeen years before *1984*. In this, human reproduction has become standardized as a laboratory process; literature, art, philosophy, and freedom of thought are totally suppressed in favor of a controlled, uniformly commonplace existence, while workers are drugged into a state of complaisance through the so-called pleasures of sexual and sensory indulgence. As in *1984*, the key characters experience the seeds of dissatisfaction. Huxley's *Brave New World Revisited* (1958, an essay on the threats to freedom of expression and the development of the mind), appeared nine years after *1984*; in it, organized distraction is used to vitiate clear thinking, and drugs are employed to alter the chemistry of the brain.

Orwell was essentially self-educated through a succession of troubling experiences—first, as an impoverished schoolboy moving in the overprivileged circles of Eton, reacting against the practice of oppressive colonialism while serving from the ages of 19 to 24 in the Imperial Police in Burma (an experience recorded in his *Burmese Days*, 1935), living voluntarily in a state of near-destitution (*Down and Out in Paris and London*, 1933), developing his own form of socialist commitment during the great depression (*The Road to Wigan Pier*, 1937), and, perhaps above all, learning at first hand how thought suppression works, both on the extreme right and on the extreme left, while serving on the Republican side in the Spanish Civil War (*Homage to Catalonia*, 1938). He was severely wounded in 1937 and developed tuberculosis, which precluded armed service in the Hitler war. He then worked for the BBC and as literary editor for the *Tribune*. His great success as a writer came with *Animal Farm* (1945) and *1984* (1949). (Both these last works were to be filmed—*Animal Farm* as an animated feature made by Halas and Batchelor in 1955, and *1984* in 1956, with a new version, starring Richard Burton, filmed just before his death in 1984 itself.) By 1950 he was dead.

During the 1930s, Orwell became both an advocate and an exponent of clear, jargon-free English style in the grand tradition established by Bunyan, Defoe, and the best of the eighteenth-century writers. He detested the political idiom adopted by fashionable communist intellectuals and the prevaricating language common among politicians and bureaucrats—what he was to term "double-think." His experiences during the 1930s led him to believe in the common decency of "ordinary" people, with their resilient, basic goodwill toward others—people uncontaminated by intellectual duplicity. He was against any form of mental enslavement through religious dogma or bureaucratic imposition achieved through documentation couched in crippling terminology. Although *1984* has been regarded as one of the bleakest novels of our time, it is surely, like *Animal Farm*, the very opposite of depressing. Rather, it is a bracing and courageous challenge to our tendencies toward doublethink and the exploitation of humankind through the misuse of the media.

The first challenge in *1984* is the exposure of the relationship of doublethink to thought control, of which it is the tool. Winston, the troubled protagonist, serves as a reprocessor of factual history in the archive department of the Ministry of Truth, ensuring with the aid of computerlike controls that the "facts" preserved in the records of the past are constantly revised to keep them in line with the ideological demands of the present:

> Some master brain in the Inner Party would select this version or that, would re-edit it and set in motion the complex processes of cross-referencing that would be required, and then the chosen lie would pass into the permanent records and become truth.[4]

The concept of doublethink is perhaps the most difficult to comprehend in *1984*, because it is the most ambiguous:

> *Doublethink* means the power of holding two contradictory beliefs in one's mind simultaneously, and accepting both of them. . . .The process has to be conscious, or it would not be carried out with sufficient precision, but it also has to be unconscious, or it would bring with it a feeling of falsity and hence of guilt. . . .Ultimately, it is by means of *doublethink* that the Party has been able—and may, for all we know, continue to be able for thousands of years—to arrest the course of history.[5]

Doublethink is represented in its crudest form by the ever-repeated Party slogans: "WAR IS PEACE; FREEDOM IS SLAVERY; IGNORANCE IS STRENGTH." But its pernicious infiltration into everyday mental experience is, in fact, far more subtle. Control through doublethink is greatly increased in the twentieth century by the existence of the new mass media, especially the domestic telescreen. Orwell points out that the powers of thought control and even the surveillance of every citizen have increased with the proliferation of the media—mass printing, radio broadcasting, cinema film and television. "The possibility," writes Orwell, "of enforcing not only complete obedience to the will of the State, but complete uniformity of opinion on all subjects, now existed for the first time."[6] In *1984*, the domestic telescreen becomes a two-way instrument—capable of watching and listening as well as of insidious indoctrination through the carefully devised propagandistic nature of its programs.

With the control of all publication in print and vision, the Ministry of Truth establishes total access to the mental process of all citizens. Dual standards operate, however, for more elite Party members as distinct from the Proles, the enslaved workers who are served by the Ministry with a branch of literature called, in Newspeak, Pornosec—a debased form of newsprint and other kinds of low-grade entertainment forbidden to Party members, who have their own more "elevated" press, books, films, teleprograms, novels, and plays.

One of Winston's colleagues is a man called Syme, whose official duty it is to reprocess the dictionary to reduce both the number of words and the range of their meaning, thus restricting their potential significance within acceptable limits. Orwell was sharply aware of how closely the concepts of human freedom are bound up with maintaining the living fluency of words—the development of language as an organic, ever-growing means of communication. Language is our most intimate medium of thought communication, kindred to though different in kind from the related but more intuitive expansion that comes from response to the visual arts and music. The control of words, therefore, is equivalent to the control of thought, and the control of thought is equivalent to the control of humanity itself. Newspeak is State language, the straitjacket of verbal communication, and Syme is an obsessive worker, the ideal bureaucrat full of goodwill and dedicated to the enslavement of his fellowmen. He says to Winston:

> Do you know that Newspeak is the only language in the world whose vocabulary gets smaller every year? . . . In the end we shall make thoughtcrime literally impossible, because there will be no words in which to express it. . . .The whole climate of thought will be different. In fact there will *be* no thought, as we understand it now. Orthodoxy means not thinking— not needing to think. Orthodoxy is unconsciousness.[7]

When the authorities finally catch up with Winston, his unorthodox thoughts lead them to regard him as insane. He is told by O'Brien, the Examiner-Inquisitor, who adopts a manner at once friendly, intimate, and persuasive, that he must become humble in the sight of the Party, and that this new humility will be the sign in him of his restored sanity. It is, indeed, an experience demanded of him that is parallel to a religious conversion, a spiritual rebirth. He must become a born-again Party convert. Unlike the heretic of the past, who clung to his heresy while being bound to the stake, clasping it to his burning bosom, the new sociopolitical convert must purge his heresy entirely before his inevitable destruction, emerging, as O'Brien puts it, with his "brain perfect before we blow it out."[8]

I was reminded of these key passges in *1984* when reading an article by Walter Reich, the American psychiatrist and student of Russian affairs, in the *New York Times Magazine*, written following an official visit to the Soviet Union:

> The charge of psychiatric abuse was a longstanding one. For years, Soviet psychiatrists had been accused in the West of diagnosing as mentally ill political dissidents they knew to be mentally well. According to both Western critics and Soviet dissidents, the K.G.B.—especially after it was taken over in 1967 by Yuri V. Andropov, now the top Soviet leader—had regularly referred dissidents to psychiatrists for such diagnoses in order to avoid embarrassing public trials and to discredit dissent as the product of sick minds. Once in psychiatric hospitals,

usually special institutions for the criminally insane, the dissidents were said to be treated with particular cruelty.[9]

A great many articles have been published during the last year or so about *1984*, most of them virtually congratulating ourselves on having reached 1984–1985, the fatal year, without having Orwell's insidious society imposed upon us. However, it is the nature of the insidious not to be obvious, to creep up on us unawares. Since Orwell's time, it is at least obvious that nuclear bombs and missiles have expanded from the kiloton to the megaton range and that they threaten human society—Orwellian or otherwise—with extinction through blast, fire, and the shrouds of radiation. It is also obvious that the expanding technical needs of modern society have placed both calculation and communication increasingly in the sphere of the omniscient and ever-present computer. The computer, in fact, is barely a generation old as a force in human society, pressured ahead by the needs of nuclear warfare, space research, and commercial expansion into competitive automation—all facilitated by the recent developments in miniaturisation through the microchip. Computer dependence is the order of contemporary advanced society, with the computer's phenomenal capacity to store and process data. We may, indeed, already be suffering from gross information overload, making choice and decision something in which the computer is forced to play an increasingly significant part, since mere human calculation falls short in both speed and capacity. There is every sign that we are moving gradually away from the book (as a static storehouse of technical information) to reading from the screen (reproducing a dynamic storehouse of information, constantly updated and ready to be conjured up at a consultant's will, like Aladdin's genie of the lamp).

It is true that in his book, *The Micromillenium* (1979), the late Christopher Evans adopted a positive view of the relationship of the advanced computer to human intelligence:

> During the 1990s computers will increasingly serve as intellectual and emotional partners. We are about to embark on a massive programme to develop highly intelligent machines, a process by which we will lead computers by the hand until they reach our own intellectual level, after which they will proceed to surpass us. In the course of this strange partnership computers will inevitably acquire ways of behaving which allow them to converse with us, exchange ideas and concepts, stimulate our imagination and so on. . . .When they *do* overtake us computers will, in my view, become extremely interesting entities to have around. Their role as teachers and mentors, for example, will be unequalled. It will be like having, as private tutors, the wisest, most knowledgeable and most patient humans on earth.[10]

At present, however, the human brain (weight about three pounds, extent about one-tenth of a cubic foot) remains preeminent in the handling and disposal of knowledge, with the computer as its tool. If anything, the computer has served so far to enhance our respect for the human brain, which is said to be capable of housing up to one hundred billion items of information. Keeping well within human terms, one is reminded of the parson in Goldsmith's poem *The Deserted Village:*

> In arguing too, the parson own'd his skill,
> For e'en though vanquish'd, he could argue still;
> While words of learned length, and thund'ring sound
> Amazed the gazing rustics rang'd around,
> And still they gaz'd, and still the wonder grew,
> That one small head could carry all he knew.[11]

Robert Jastrow, however—professor of astronomy and geology at Columbia University and founder of NASA's Goddard Institute for Space Studies—in his remarkable book,*The Enchanted Loom* (1981), insists on behalf of our human freedoms that "computers . . . are not biological organisms." He adds:

> The qualitative superiority of the brain over today's computers is even more striking than its compactness. Every cell, or gate, in the brain is directly connected to many other cells, in some cases to as many as 100,000. As a result, when we send a conscious impulse down to the recesses of the memory to summon forth a point of information, the cells in which this information is stored communicate on a subconscious level with thousands of other cells, and a wealth of associated images pours out at the conscious level of thought. The fruits of the subconscious activity are intuitive insight, flashes of perception and creative inspiration, all made possible by countless connections among the cells of the human brain.[12]

However, he also suggests that the human brain may have reached its maximum potential and therefore not only has invented the computer as a necessary adjunct but has rapidly come to rely upon it as an extension of itself. The dangers of this new dependence on a purely mechanical aid must be only too obvious to readers of *1984*. In a survey of the invasion of the computer into our homes published in *Time* magazine, the compilers wrote: "Computers do not think, but they do simulate many of the processes of the human brain: remembering, comparing, analyzing. And as people rely on the computer to do things that they used to do inside their heads, what happens to their heads?" And they quote MIT computer professor Joseph Weizenbaum's description of the new computer generation—"bright young men of disheveled appearance playing out megalomaniacal fantasies of omnipotence."[13]

Negative, too—and closer still to Orwell's *1984*—is John Wicklein in his book, *Electronic Nightmare: the New Communications and Freedom* (1981).[14] He writes, first, of the danger of increased mechanization in the media and in their sources of information; he fears an increasing control of their output by powers that are opposed to freedom in the media and in human expression. He exposes the ever-present issue of what he terms "invisible censorship," exercised through behind-the-scenes policy controls, such as the purposeful avoidance of controversial programming on the insistence of sponsors—that is, thought control by deliberate omission of information the public has a right to possess. He fears, too, the danger of governmental or commercial control of the liberty of the individual through the increasingly complex mechanization of personal data. We are moving toward a form of society in which there will exist computer-assembled dossiers on us all.

So, before we overcongratulate ourselves that 1984 has come and gone without subjecting our society to the more obvious threats that Orwell's fable projects, it may be salutary to consider to what extent our basic human rights are in fact being eroded through various forms of insidious encroachment, not only through the handling of our personal data (by the computerized records compiled by our employers, by our banks, by our medical services, by our tax gatherers, and so forth), but also through the restrictive handling of our sources of information through the news media (print and broadcasting), whether as a result of state intervention or the private considerations of those who own or control newspapers, magazines, and broadcasting stations. To what extent are we aware, too, of other forms of control over our increasingly automated information resources—controls the nature of which are not always easy to trace? As for the "Proles," commercialized "pornosec" has existed for some while to a phenomenal extent, enriching its purveyors just as it inevitably degenerates the mentality of its consumers.

Orwell did not—could not in 1948—have all this in mind. But intuitively he appears to have understood the danger signals, and in both *Animal Farm* and *1984*, through the smoke signals of fable, he put us on our guard in uncompromising terms.

# 7
# A Spectrum of Press Watchers

*Tenney Kelley Lehman*

P ress freedom is a person. It is the Asian reporter sharing breakfast with a friend in a Washington hotel. Two days ago, the journalist had fled his country when his newspaper was seized and his job became nonexistent. Now he cannot go back home, and he wonders how to find a job and start over in a strange land. He is 58 years old, and his entire professional experience has been with the newspaper that now is shut down.

Press freedom is the Iberian editor kidnapped in front of his house as he was departing for work. Tortured and left for dead on a mountainside, he stumbled miles before reaching a village to call for help. Hospitalization and a long convalescence restored his health. Months later, he was able to return to his job.

Press freedom is the Middle Eastern correspondent on sabbatical leave in the United States. At the university where he is in residence, his studies compete for his attention with news from abroad, which he hears over a small shortwave radio that fits into his pocket. Relatives and colleagues are being jailed; some have disappeared. Later, asked to address an international gathering of press people, he stays awake all night to plan what he must say. He knows that after giving his talk and telling the truth, he never can go back home.

Press freedom is the Far Eastern political columnist who for eight years has had a secret plan with a colleague in the United States. When his sources warn him that the government is poised to pick him up, he will telephone his American friend, using prearranged code words to set in motion his clandestine departure to safety.

Press freedom is also a subtlety. The politics of type size allow a nation whose official policy is apartheid to run a half-page ad in the *Wall Street Journal*, with a caption in 72-point type reading "The Changing Face of South Africa," under two photographs of racially mixed teams of soccer players. A sentence above the pictures says, in 6-point type, "These photographs portray the reality of equal opportunity in South Africa."[1]

To one who watches international press developments, it appears that the media are being attacked at every turn. What else can explain the proliferation of protective and/or investigative groups that seem to have sprung up overnight?

None has been created on a whim. Each is a serious undertaking. The roll calls are lengthy with cases of need, peril, and injustice. Aid from more fortunate—that is, freer—colleagues has been prompt and heartening.

And yet the cries for help continue—or, to put it more accurately, the silences deepen. Speech is lost to journalists who "disappear," who are harassed, kidnapped, or imprisoned, but their predicament is heard through the mouths of others pleading for justice, release, human rights. The files of press organizations are crammed with documentation for such cases, but they are the known; many are unknown, despite outside vigilance.

If there is danger—and there is—and if there is inequitable treatment—and there is—the question becomes one of accountability. Where is the integrity of lawyers and government officials? The query is simple and forthright, coming from a U.S. citizen asking within the comfort of the First Amendment guarantees. Safe in the armor of free speech and the right to know, most Americans are eager to do battle on behalf of beleaguered colleagues everywhere.

To fight well requires knowledge of the enemy, but already the troops are groping their way through thickets. To some, the foe is seen clearly as government control of the media—suppression, censorship—situations to be vanquished. To others, the enemies are the ones who decry government-supervised news and do not recognize the authority of an absolute system.

The nationalism of developing countries swells patriotic pride until no room is left to tolerate criticism. As a result, any adverse comment or casual remark—even a constructive observation—is viewed as disloyal to the regime and becomes an attack or even an act of treason. Leadership reacts accordingly and isolates or destroys the source. Hence, the global battlefield becomes the ground of human rights and the right of the press to report freely and responsibly.

Within this arena, another jousting is taking place. The developing countries have joined forces against the Western concept of a free press. UNESCO is the guidon, and the New World Information Order (NWIO) is their rallying cry—or so it sounds to democratic ears. The NWIO calls for control of the flow of information and the licensing of journalists, both anathema to the Western press. Understanding is fragile when a journalist from the democratic West praises the practice of investigative reporting to another reporter from an Eastern Marxist country. This concept is unknown to a loyal citizen; in fact, it sounds like treason. Thus, confrontation is foreordained, and conflict is unavoidable. When violence follows, the temperate forces redouble conciliatory efforts. Their banner is the absoluteness of the First Amendment; its guarantees remain nonnegotiable.

Chief among the many institutions for press freedom that have been created in this atmosphere are eight organizations whose origins span the forty years between 1941 and 1981: Freedom House, the Inter American Press Association, the International Press Institute, Amnesty International, the Reporters Committee for Freedom of the Press, the Index on Censorship, the World Press Freedom

Committee, and the Committee to Protect Journalists. Although their purposes and operations may vary, the armature of each remains the basic premise that there should be press freedom for all—freedom for reporters to report accurately, for publishers and editors to print complete information, and for readers to have access to that news. Whatever the structure of the society, each nation recognizes the importance of its press, whether that recognition takes the form of suppression or laissez-faire.

## Freedom House

Freedom House, the oldest of the organizations, was founded in 1941, a year preceded by convulsive events in the West, as Germans marched across neighboring borders and their U-boats prowled the North Atlantic. The upheavals of those twelve months culminated in the Pacific with the Japanese bombing of Pearl Harbor in December and the U.S. declaration of war against Japan, followed almost immediately by declarations of war against the United States from Germany and Italy.

From its headquarters in New York, Freedom House carries out its credo to support civil rights and equal opportunity at home and to advocate human rights abroad. The latter charge was blunted after the outbreak of World War II, when the efforts of Freedom House were channeled exclusively toward the support of the United States and its Allies against the Axis nations.

In its initial stages, Freedom House launched its campaign to uphold civil rights everywhere—a formal commitment made seven years before the United Nations adopted its Universal Declaration of Human Rights. Today the global organization is well established in many activities, as proclaimed on its letterhead: "Freedom's Advocate the World Over."

Leonard R. Sussman, executive director of Freedom House since 1967, introduced a media watch that continues in diverse forms. One effort is publication of a yearbook, *Freedom in The World: Political Rights and Civil Liberties,* which lists the levels of print and broadcast press controls in every country. In addition, the forum of the United Nations Educational, Scientific and Cultural Organization (UNESCO) is fully reported on and analyzed. As Mr. Sussman writes:

> We were the most active source of information on the mass media debates at UNESCO from 1976 on. We first alerted the U.S. media to the issues, and we have stayed with the debates. We have been an active participant at several points. [We] made the only non-governmental U.S. press-freedom address before the UNESCO plenary at Belgrade in 1980. Having been a persistent critic of many of UNESCO's mass media activities, I nevertheless believe the U.S. should remain in the organization to provide intellectual leadership. That American contribution has been lacking for 15 years at UNESCO, and we have suf-

fered the consequences of others filling the vacuum. Last November at Paris as a member of the U.S. delegation to the General Conference of UNESCO, I negotiated the communications issues. We made significant gains in the view of most observers because we demonstrated we were taking the forum seriously, and working at it.

Freedom House is a member of the U.S. Commission for UNESCO (and I am its vice-chairman) mainly because of our long-time role in the news media field. . . .We produce a steady flow of analyses of the international issues, as well as the domestic aspect of the press/government relationship.[2]

Another facet of Freedom House effort is a bimonthly magaine, *Freedom at Issue,* which covers domestic and foreign issues and carries a special section, "Freedom Appeals," presenting work from writers in repressed countries, translations of selected documents, and reports of recent events. For example, the May–June 1984 issue reported on the Ukrainian journalist and scholar Valery Marchenko. In March, he was sentenced by a Kiev court to ten years in a "strict regime labor camp" and five years of "internal exile as a 'repeat offender.'" Marchenko worked for the *Literary Ukraine,* a major newspaper, from 1970 to 1973, the time of his first arrest. His reports, reviews, and essays appeared frequently in the newspaper, as he continued his research and writing on Azerbaidzhan culture (his college major), and his work was printed in the Azerbaidzhani press as well. One essay called for the preservation of that nation's historical landmarks. Marchenko had also translated plays and a collection of fairy tales into Ukrainian, but a KGB charge against him in 1973 was based on three of his essays that were never published. At that time, a Kiev court sentenced him to "six years' strict regime labor camp and two years of exile for 'systematically participating in activities which are hostile to Soviet society.'" At present, Marchenko suffers from several medical problems, including a serious kidney ailment. Two days after his most recent sentencing on March 14, his mother visited the jail, but he was too ill to see her. She then sent a telegram of appeal to Pope John Paul II. A few days later, German authors Heinrich Böll and Günter Grass were among those who wrote messages of protest to the Soviet government.

A recent "Freedom Appeals" section informed readers of the detention of the Nicaraguan journalist Luis Mora Sanchez, a reporter with the Nicaraguan independent newspaper *La Prensa* and correspondent of *Radio Impacto* of San Jose, Costa Rica. Sanchez had filed a report for *Radio Impacto* describing how a group of Nicaraguan mothers had appealed unsuccessfully to the Sandinista government for news of their sons, who had been drafted earlier and not heard of since.[3]

"Freedom Appeals" also reported on the sentencing by a Kiev court of Irina Ratushinskaya, a poet and physics teacher. She is in a strict regime labor camp for seven years to be followed by five years of internal exile for "anti-Soviet agitation and propaganda." She had participated in a Moscow demonstration in 1981, but she has been deprived of twelve years of liberty especially for "preparing and distributing her poetry," an example of which follows:

Who's fated to know what parting is—
The parting of the bridge-halves, as they lift.
Who can know just why it is
At night, despair of silence lies
On the white guard of the snowdrift?
Why name love—the word's bereft.
Better there were no name for it.[4]

Freedom House's project Books USA is an endeavor whereby 120 different titles of historical, literary, and resource books are donated to potential leaders of developing countries in Asia, Africa, and Latin America. These shipments total thousands of tons annually.

The Freedom Award has been given annually since 1943 in public recognition of outstanding contributions to the cause of human liberty. Among writers or news organizations that have been cited are Walter Lippmann, the first recipient in 1943; Edward R. Murrow (1954); the *Arkansas Gazette* (1958); Alan Paton (1960); Dong-A Ilbo, South Korea (1975); the "responsible journalists of South Vietnam" (1975); and Cushrow Irani, editor of *The Statesman*, India (1977).

In an attempt to make discourse between citizens of different nations as effective and fruitful as possible, Freedom House has published the *Glossary for International Communications*, in which Leonard Sussman introduces commonly used words that vary in meaning according to the background and politics of the person speaking, since people hear and conceptualize within their own frames of reference. To clarify the semantics of different cultures, four definitions are given for each word or phrase, according to its use in the First World, the Second World (Marxist), the Third World, and UNESCO. For example, the debates in UNESCO concerning the proposed New World Information Order provide endless opportunities for misunderstanding, including varied definitions of *detente, journalistic code, news monopoly, and protection of journalists*.

Some examples of the multiple definitions in Freedom House's Glossary are as follows:

**"Access"**
(First World)
Open access to sources of news. Sources that substantiate information are essential to support credibility of news reports. Access to such sources is, therefore, essential. To assure the accuracy and the perception of veracity of a report, one or more kind of verification by sources is desirable. The free and easy access to diverse sources is therefore essential to provide accurate and balanced reporting.

(Second World—Marxist)
Access to official news only. Marxist countries generally permit access by journalists only to official sources or officially designated sources. These nations also severely limit the right of the foreign journalists to travel outside the country to

consult sources or seek information. The right or access to some few sensitive places may be restricted in even the most democratic countries; there it is the rare exception; in Marxist countries it is the rule, invoked as a matter of national sovereignty to prevent "interference" by foreign journalists in the country's internal affairs.

(Third World)
Right of access to sources varies with the political structure of the country. Very few developing countries, however, permit free access by journalists or others to official and unofficial sources of information. Even when free access is not barred as a matter of ideology, it is argued that the fragile structure of the society or the poorly trained press demands control of information at the source.

(UNESCO)
Access to news media for messages governments want. One of the most important rights of journalists is to seek information freely with access to both official and unofficial sources. UNESCO documents support liberal access to sources, but add the right cannot be totally unqualified; sovereign states restrict it when military or diplomatic considerations are involved. Yet the rule of "official secrecy" has been invoked, even in democratic societies, where it cannot be justified by such consideration.

**"Freedom of the Press"**
(First World)
The freedom of news media is a fundamental pillar of a free society. Press freedom may be defined as independence from ownership, control or influence by the government; or, even if a medium such as a broadcast facility is government owned, the independence of the communicators to provide balanced programs reflecting more than an official viewpoint. Press freedom permits the independent media to be wrong or biased. Professional ethics, a sense of social responsibility and diversity of views and reports provide the correctives.

(Second World—Marxist)
Within the confines of government policy, party interpretation, and fixed ideological commitments, the press and other media may select current examples of events and personalities that illuminate established policies. There is no freedom to see or report other than official policies, or speculate on possible implications of present policies. Journalists are permitted only to use variations on established themes. There is no press freedom.

(Third World)
Press freedom varies widely in the developing—as in the developed—world. Print media are free in 34% of all nations, partly free in 24%, not free in 42%. Broadcast media are free in 23%, partly free in 22%, not free in 55%. The difference: press-controllers in industrialized countries cannot use the excuse of Third World nations that they are too poor to afford independent media. Several of the poorest countries have a free press with diverse, often anti-establishment views published. Most developing-country leaders are either impatient with media that permit diversity, or fear political instability presumed to follow journal-

istic pluralism. In the name of advancing the development process, then, freedom of the press is often restricted.

(UNESCO)
UNESCO documents oppose censorship, harassment and imprisonment of journalists. UNESCO meetings, papers and statements of representatives often raise questions about press practices, and consider or recommend state actions that may eventually inhibit press freedom. UNESCO, for example, has not formally recommended the licensing of the press but since the issue has been repeatedly raised under UNESCO's auspices, a number of countries have begun the licensing of the press.[5]

Through its well-established endeavors of publications, conferences, programs, and projects Freedom House provides a comprehensive picture of political rights and civil liberties the world over. Its annual publication of the survey *Freedom in the World* presents a continuing record of the levels of democracy in the world's governments, thus furnishing a wide frame of reference and a background against which indicators of press conditions clearly emerge.

## Inter American Press Association

From turbulent beginnings and stormy adolescence, the Inter American Press Association (IAPA) has matured into strong, responsible adulthood. It came into the world in 1926, when the First Pan American Congress of Journalists convened in Washington, D.C. Under the auspices of the Pan American Union, the gathering called for the creation of a permanent inter-American organization.

For the next sixteen years, congresses met randomly, at the convenience of governments who paid the expenses of delegates—many, such as senators, ambassadors, and typographers, at the periphery of the press. Allegedly, the purpose of the meetings was not only to promote continental unity but also to provide a counterbalance to communist propaganda. In practice, delegations sat and voted by countries.

As Mary Gardner writes in her history of the IAPA:

> There were other difficulties also. Many Latin American editors and publishers were politically ambitious and saw no conflict in serving as a public official while still active in the newspaper business. They used their editorial columns to attack the opposition and to advance their own political causes. Then, once in power, they would often go so far as to imprison editors of the opposition papers.[6]

In 1942, the Mexican government arranged and financed the second congress. Held in Mexico City, the meeting abounded in hecklers and communists who tried to get control of the sessions. One year later, at the Second Pan American Congress in Havana, the association was given the Spanish name it retains, Sociedad Interamericana de Prensa (SIP). In his account of the proceedings. Lee Hills writes:

> Only 12 United States publications sent delegates. These included . . . Ralph McGill, Robert U. Brown, and myself. We were fascinated but dismayed by the proceedings. Cuba and Mexico were then the centers of Communist power in Latin America, and between them sent delegates from 130 publications. The Cuban government paid all the bills. . . . Many of the delegates were not journalists, but simply propagandists.
>
> Numerous resolutions were strictly political, having nothing to do with the press. The Communist thrust was openly directed at the United States. The enthusiasm of Latin American newspapermen for an inter-American organization was obvious. . . .
>
> The reaction began in 1945 at the Caracas congress against the way the SIP was constituted—political, non-professional, government-subsidized, Communist-infiltrated. The revolt grew at the 1946 Bogota meeting and jelled into action in Quito in 1949. With the aggressive backing of North Americans and a group of influential Latin American publishers, the Quito congress voted to reorganize the association.
>
> This was done at an historic meeting in New York in 1950 which changed the basic character of IAPA, made it totally independent, sustained entirely by dues of its own members. For the first time it occupied itself predominantly with freedom of the press. This marked the end of government-sponsored congresses. The freedom of the press report that year denounced repressive measures against the press in 15 nations in the Americas.[7]

Over the years, the tempestuous history of IAPA reads like the scenario for a series of melodramas. For example, Carlos Mantilla Artega, the presiding officer of the 1949 meeting in Ecuador, had to shout to be heard above the unruly delegates. At one point he stepped down from the chair and used force to maintain order, shaking one Latin American delegate to silence him. In Montevideo in 1951, the IAPA president suffered a heart attack when Peronistas attempted to gain control of the sessions. Two years later, a delegate from the Dominican Republic took offense when a Peruvian called Trujillo's regime a "stomach turning" dictatorship. For voicing his opinion, he got swatted with a 300-page, one-pound "Freedom of the Press" report.

When conditions warrant, the IAPA sends out envoys to conduct on-the-spot investigations in various countries and to report on incidents of press suppression. Few can claim as dramatic an entrance as that of the IAPA president in 1954, Miguel Lanz Duret of Mexico. He jumped through a window in the Costa Rican embassy in Managua, Nicaragua, to talk with a publisher who had taken refuge there.

When the annual IAPA meeting was held in Havana in 1956, Rojas Pinilla, the Colombian dictator, sent emissaries to Cuba to sabotage the gathering. Three officers of the IAPA, as well as the general manager, had received threats, and the hotel where the meeting took place was patrolled by armed guards and Cuban plainclothesmen. During the session, Jules Dubois of the Chicago *Tribune* was challenged to a duel by one of Trujillo's strongmen. The Rojas Colombians screamed themselves hoarse for a day and a half but finally were fought down by the General Assembly.

Today, IAPA membership totals more than 1,000 and represents thirty-three countries in the Americas, in addition to Canada. The society concentrates its activities in well-defined areas. For example, with funding from private organizations, members, and other friends, the society set up the Inter American Press Association Scholarship Fund in 1954. This fund enables North Americans to study and work for a school year in a Latin American Country, while Latin Americans or West Indians spend a year in a U.S. or Canadian journalism school. Approximately ten scholarships are awarded annually; to date, more than 2,000 men and women have been recipients.

The IAPA established its Research and Information Center that same year (1954), making it a forum for the exchange of information and ideas. Under its auspices, seminars and roundtable meetings have been held in the United States and in Latin America. The Center also provides a consulting service for Latin American newspapers and publishes books and monthly bulletins.

The IAPA's Freedom of the Press Committee overtly fights for newspapers and journalists tyrannized by repressive regimes. It has helped effect the release of editors and publishers from Latin American prisons; it has battled to reopen closed newspapers; and it has aided in restoring confiscated publications to their legal owners. Among the first to benefit from the IAPA's efforts was Demetrio Canelas of Los Tiempos, Cochabamaba, Bolivia. He saw his newspaper destroyed by government mobs, and because he had not supported the government in editorials. he was jailed as a traitor and threatened with execution. Protests from the IAPA saved him, and Canelas expressed his gratitude: "I owe not only my freedom but my life to the Inter American Press Association."

The IAPA gives awards annually to publications or individuals for their efforts to maintain a free press in the hemisphere. Three newspapers and four journalists from the United States and five dailies or newsmen from Latin America were recipients of the 1984 awards.[8]

The society publishers *IAPA News* monthly and as needed, sends out an urgent-alert newsletter, the "IAPA Updater." An "IAPA Updates" in 1984, for example, called attention to an urgent alert in Paraguay, where the country's only independent daily newspaper, *ABC Color,* was closed by the government in March.

When appropriate, the IAPA also issues statements of formal protest to repressive governments. The association continually monitors editorials and news columns in U.S. and Latin American publications and calls public attention to cases of press restraint. Conceived during the early years of World War II, and often a victim of inner conflicts, the IAPA has emerged as a vital member of the Western world's press watchers.

## International Press Institute

In the same year as the IAPA's landmark New York meeting in 1950, Lester Markel, the Sunday editor of the *New York Times* and a prominent member of the American Society of Newspaper Editors, met in New York with thirty-three other editors from fifteen countries to consider forming an organization run by and for the press.

In line with Lester Markel's belief that accurate information is basic to understanding among individuals and races, and that the first step toward that ideal is understanding among journalists, the decision was made to form an association of international newspeople. It was recognized that the effectiveness of such an organization would depend on a certain discrimination in its formation; that is, in countries where political systems precluded freedom of the press, governmental pressure not only on delegates but also on the sessions themselves would be damaging and inhospitable. (The early years of the IAPA are a case in point.) Nonetheless, a practicable formula was found by the group of organizers, and the International Press Institute (IPI) became a reality. As far as possible, its executive board was representative of the broadest geographical range.

A summary of its objectives is listed in the preamble to the constitution of the IPI, written by Lester Markel:

1. The furtherance and safeguarding of freedom of the press, by which is meant: free access to the news, free transmission of news, free publication of newspapers, free expression of views.

2. The achievement of understanding among journalists and so among peoples.

3. The promotion of the free exchange of accurate and balanced news among nations.

4. The improvement of the practices of journalism.[9]

To accomplish the goals of the IPI, national committees were set up in countries where the Institute would be active and where the press was free. These committees have proved to be the lifeblood of the IPI, as Lester Markel must have known they would be. Realizing that it probably never would be possible to have the entire membership assembled in one place—for reasons of finances and members' professional commitments—Markel defined the role of the national committees in a 1951 letter to Ed Law Yone, chairman of the Burmese National Committee:

Each national committee can present to the Secretariat for study, problems it considers important to the world's press, keep it informed about important events concerning the press in its own country, participate in regional conferences and international seminars organized by the Secretariat, and recommend journalists for exchange schemes.[10]

The IPI's administrative center originally was in Zurich; it is now located in London. The neutrality in Switzerland made it an appropriate site, particularly in the cold war era of the Korean War, Stalin's rule of the Soviet Union, and his permeating influence on Eastern Europe.

In 1952, the first General Assembly of the IPI met in Paris, with 101 editors from twenty-one countries attending. By the time the pounding gavel signaled the opening session, the agenda was thick with reports on projects either in progress or completed, and the IPI was launched. By 1955, the focus of the Institute was on the safeguarding of press freedom; from then on, the assemblies effected policy decisions and publicized violations of press freedom.

In 1974, an American editor addressing the assembly in Kyoto said that the IPI's activities in this matter were insufficient:

> IPI has talked about and done a great deal on the freedom of the press but it has virtually ignored what the press does with the freedom it has. I think IPI should start talking about the quality of our performance . . . how we focus on the news, report it, analyze it, write it and how we display it. We would get bruised a bit.[11]

In its first quarter-century, the IPI Secretariat arranged about forty bilateral meetings and fifteen Asian seminars among editors of countries with common problems. The first series was between French and German editors; another meeting took place with editors from Japan and editors from Burma, Indonesia, and the Philippines—three of the countries Japan had occupied during World War II. It took the IPI seven years to arrange a meeting between newspeople from Greece and Turkey, and setting up a session between Austrian and Italian editors took twice as long. Other gatherings included discussions between British and West German journalists between the Dutch and Indonesians, and between the Japanese and the Koreans. The most significant pairings were the talks between Japanese and American editors. Two years after the sessions started in 1970, agreement was reached on a scheme for exchange visits, which continue to this day.

Other IPI activities include field programs whereby Asia and Africa are provided with consultants. Workshops and seminars have been organized for the purpose of using clearer language in reporting and making better newspaper layouts. After eight years, the Asian program was deemed a success; the distance had proved not so far between today's printing technology and movable clay type, invented in eleventh-century China, and movable metal type, used two centuries later by Koreans to print books. In countries with traditions of written history and literature, the word in print was at home.

Africa was a more complex challenge. According to the German sociologist Janheinz Jahn, Africans "did not need an alphabet to convey information; instead they developed the drum language, which is superior to writing for that purpose . . . [and] can convey its message to a greater number of people at one time than telegraph or telephone. Only recently has the wireless come to excel in this respect the language of the drum." Jahn was quoted by Lateef Jakande, a former chairman of the IPI and one of Africa's leading journalists, when he addressed the Nigerian Institute of Journalism in 1974. He added that the drum is the traditional newspaper of Africa, the drummer its journalist.[12]

In due course, the IPI's training program in Africa became so popular that it was made competitive. Employers or editors had to write recommendations for nominees, who were required to submit an essay with their application stating why their country was in need of trained journalists. Applicant Ajwando Abour, born on the shores of Lake Victoria into a tribe of cattle herders, wrote:

> I used to spend a lot of time writing with a twig on my arms and thighs as I herded our cattle. Full of enthusiasm and urge to write, I decided to open up a News Agency. The first of its kind.
>
> I came across a book in which a line suggested that all one needed to become a writer was a writing table, pens, a notebook and ink. Using a small amount of working capital I decided to open a News Agency in Mombasa. That is how I got into the print.

After he graduated from IPI's course of instruction, Abour became information officer for a region of approximately 100,000 square miles.[13]

Today, IPI membership numbers more than 2,000 editors and publishers, representing sixty-eight countries. *IPI Report*, a monthly bulletin (with a circulation of 2,500) keeps members and affiliates up to date on media issues, especially incidents of press repression and the Institute's official statements. Peter Galliner, director of the IPI since 1975, writes:

> I do not keep a note of how many formal protests we make but it would be true to say that we make at least one or two protests in some form or other a week, if not more. . . . I think that we have been very successful, particularly in recent times, in dealing with situations in Greece, Turkey, Nigeria, Kenya and Pakistan, but there are many other countries as well.
>
> We watch the situation throughout the world, but of course tend to keep a special watch in those countries where there is or has been press freedom as we know it. . . . We also have special observers in South Africa, Asia, and Africa and to a certain extent also Latin America.[14]

At the 33rd IPI Assembly in Stockholm in June 1984, Richard Leonard, editor of the *Milwaukee Journal,* was elected IPI chairman. He is the fourth American to hold that office. In a recent interview, he commented:

> We have some real heroes in IPI. There's an editor in Greece who closed his paper rather than be under the [previous military] government's control. And an editor in an Asian country who spent 10 years in jail rather than knuckle under. . . .
>
> I asked the South Korean members one time why they never bring their wives. The reason is that they are hostages.[15]

The IPI's 1983 "World Press Freedom Review" states in its opening paragraphs:

> Throughout the world press freedom continues to take a turn for the worse. This year the International Press Institute issued more protests than at any time during its history.
>
> Each year the Institute publishes its annual World Press Freedom Review and each year the situation continues to grow worse. . . . 1983 has been no exception.
>
> Highest on the list of protests has been Turkey. Journalists and editors too numerous to mention have been brought before the courts and sentenced to heavy fines or stiff jail terms, charged with offences that most people in the free world would not even consider crimes.
>
> Throughout the world newsmen and publishers have found that speaking the truth is not a guaranteed right of the individual but something to be suppressed or distorted. The majority of signatories to the U.N. Charter on Human Rights or the Helsinki Agreement are breaking their word.
>
> Today only a small part of the globe can boast that free speech is respected and honored. The rest of the world is "gagged."
>
> Most of the Eastern European countries continue to jail journalists and writers, as does most of Africa, the Middle East, South, Central and Latin America and Asia.
>
> Some do not even bother with the luxury of prisons, some prefer more direct measures like the bullet.
>
> During 1983 many journalists died around the world. Newsmen, as always, have been at the front lines of all major conflicts. Some of the worst places to be a reporter . . . are Central and Latin America. Overseas and domestic correspondents have faced danger daily from a variety of sources. . . .
>
> The role of the journalist has never been harder than it is today.[16]

## Amnesty International

The year 1961 was one of momentous headlines: the Bay of Pigs disaster; the U.S. sending guerrilla warfare specialists to train South Vietnamese soldiers; the

Union of South Africa becoming a republic; and, in Europe, the Berlin Wall cutting a city in half. A single article in a magazine provided the impetus for the founding of Amnesty International. In May 1961, *The Observer* published a piece entitled "The Forgotten Prisoners," by British lawyer Peter Benenson.[17] He appealed to the general public and urged that work begin peacefully and impartially for the release of thousands of prisoners throughout the world. Jailed for their religious and political beliefs, these men and women were described as "prisoners of conscience," a phrase that has become part of the international vocabulary.

Less than month after Benenson's article appeared, he had heard from more than a thousand people, all offering to collect information on cases, to publicize them, and to get in touch with governments. Two months later, citizens of five countries helped establish the beginnings of Amnesty International (AI). Among its early supporters were humanitarian Dr. Albert Schweitzer and artist Pablo Picasso.

AI's purpose is to defend specific human rights, based upon the provisions of the Universal Declaration of Human Rights, as adopted by the General Assembly of the United Nations in 1948. This document states that the foundation of world freedom, justice, and peace depends on recognition of the inherent dignity and the equal and inalienable rights of all members of the human family.

Today, AI remains unique, with more than 350,000 members, subscribers, and supporters in more than 150 countries territories and organized sections in more than 40 of them. Its International Secretariat in London has a staff of about 150. Each year, the movement handles an average of nearly 5,000 individual cases, regardless of the ideology of either the victims or the governments concerned.[18] AI has formal relations with the United Nations, UNESCO, the Council of Europe, the Organization of American States, and the Organization of African Unity.

The role of Amnesty International is exact; its activities focus on prisoners:

—It seeks the release of men and women detained anywhere for their beliefs, color, sex, ethnic origin, language or religion, provided they have not used or advocated violence. These are "prisoners of conscience."

—It advocates fair and prompt trials for all political prisoners and works on behalf of such people detained without charge or without trial.

—It opposes the death penalty and torture or other cruel, inhuman or degrading treatment or punishment of all prisoners without reservation.[19]

AI does not support or oppose any government or political system. Its members around the world include advocates of different orders, yet they agree on the need to protect all people in all countries from imprisonment for their beliefs, and from torture and execution. Throughout most of the world, the victims are often from the working press. Even in many countries where there is no overt government control of the media, there is a pattern of imprisonment and ill treatment of journalists and writers who report on politically or socially sensitive issues. The records of Amnesty International bear this out; therefore, in 1974, AI created a new program for the especially vulnerable group of writers and journalists. Called the Urgent Action Network, this program enables persons to respond immediately on behalf of cases of arbitrary arrests, disappearances, torture, or impending death.

A list published in March 1977 contained the names of 104 journalists who had been imprisoned or who had disappeared in twenty-five countries. By mid-1981, members of the Urgent Action Network had worked on behalf of 214 arrested or abducted journalists and writers in thirty-five countries. In approximately half of the cases in which letters and telegrams were sent from the outside, torture stopped, prison conditions improved, or prisoners were released. It should be noted, however, that the lists are not all comprehensive; they include only the cases that are known. Virtually all of the involved journalists have been detained in violation of Article 19 of the United Nations Universal Declaration of Human Rights, which asserts the right of everyone to "receive and impart information through the media" as an integral part of the right to freedom of expression. Many of these journalists and writers have been held without charge or trial. Others have been subjected to "torture or to cruel, inhuman or degrading treatment or punishment," in violation of Article 5 of the declaration.

Over the years, AI has developed an extensive publications program, including books, newsletters, leaflets, posters, films, tapes, and slides. All materials reflects AI's philosophy of nonpartisanship, as spelled out in the *Amnesty International Handbook*.

AI's reports and public statements must be worded so as to be consistent with its policy of impartiality. For example:

(a) it does not label governments "regimes" or "dictatorships," or describe them or their leaders as "reactionary," "fanatical" or "despotic";

(b) it does not use vague labels when describing political parties, opposition movements or other organizations. It describes their policy and avoids interpretations;

(c) it does not use unnecessary adjectives and adverbs for extra effect. The facts themselves are usually sufficiently shocking: additional emphasis is unnecessary and can undermine AI's credibility as an impartial and reliable source of human rights information.

Graphics, cartoons and photographs used in reports and public statements must conform to the same standards of accuracy and impartiality. They should be used because they are directly relevant.[20]

The *Amnesty International Report*, an annual country-by-country survey of the association's work, covers developments in at least 100 nations. Its findings are quoted widely in the Western World:

Accurate information based on honest, painstaking research is vital to the human rights movement. Unbiased evaluation of that information can be achieved only by an approach that is scrupulously non-partisan, and that applies a single, universal standard for the protection of rights everywhere, regardless of politics or nationality.

Amnesty International tries to apply these principles in its work. It addresses all governments openly and seeks to disseminate its information as widely as possible. The organization attaches paramount importance to accuracy and is prepared to correct any errors it has made. Before publishing major country reports Amnesty International asks the government concerned for its comments and has often abstained from immediate publication in order to give those in authority an opportunity to clarify the facts. But ultimately the organization must make its information public. The publication of this annual report is one such moment.

Amnesty International is in fact rarely shown to have reported incorrectly. Many complaints from governments are not about *what* has been published, but about the very fact of publishing, or about the timing of publication. The organization is often accused of failing to appreciate the background to abuses or of giving, at least indirectly, support to the political opposition. This is a misconception. Amnesty International does not work against governments, but against human rights violations. It compares actual practice in a country with internationally accepted standards and demands compliance with these where they have not been respected.[21]

The *Amnesty International Newsletter,* printed in three languages, is sent monthly to members and subscribers. It gives news of AI concerns in individual countries and includes feature articles and details on "Prisoners of the Month."

Starting as a brief publicity effort twenty-three years ago to aid prisoners of conscience, AI has evolved into a global organization. Since its inception, a total of 5,557 prisoners have been "adopted," or investigated as prisoners of conscience. Since 1982, 1,743 new cases have been taken and 1,022 prisoners have been released.

So long as the German city is divided, the Berlin Wall remains a symbol of humanity at war with itself. Meanwhile, Amnesty International continues to surmount all barriers of political, ideological, and geographic boundaries and brings hope and, sometimes, release to those behind prison walls.

## Reporters Committee For Freedom of the Press

In 1970, at Kent State University, a campus demonstration against the Vietnam War ended with the killing of four students by the Ohio National Guard, and in the Far East, U.S. and South Vietnamese troops invaded Cambodia. The American press and the U.S. government were on a collision course. Foreign correspondents reported what they saw and Washington officials denied the accounts.

Journalists at home were subject to subpoenas to reveal their sources; gag orders increasingly fettered the media; and Mark Knopf, a reporter with *Kaleidoscope* in Madison, Wisconsin, was jailed for contempt of court after he refused to disclose confidential sources to the grand jury.

Concerned with the trend toward repression in their own country, a group of Washington journalists met to discuss the possibility of an organization that would provide information and practical help to reporters needing legal aid in the United States. Within twelve months, the Reporters Committee for Freedom of the Press was established by the press and for the press. This unique joint legal defense and research effort is devoted to protecting the First Amendment rights of the media to gather and publish news. The Reporters Committee is accountable to its Steering Committee, a group of thirty news reporters from around the country. The Committee's day-to-day operations are supervised by director Jack Landau, a journalist, a lawyer, and a founding member of the Reporters Committee. Three attorneys are on the staff as well.

After fourteen years, the Committee's accomplishments include the creation of the News Media Law Center in Washington, D.C., and efforts in four areas: legal defense, research, education, and publications.

The Reporters Committee's legal defense efforts on behalf of the press involve litigation, congressional testimony and various special projects to educate journalists about their legal rights and responsibilities.

Litigation initiated by the Reporters Committee includes:

Reporters Committee v. Civiletti: Challenging the Justice Department's refusal to release, under the Freedom of Information Act, documents showing the prior criminal records of several organized crime figures.
Status: awaiting decision in federal district court.

William P. Tavoulareas v. The Washington Post Co.: The Committee intervened to challenge the broad judicial order which sealed from public disclosure all documents produced by the Mobil Oil Co. during discovery in the Tavoulareas libel case.
Status: on remand to the federal district court.

Nixon v. Reporters Committee et al.: Asserting that 42 million documents and tapes amassed by former President Richard Nixon during his presidency were government rather than personal property.
Status: U.S. Supreme Court ruled that the Nixon presidential material belonged to the government under the Presidential Recordings and Materials Act (passed subsequent to the initiation of this lawsuit).

Reporters Committee v. Kissinger: Asserting that transcripts of telephone conversations by Henry Kissinger, while he was Director of the National Security Council and Secretary of State, were government property under the Freedom of Information Act and not personal property as Mr. Kissinger alleged.
Status: U.S. Supreme Court ruled that journalists have no rights under the Free-

dom of Information Act to force the government to retrieve documents removed from agencies by government officials.

Among the recent amicus briefs prepared by the Reporters Committee:

Carol Burnett v. National Enquirer, Inc.: Challenging a trial court ruling that the Enquirer was not a "newspaper" in a $1.6 million libel case filed by Carol Burnett.
(Appellate Court in California)

Richard Beach v. New York: Asserting the constitutionality of the New York shield law when applied to protect a television reporter from being subpoenaed by a Grand Jury investigating the leak of a sealed Grand Jury document.
(Appellate Court in New York)

Branan v. Hayes: Challenging the exclusion of videocameras from a Food and Drug Administration public hearing.
(U.S. district court)

Recent legislation for which the Reporters Committee has prepared and delivered testimony before Congress includes:

Freedom of Information Act: Testified against proposals to restrict press and public access to government information through broad-reaching amendments to this Act.

Agents Identities Bill: Testified against proposal to make it a crime for members of the news media to disclose the identity of covert U.S. intelligence agents and sources.

S. 855: Testified in favor of several proposals to reverse the Supreme Court decision in Zurcher v. Stanford Daily which authorized police searches of newsrooms.

Washington State Shield Law: Testified in favor of state legislation providing an absolute privilege for reporters to protect both their confidential sources and unpublished information.[22]

The Committee's research interests fall into the following major areas:

Prior restraints on publication and distribution

Gag orders, judicial secrecy, and access to courts

Protection of confidential news sources

Access to legislative and executive branches of government (federal and state freedom of information and open meetings acts)

Privacy (statutory and common law problems)

Libel

Broadcasting

These research projects are undertaken in cooperation with one or more press groups, such as the American Newspaper Publishers Association, the American Society of Newspaper Editors, the National Association of Broadcasters, the Associated Press, United Press International, and the Radio and Television News Directors Association, among others.

Through a clinical internship program for credit each semester, the Committee offers eight qualified law students study in the legal problems of the press. The interns assist the staff attorneys in their response to the more than 2,000 annual inquiries from press and media lawyers concerning First Amendment and freedom of information problems. Many major law schools recognize this internship program.

The Reporters Committee publications include a quarterly magazine, *The News Media and the Law* (circulation 9,000), which presents the latest cases and laws and trends in press law, and an eight-page biweekly newsletter, "News Media Update," which carries summaries of latest First Amendment and business news. "FYI Media Alert," another newsletter that provides analyses of urgent opinions and legislation, is circulated as needed. In addition, a guidebook for the media, *How to Use the Federal Freedom of Information Act,* is revised and published annually.

The Reporters Committee provides the Hot-Line Service for the national news media. Calls to this resource, which have increased recently, most usually involve questions about freedom of information, libel, confidential sources, and secret courts. The Committee also supports the Freedom of Information Service Center:

> The Freedom of Information Service Center was created in 1979 as a joint project of the Reporters Committee and the Society of Professional Journalists, Sigma Delta Chi. Its purpose is to assist journalists, authors and scholars in gaining access to government records and government meetings on federal, state and local levels.
>
> During its first year, it had assisted approximately 200 journalists. In 1983, it helped more than 1,000.[23]

## Index on Censorship

The origins of *Index on Censorship* are similar to those of Amnesty International; that is, an individual became so outraged by flagrant injustice that he appealed to the public through the pages of a newspaper. Soviet dissenter Pavel Litvinov joined with his colleague Larisa Bogoraz Daniel to write an open letter to the West. Printed in the *Times* of London and elsewhere in January 1968, the appeal in the Litvinov-Daniel letter described in detail the trial of four Soviet citizens:

The judicial trial of Galanskov, Ginsburg, Dobrovoisky and Lashkova which is taking place at present in the Moscow City Court is being carried out in violation of the most important principles of Soviet law. The judge and the prosecutor, with the participation of a special kind of audience, have turned the trial into a wild mockery of three of the accused—Galanskov, Ginsburg, and Lashkova—and of the witnesses unthinkable in the twentieth century. . . .

The case took on the character of the well-known "witch trials" on its second day, when Galanskov and Ginsburg—in spite of a year of preliminary incarceration, in spite of pressure from the court—refused to accept the groundless accusations made against them by Dobrovoisky and sought to prove their own innocence. Evidence by witnesses in favor of Galanskov and Ginsburg infuriated the court even more.

The judge and prosecutor throughout the trial have been helping Dobrovoisky to introduce false evidence against Galanskov and Ginsburg. The defense lawyers are constantly forbidden to ask questions, and the witnesses are not being allowed to give evidence which unmasks the provocative role of Dobrovoisky in this case.

Judge Mironov has not once stopped the prosecutor. But he is allowing people who represent the defence to say only that which fits in with the program already prepared by the KGB investigation. . . .

The courtroom is filled with specially selected people, officials of the KGB and volunteer militia, who give the appearance of an open public trial. These people make a noise, laugh, and insult the accused and the witnesses. Judge Moronov has made no attempt to prevent these violations of order. Not one of the blatant offenders has been ejected from the hall.

In this tense atmosphere there can be no pretense that the trial is objective, that there is any justice or legality about it. The sentence was decided from the very start.

We appeal to world public opinion, and in the first place to Soviet public opinion. We appeal to everyone in whom conscience is alive and who has sufficient courage. . . .

Demand public condemnation of this shameful trial and the punishment of those guilty of perpetrating it. Demand the release of the accused from arrest. Demand a new trial with the observance of all legal norms and with the presence of international observers.

Citizens of our country, this trial is a stain on the honor of our state and on the conscience of every one of us. You yourselves elected this court and these judges. Demand that they be deprived of the posts which they have abused.

Today it is not only the fate of the three accused which is at stake—their trial is no better than the celebrated trials of the 1930's which involved us in so much shame and so much blood that we have still not recovered from them.

We pass this appeal to the western progressive press and ask for it to be published and broadcast by radio as soon as possible—we are not sending this request to Soviet newspapers because that is hopeless.

Signed:
Larisa Bogoraz Daniel, Moscow, V-261, Leninsky
Prospect 85, Flat 3
Pavel Litvinov, Moscow, K-1, Ulitsa Alexei
Tolstoy 8, Flat 78

Among readers who responded to the plea was Stephen Spender, who sent the two letter writers a telegram, signed by prominent Western intellectuals:

> We, a group of friends representing no organization, support your statement, admire your courage, think of you and will help in any way possible.
>
> Signed:
>
> | | |
> |---|---|
> | Cecil Day Lewis | Mary McCarthy |
> | Yehudi Menuhin | J.B. Priestley |
> | W.H. Auden | Jacquetta Hawkes |
> | Henry Moore | Paul Scofield |
> | Stephen Spender | Igor Stravinsky |
> | A.J. Ayer | Stuart Hampshire |
> | Bertrand Russell | Maurice Bowra |
> | Julian Huxley | Mrs. George Orwell |

Pavel Litinov then wrote:

> Moscow, 8 August 1968
> Dear and Respected Stephen Spender,
>
> Larisa and I are very grateful to you for your January telegram. Please convey very warm gratitude also to your friends who signed it with you. Your telegram was not only a source of enormous moral support to us, it only made us aware that our appeal had not gone unanswered, but we are convinced had a good deal to do with saving us from the repressions which might have been expected. We ought to have thanked all of you immediately, but rather stupidly waited for a long time, expecting to be given your telegram officially—we never did receive it, but only heard its text from a BBC broadcast. . . .
>
> You write that you are ready to help us "by any method that is open to you." We immediately took this not as a purely rhetorical phrase, but as a genuine wish to help us. Help and understanding on the part of progressive circles in the West is what we need more than anything else. . . .
>
> My friends and I think that it would be very important to create an international committee or council, that would make it its purpose to support the democratic movement in USSR. This committee could be composed of universally respected, progressive writers, scholars, artists, and public personalities from England, the United States, France, Germany and other western countries and also from Latin America, Asia, Africa, and, in the future, even Eastern Europe.[24]

Thus began Writers and Scholars International Ltd., publishers of the magazine *Index on Censorship*, with headquarters in London. George Theimer is editor of the six-issues-per-year periodical, which has a circulation of 4,000, and Stephen Spender is a director. Among the patrons are Yehudi Menuhin, Henry Moore, Iris Murdock, Alan Paton, I.F. Stone, and Morris West.

The work of this twofold organization is carried on primarily by its publication *Index on Censorship*, which reports on the persecution of writers and journalists and prints the work of banned writers. In addition, "Briefing Papers," urgent one-page reports issued approximately every month, give details of harassment, arrest, detention, and disappearances of journalists and writers the world over. For example, four "Briefing Papers" were circulated in September 1984. In Peru, Jaime Ayala Suka, a 22-year-old journalist, has been missing since August 2, when he visited police headquarters in the town of Huanta to complain about an earlier armed police raid on his mother's house. In Morocco, Abd Al-Salam Yassin, a writer and publisher, was sentenced to two years' imprisonment because of a political review he published in *Al-Subeh*. In Thailand, Sulak Sivaraksa, a social critic and noted writer, was arrested in August, and thousands of copies of his latest book have been seized by police. The book, *Interviews with S. Sivaraksa: Unmasking Thai Society,* is alleged to contain passages defaming the Thai monarchy. In Zimbabwe, the prize-winning author Dambudzo Marechera was detained on order of the Central Intelligence Organization after he gave an outspoken interview in August at the International Book Fair in Harare.

Other publications are also available, including two books that have been produced to introduce young people to the concept of human rights. *Your Life My Life,* by Sarah Woodhouse, written especially for 11- to 14-year-olds, is one of the first of its kind for secondary schools. It was written in consultation with the British Council for Education in World Citizenship.[25] A sampling of chapter headings includes "How Small Is the World," "Things that Go Wrong," "War and Refugees," "When Human Rights are Lost, What Then?" and "Freedom Inside Ourselves." The author adds that it "was part of the present search to find other ways than violence to solve our world-wide human problems." *Human Rights and Wrongs,* by Jeremy Cunningham, is aimed at 14- to 18-year-olds. It introduces some of the political rights affirmed in the United Nations Declaration of Human Rights and provides stimulus for thought and discussion about individual rights and responsibilities.[26] Both books are suitable for classroom use and include resource guides.

*Index on Censorship* research on censorship continues. Representatives report on conditions in Latin America, the Middle East, Asia, Africa, and Central and Eastern Europe. In addition, Friends of Index committees are active in Holland, Finland, India, and Sweden. In the Annual Report for 1983–1984, chairman Mark Bonham-Carter wrote:

> As we now turn to expanding our work, we should be under no illusion how damaging censorship can be. One writer described its effect his way: "It keeps people apart; it promotes ignorance; but primarily it works to preserve the monopoly of power."

## World Press Freedom Committee

The World Press Freedom Committee (WPFC), activated in 1976 by a group of international journalists, is based in Washington, D.C. Its goal is to unify the free world media against major threats. To date, thirty-two journalistic organizations on five continents march under the WPFC banner to raise a strong voice in protest of those who advocate a state-controlled media, who seek to deny truth in news, and who abuse newspeople. The WPFC is formally dedicated to (1) a media free of government interference; (2) a full and free flow of international news; (3) a responsible and objective media; and (4) providing technical assistance to media in need. WPFC affiliates include the major press organizations in the United States and a wide range of societies abroad, based in such disparate areas as the Asia-Pacific, Argentina, Venezuela, the Caribbean, Australia, and Canada.

Dana Bullen, executive director of WPFC, comments:

> Our program is rather evenly divided between activities in support of press freedom and helpful assistance to media in developing countries. . . .
>
> According to annual Freedom House surveys, governments in two-thirds to three-fourths of the nations of the world have a significant or dominant voice in determining what does or does not appear in the media.
>
> And in about two-thirds to three-fourths of the nations of the world—a great many of them precisely the same countries—there is a serious lack of needed development.
>
> One might well reflect on this "coincidence."[27]

To meet some of the media needs in developing nations, the WPFC undertook a fund-raising campaign. Contributions came from large print and broadcast organization as well as from small dailies and broadcast stations over the world. All donations were from nongovernmental media sources. As a result, the press has been helped in Asia, Africa, Latin America, and the Caribbean with sixty-six funded grants and projects. The following is a random sampling of allocations:

—Organizing and conducting two training schools for reporters in Trinidad and a four-month training course in Barbados.

—A two-week print and broadcast seminar at the University of Khartoum in Sudan.

—Conducting a seminar for newspaper editors from 18 African nations at the University of Nairobi.

—Underwriting four regional training seminars by the Asia-Pacific Institute for Broadcasting Development.

—Two world conferences in Talloires, France, with independent media leaders.

—Textbooks for journalism students in Kenya, Nigeria and Nepal.

—Workshops for bureau chiefs, correspondents and stringers, the Caribbean News Agency and the Central American News Agency.

—Six-week journalism training program for mid-career newsmen in Nepal and Bangladesh; a seminar for Asian-Pacific business writers in Kuala Lumpur.[28]

A WPFC newsletter, distributed approximately every month to its affiliates and contributors and to other media leaders, reports on global press developments. Another WPFC publication is the book, *The Media Crisis: A Continuing Challenge,* which covers the broad issue of news media freedom—or its lack—across the globe.[29]

Through its program to provide technical assistance to the media in developing nations, the WPFC has served as a clearinghouse for equipment donated by print and broadcast media of the United States and Canada. Most of this equipment has gone to the Caribbean and Central America. Although the WPFC has received numerous requests for equipment from the Asian and African media, shipping costs and excessive governmental duties have prevented shipment of equipment. (The WPFC hopes to get governments to reduce fees and shipping forms to reduce costs.)

In August 1984, the WPFC added nine new assistance projects:

—Provision of books on print and broadcast journalism for journalism schools in Liberia, Tanzania and Kenya.

—Print and broadcast instructional equipment for the Department of Communication at the University of Liberia in Monrovia.

—Providing resource person for seminar on agricultural journalism at the Tanzania School of Journalism.

—Print and broadcast equipment for the School of Journalism at the University of Nairobi in Kenya.

—Providing help to print FIEJ/IPDC kenaf newsprint production report.

—Support for the Committee to Protect Journalists.

—Grant to Asia-Pacific Institute for Broadcasting Development for a regional course on radio and television news in Colombo, Sri Lanka.

—Training course for mid-career journalists on Fiji newspapers.[30]

The World Press Freedom Committee continues to monitor issues on press freedom and maintains a press watch in Paris to observe UNESCO and other major international organizations.


## Committee to Protect Journalists

The most recent of the press-watching organizations, the Committee to Protect Journalists (CPJ), was founded in 1981. That year's news was cataclysmic: Iran released the U.S. hostages; Egypt's President Anwar Sadat was assassinated; the government imposed martial law in Poland; and the United States orbited Columbia, the world's first space shuttle. Meanwhile, in many countries, journalists working at their craft discovered how routine assignments could turn into perilous undertakings.

The CPJ is a New York-based nonprofit organization of working journalists, fighting censorship and abuses suffered by their colleagues worldwide. To carry out its directive, the Committee investigates, protests, and publicizes the plight of reporters, editors, newscasters, and the press by the following means:

—Gathering data about arrested or imprisoned journalists

—Sending delegations of prominent journalists to countries where repression is rampant

—Publishing a newsletter that highlights recent cases

—Marshaling its forces to pressure governments to free jailed journalists and re-open banned media

—Alerting press and media in the U.S. and abroad to breaking events and trends, so the public can be informed

—Running seminars and forums for universities, journalism schools and groups of citizens.[31]

The Committee issues more than 100 formal protests to heads of state around the world annually; this averages out to approximately two protests each week. Copies of these protests are routinely sent to other pertinent officials of offending governments (including ministers of interior, justices, and ambassadors to the United States). It should be noted that the Committee investigates far more cases than those upon which it takes formal action. The CPJ believes that inquiries made to the State Department and to foreign governments' officials in Washington in the course of these investigations also have a positive effect in many cases of press abuse.

The CPJ's executive director, Barbara Koeppel, writes:

It is difficult to assess the specific number of cases CPJ has worked on that have resulted in positive outcomes. However, working either alone or in concert with other human rights and press organizations, the Committee's work has contributed to some important successes over the past year. Among them:

In Bangladesh, Sunil Kanti De, a reporter with the daily, Sangbad, imprisoned for nearly three years for his active investigating and reporting of army activities, was freed.

In Liberia, Willis Knuckles, a journalist with the Daily Observer and correspondent for the BBC, detained for two months for broadcasting a report of the government closure of his newspaper, was released. Just recently the Daily Observer was allowed to resume publication.

In Turkey, Ismet Imset, a UPI correspondent, has been harassed by police and threatened with arrest since March 1983 when he applied for a passport to attend a UPI workshop in London. Efforts by CPJ have certainly been effective in interesting American Embassy officials in his case. As a result, we believe, Turkish authorities have stopped short of arresting the journalist, and conditions have improved. As yet, however, authorities have refused to grant Imset a passport.

In Ghana, Thomas Quarshie Thompson, John Kugblenu and Mike Adjei, three journalists who worked for The Free Press, arrested apparently for publishing articles critical of the government, were released after being held for a year without charge or trial.

In South Africa, Sowetan reporter Joe Thloloe, who was sentenced to two and one-half years' imprisonment in April 1983 for possessing a banned book, was released.[32]

Figures given by the CPJ in April 1984, covering the period since January 1981, account for the following:

—76 journalists have died violently or disappeared

—194 journalists have been detained or jailed

—54 journalists are at this moment imprisoned in 16 countries

—33 journalists were forbidden to publish or were expelled from countries

—14 publications or media were permanently shut down

—48 issues of publications were confiscated.[33]

Barbara Koeppel comments:

Although other human rights and journalists' associations exist in the U.S. at the present time, there is none that is involved full-time in the activities undertaken by the CPJ. Moreover, we believe that, due to their prominence in the profession, U.S. journalists can have a major impact when they intervene around the world on their colleagues' behalf.[34]

## Summary

The international press associations cooperate with one another in the exchange of information and discussion of common goals, so duplication of effort is at a minimum. Put in medical terms, some press organizations practice "preventive medicine"—that is, education before repression; others "diagnose" cases and administer "treatment" by issuing formal protests to governments, alerting the public to violations of human rights, and providing legal counsel and advice; and still others supervise "intensive care," such as actions on behalf of prisoners of conscience.

Freedom House and Amnesty International cast the widest nets, monitoring human rights violations around the globe. Suppression of journalists and the news flow is simply one aspect of their multiple endeavors. Freedom House is an advocate for human rights at home and abroad; it directs its efforts through a number of programs. Its emphasis on press freedom goes hand-in-hand with other basic freedoms. Amnesty International's mandate is summed up as "the worldwide movement that works for the release of prisoners of conscience, fair trials for political prisoners, and an end to torture and executions." The large number of journalists and writers detained in recent years has caused AI to initiate its Urgent Action Network for prompt response on behalf of these men and women.

The Inter American Press Association, the International Press Institute, and the Committee to Protect Journalists have functions consistent with their nomenclature. *Index on Censorship* monitors the restriction of writers and journalists, particularly in European, African, and Eastern countries. The World Press Freedom Committee, in addition to administering its own global program of outreach to aid the press, is an active participant in international press meetings and coordinates many of their projects. The WPFC, like Freedom House, keeps close to UNESCO proceedings and the New World Information Order, with all their ramifications. The Reporters Committee for Freedom of the Press has the United States as its bailiwick—a jurisdiction of ever-increasing demands.

To U.S. journalists, the shield of the First Amendment should bring more appreciation than comfort. It should not act as protection against outrage at the assaults suffered by colleagues in other countries. A policeman's club cracks a skull in Chile with the same resonance as one wielded in Turkey or Africa. The closed door of censorship forbids dissemination of information and impoverishes growth of the intellect in India just as it does in Morocco or the kingdom of Thailand. The "disappearances" of working journalists in Latin America is as final as any in Europe or on the continent of Africa.

The challenge posed to international press organizations is not only to bring succor to the beleaguered media in foreign countries, but also to sound the alarm in U.S. newsrooms. Journalists working under the privilege of the First Amendment can keep that freedom only by battling for it on all fronts. Freedom of the press must fly its own flag, near and far.

# 8
# Irreplaceable Experiences

*Deac Rossell*

There is an essential conflict in discussing the roles of minorities in motion pictures, for the movies are a mass medium, by definition, and not, therefore, a vehicle for ethnic or ideological minorities. Most recent studies of ethnic minorities in American films, including those by Woll, Pettit, Cripps, Bogle, and others[1] have enlarged the general consciousness of the struggle of a variety of ethnic groups to overcome stereotyping in motion pictures and have recounted in detail the individual battles fought by performers, writers, directors, and pressure groups to achieve, as some were able to do in some circumstances, a respectably honest portrayal on the big screen. Other studies, including those of Smith, Richards, and Isaksson and Furhammar[2] have defined and analyzed Hollywood's treatment—or lack of same—of ideological minorities, which have been handled in remarkably similar ways to ethnic minorities. A minority group is a state of mind as much as it is a demographic or statistical fact, and undervalued in the literature on minorities in the American cinema is the industrial nature and purpose of the American moviemaking system itself.

From the period just after World War I, when the first generation of movie moguls began assembling the vertically integrated monopoly of production distribution, and exhibition that would collectively become known as Hollywood—in the process replacing the pioneering inventors of the cinema and the early generation of film artists who elaborated the vocabulary of pictorial storytelling, from Griffith to Stroheim to Tourneur—American movies have been a one-dimensional industry aimed overtly and specifically at reaching the largest possible numbers of people with a steady and unbroken supply of narrative films. Along with the rise of inexpensive daily newspapers, Hollywood's movies were the first mass medium of the twentieth century. Today, they remain a mass medium, notwithstanding the famous 1948 consent decree that broke up the ownership monopoly.[3] The oligopoly that is Hollywood has extended its penetration of visual culture by becoming the major supplier not only of movies but also of series programming for the now-universal new dissemination technology of television.

For the public at large, the monopoly/oligopoly of Hollywood has several important corollaries. First, until very recently, control of production meant control of the cameras, laboratories, lights, and devices of filmmaking. By maintaining control of the "secrets" of filmmaking, Hollywood promoted the idea that only this system knew how to produce a satisfying feature-length narrative film. Concomitantly, only technicians trained within this system and knowledgeable about it possessed the requisite skills to work on the highly "professional" plane demanded by the Hollywood system. Second, by implying that only this system could produce mass-audience or audience-satisfying films—an idea ruthlessly proselytized during the thirty-five years of monopoly control—the system virtually precluded the investment of private or institutional capital in feature films, except from time to time as the system itself accepted the necessity of outside investment. As a largely self-financed industry, Hollywood effectively precluded the potential incorporation of outside ideas of what an audience-satisfying film might be. Third, monopoly over distribution carried with it a monopoly of access to newspapers and the information media for the promotion, selling, and public relations of narrative films. The professional career of nearly every magazine or newspaper editor or writer is lived within an information tradition and an actively manipulated mythological context invented and controlled by Hollywood. Fourth, monopoly over exhibition, particularly given the vigorous movie-going habit of the mass public from 1920 through the 1950s—which remains vestigially in a smaller audience (though a larger audience is connected through television)—extended the dominance of Hollywood dramatic and stylistic precepts to the audience at large. Hollywood produced a closed, self-referential system; the phrase "going to the movies" came to mean going to one kind of movie.

At the other end of the spectrum, the movie colony itself was, and is, a tightly knit, homogeneous community, with few links to the heterogeneity and diversity of American culture as a whole. When anthropologist Hortense Powdermaker went to Hollywood to conduct a professional study of its inhabitants, she conceded that it was a part of the United States but contended, with good reason, that "Hollywood is no mirrorlike reflection of our society, which is characterized by a large number of conflicting patterns of behavior and values. Hollywood has emphasized some, to the exclusion of others."[4] Recounting that Hollywood has often been described as a state of mind, existing wherever people connected with the movies live and work, Powdermaker found:

> For the most part, people work, eat, talk and play only with others who are likewise engaged in making movies. . . .Hollywood was like a "sealed chamber" and one gradually accepted its standards and values, forgetting about others. . . .The producers and executives seem somewhat unbusinesslike in not recognizing the true nature of their medium and exploiting it to the utmost. To be sure, they employ artists and pay them high salaries, but instead of permitting them to function as such, they insist that the work be done according to the businessman's formula.[5]

In 1981, writer-director John Sayles (*The Return of the Secaucus Seven, The Howling*) described the Hollywood system in much the same terminology:

> Some movies just won't survive the studio system. I meet very good people who work in movie studios. Their problem is that they are not independent opera-tors. One of twenty pictures, one of thirty, gets made. There is a whole system of cut-off deals, approval in stages, from idea to treatment to first draft, through more drafts, final draft, production approval, etc. Any idea that starts through this system may not happen. The studios work by committee; in some ways this is because of the huge amounts of cash involved. It's very much like getting a bill through Congress. You start off with something that is needed, and then during the process of reviewing the bill, you have to say "I'll do this and this and this" to protect your constituency, and yours, and yours, for various special interest groups. Then as the bill comes up for a vote, riders are attached to the bill giving more limitations and making more exceptions. At the end the bill is so watered down that what comes out the other end of the process is the opposite of what you started with. It's just the opposite. And the same thing happens to movies.[6]

On its own terms, Hollywood has always felt it had good and sufficient rea-sons for how minority groups and minority views appeared in the movies. If Lena Horne never got a real acting role but was always to be found leaning against a column draped in a long gown for a single musical number, it was so that exhib-itors in the South could easily cut her role from prints of the film and not offend their white patrons. The feeble beginnings of a responsibly ethnic Hollywood cinema came out of the experiences of the U.S. Army in World War II, when troops of varying ethnic backgrounds relied on each other in life-and-death situ-ations. The war movies began to use ethnic characters in a carefully balanced blend that reflected the diverse populations of the military services: the platoon in Howard Hawks's *Air Force* (1943) is made up of men named Weinberg, Cal-lahan, McMartin, Peterson, and Winocki; for Raoul Walsh's *Objective Burma*, Errol Flynn is assisted by Jacobs, Miggleori, Brophy, Negulesco, and "Ne-braska"; for *Action in the North Atlantic*, directed by Lloyd Bacon, Humphrey Bogart (as Joe Rossi) is supported by characters named Abrams, O'Hara, and Pulaski.

The inbred distance of the moviemaking system from real-world struggles can be seen by an analysis of the 1981 film *Borderline*, directed by Jerrold Freed-man and starring Charles Bronson. Made for Lord Lew Grade's international conglomerate, *Borderline* is one of a flock of several recent pictures to take up the subject of illegal immigration across the U.S. border with Mexico. In Holly-wood terms, it is by all means a "small" picture, budgeted at about $8 million and dealing with an important social subject. In the role of a Border Patrol sta-tion chief, Bronson investigates a highly organized and well-financed gang importing farmworkers across the border. The gang, led by an important produce grower with powerful political connections, distributes its human cargo across the entire country, where the virtually helpless Mexicans are delivered into a modern form of slavery. However, the focus of the film is not on the Mexicans but on the chase: the clues leading up to the proof against the gang, the technology used to gather the evidence, and finally the extended suspense of the gang's capture at the film's climax.

In essence, the construction of this film is precisely the same as that of any big-caper suspense film, except that Mexican farmworkers substitute for the jewels or paintings or gold bullion that is the usual object of the gang of crooks. During the film, Bronson and his widowed girlfriend talk a lot about the plight of the illegal farmworkers and their exploitation. And the gang brags about filling orders for a thousand bodies a month in Chicago, Boston, and Philadelphia, while delivering 4,690 "units" in California's Imperial Valley. At the end, we find out that the Border Patrol arrested 1,069,400 illegal Mexicans in 1979 alone, an estimated one-fifth of those who cross the border annually.

But there are barely any Mexicans shown in the film. In the opening sequence, one group of illegals scurries through a wire fence and in short order is packed away in the back of a fruit truck. Later, Bronson visits a farmworkers' encampment, silent and sullen at his appearance, and the camera pans across a picturesque row of weathered, leathery faces reminiscent of Dorothea Lange's Depression photographs—a beautifully picturesque gallery of portraits. The movie shows the hovels provided for living and emphasizes the violent ruthlessness of the foremen, along with the callous indifference of the boss, but it never comes close to the Mexican workers. All sense of dignity and character is channeled into the immense presence of Bronson, bucking the system to bring down the boss, speaking out of his own sense of justice about the exploitation of the workers. The audience's emotions are channeled toward applauding Bronson's heroism and tenacity, not toward sympathy with the chattel he frees or toward the overall situation the movie describes in such satistical exuberance. The film is a classic struggle between evil criminals and dogged, triumphant forces of law and order, personified by Bronson. The farmworkers are incidental. They could just as easily have been Portuguese from the Azores working in Cambridge, or Puerto Ricans in the garment industry in New York—or a bundle of jewels, a stack of bullion.

Yet without overstating the case, it is most likely that everyone involved in making this minor film was quite proud of the association. The film dealt with an important social subject. Bronson's role gave him a chance to shift slightly away from his usual superviolent, macho image. He expresses a concern for other people in the movie, if only verbally and without interacting with them. He shed a bit of Herculean ruggedness to expose a more intimate, vulnerable persona. In star terms, it is the kind of shift that John Wayne tried in *McQ* and Clint Eastwood in *Bronco Billy*. So the risks undoubtedly seemed great: a contemporary social problem, a risk of the carefully developed star personality. But the insurance was also great: exploited Mexicans so hesitantly brought to the screen as to be almost invisible to the mass audience, a major star who is the center of all emotional attention, a cops-and-robbers plot outfitted with high technology and high suspense.

When films are made inside the Hollywood system, especially if any minority issue is present, the insurance is always high. Paul Muni plays Juarez and Henry Fonda plays the whiskey priest in *The Fugitive*. If Stanley Kramer's finely cast *Guess Who's Coming To Dinner?* carried a theme of interracial message out to a broad public, Sidney Poitier's role as the smarter, cleaner, politer, wittier groom made the film classically unrealistic. The only Hollywood film about Vietnam made during the war, *The Green Berets*, was fully structured as a typical World War II action picture, with planned engagements fought for specific territory; this provided secure insurance for the producers, albeit giving a wholly inaccurate image of the ongoing, amorphous conflict.

An American film released at the same time as *Borderline*, although not made in Hollywood, provides a clear contrast in the handling of minority subjects. Robert M. Young's *Alambrista!* also depicts the situation of Mexicans illegally crossing the U.S. border in the Southwest. The film opens in Mexico, where a young man is about to follow his father to America; the family has not heard from the father in two years, and everyone is nervous about the fate that may await the young man who is now the *de facto* head of the household. After a series of harrowing adventures crossing the border, the new immigrant, friendless and unable to speak English, is herded from farm to farm by an unending succession of fast-talking foremen who buy and sell his daily work at prices far beyond those he will ever receive. He has little or no idea of where he is as he works across the strawberry fields and grape arbors of the Southwest, and the audience is kept equally uninformed, adding to the sympathetic tensions of the film. The hot landscape of his long trudge across the border and the grimy trucks in which he is packed for nocturnal shipment from farm to farm are both captured with compelling realism. The film never loses its emotional contact with the fright and loneliness of a young boy in a foreign land, as it keeps in the foreground a sense of the personal and individual tragedy of a blasé traffic in lives.

*Alambrista!* is a film that could only have been made outside Hollywood, for it contains no major stars, follows no predetermined genre patterns, and carries no heavy insurance to ensure snagging a substantial portion of the identifiable movie-going market. It is a film made out of the commitment of the director and his backers, the same commitment that sent Robert M. Young and Michael Roemer to the South in 1963 to independently make *Nothing But a Man*, one of the very few honest portrayals of a southern black family on film. Both pictures were minority films because they fully expressed a minority viewpoint, not needing to purvey a mass-public conception of a minority.

The distinction is significant. One of the legacies of the long reign of the monopoly/oligopoly system has been that no secondary system or channel for the dissemination of motion pictures has appeared in the United States until recently. In every other major filmmaking country—including France, Germany, Italy, Brazil, India, and Japan, to name but a few—there have always been double-level movie production systems. One level provides the constant stream of mass-public "entertainment" or "commercial" films, which seem to be a necessary industrial component of a flourishing cinema industry; the other level provides, in some cases erratically and spordically, the "artistic" or minority point-of-view productions. Called variously a "parallel cinema," "art cinema," "second cinema," or even "minority cinema," this cultural phenomenon is the source from which most of the foreign films seen in America are drawn. It is this level of production that produced Luis Buñuel's *L'Age d'Or;* the Jean Renoir films of the 1930s, including *Boudu Saved from Drowning* and *Toni;* the Brazilian political and multiethnic films of Carlos Diegues and Glauber Rocha; the humanist films of Satyajit Ray; and many others.

It is this "second cinema" that provided the potential for expressing minority views, whether ethnic, ideological, or artistic. Until approximately the mid-1970s, it was an alternative that did not exist in America. Hollywood had been so successful in creating a product for a mass audience that although isolated independent narrative films had occasionally been produced (at great effort) by passionate individuals or groups, there was never enough independent activity to establish anything resembling an alternative to the oligopoly.

Until now. At their sixth annual market in 1984, organized to allow foreign buyers access to the growing span of independently made feature films, the Independent Feature Project in New York offered a selection of 110 titles in scheduled screenings. In 1983, at the fifth market, there were 84 films. More important, the backup business and industrial systems that can support this independent flowering of cinematic diversity are beginning to fall into place. Apart from the Independent Feature Project, itself a filmmaker-founded center for technical information and assistance, and First Run Features, a distributor for many of the pioneering works of this new American film movement, other new distributors like Cinecom and Pickman Films, along with specialized foreign film distributors like Almi and Kino International, are active in acquiring films from this new American source. Agents like Affinity Enterprises and others have sprung up quickly to service the important foreign markets for the films. Slowly, a support system that is open to diversity, encourages the minority view, and fiercely defends its independence is growing around the filmmakers themselves.

And what kinds of films are coming from the independents?

*Northern Lights,* by Rob Neilsen and John Hansen, the story of a movement to begin a farmer's union in North Dakota in 1910.

*Killer of Sheep,* Charles Burnett's uncompromising yet warm look at ghetto life in the Watts section of Los Angeles.

*Chan Is Missing*, by Wayne Wang, a suspenseful and energetic look at friendship in the Chinese community in San Francisco.

*Gal Young 'Un*, a period film set in the Florida interior, made by Victor Nuñez.

*Best Boy*, Ira Wohl's documentary about the future security of his 54-year-old autistic uncle.

Among the many other films coming out of this vital new segment of American filmmaking are Robert M. Young's aforementioned *Alambrista!*, and *The Return of Gregorio Cortez*, John Sayles's tale of a group of aging 1960s radicals, *The Return of the Secaucus Seven*, *The Killing Floor*, *Smithereens*, *Testament*, and *Tuck Everlasting*. Characteristic of these titles is the regional quality of the films: they are dramas that speak in the quiet dignity of the Florida interior, in the incessant chatter of the intellectual East, in the energetic rhythms of the New York City streets, and in the stunted hesitations of the physically handicapped. Each and every one is made by a minority and/or from a minority viewpoint. Without exception, they present their people and their human interactions within an honest and appropriate context: the dramatic form of the film is dictated by the needs of the characters and the setting, not by the magnetism of the mass-public marketplace. None of them went through the system.

One film that did go through the system is Laurence Kasdon's major production *The Big Chill*, which bears an uncanny resemblance to Sayles's *Secaucus Seven* in its theme and characters. Both films are about the midlife crises facing an assorted group of former members of the alternative culture of the 1960s. But the two films deliver very different impressions. *The Big Chill* has moments of great exuberance for its audience while in the theater—especially in the kitchen dishwashing scene, which turns into an at-home disco dance, wonderfully choreographed. There are no such scenes in *Secaucus Seven;* Sayles's one attempt to lift the film above the incisive dialogue of his characters, in a pick-up basketball game in town, does not work. On the other hand, Sayles's characters come to life with a strength and involvement that is missing from the quick repartee of the players in Kasdon's movie. While you are in the theater, *The Big Chill* makes a bigger impression. It does what system movies have always been able to do best—create a momentary illusion of substance, two hours of emotional catharsis, and a sense of being in the midst, however briefly, of people with strong commitments who are actively solving their problems. *Secaucus Seven* works very differently. It starts very slowly and, in fact, hesitantly. But by midfilm both the characters and the unforced style of the film begin to work. There are few high points, rarely a striking quote. But the honest core of the film is insidious, by the end compelling. And six months later, it is *Secaucus Seven* that remains in the memory, that has been incorporated into the permanent cultural/literary files, while it only takes six weeks for *The Big Chill* to be replaced by the next new film experience.

What a true minority film presents is an irreplaceable experience—created and produced by the vision of a single artist reaching through his or her passions to bring vicariously to an audience the texture, rhythm, and drama of a particular place, particular people, a particular event. It stands alone, unvarnished and unsupported by the hidden helpers of the Hollywood system, with its technicians, its leveling committee decisions, and its long development of the audience's own expectations. If it is a minority film that reaches you, it will reach into your heart and mind with uncommon boldness. It may not be the film that all your neighbors are talking about, but it will be the one you will always remember.

# 9

# Cameras in the Courtroom: Education or Entertainment?

*T. Barton Carter*

> But she wasn't alive when Frank Wilson got there, was she? She wasn't alive because you killed her. The thought of her leaving you was just too much to bear. So you picked up the poker and you killed her. Admit it, Mr. Johnson. You killed her.
>
> Yes, yes. I killed her. I loved her, but she didn't care. She just stood there and laughed at me. To her I was nothing. . . .
>
> Typical TV drama dialogue of fictional lawyers.

For many years, this was the typical picture of the courts broadcast by U.S. television stations. Dramatic network series such as "Perry Mason," "Judd for the Defense," and "The Defenders" portrayed courtrooms as seething caldrons of emotion, full of constant drama. Of course, television portrayed everything from operating rooms to boardrooms in this manner.

What made courtrooms different was that for many years, cameras were banned from most courtrooms in this country. Thus, the general public was captivated by the fictional depictions of the bench and bar. Anyone who wanted to know what actually occurred in a real-life courtroom had to depend on written descriptions, ranging from civics texts to newspaper accounts, or was obligated to attend a trial in person.

Recently, this has all changed. Many states have new laws allowing cameras in the courtroom, and it is possible to see portions of or even complete trials in the comfort of your own living room. This new freedom has certainly introduced some dramatic moments to television. More than 200 million viewers saw *Florida v. Zamora*, the trial of Ronny Zamora, a teenager accused of murder whose defense, ironically, was that his actions were the result of watching too much violence on television.[1] In 1983, viewers in Massachusetts were able to watch policemen from a Boston suburb as a jury found them guilty of assault and battery charges in *Commonwealth v. McCluskey et al.*[2] More recently, the cases of *Commonwealth v. Corderio et al.* and *Commonwealth v. Silvia et al.* showed six men from New Bedford, Massachusetts, being tried on charges of gang-raping a woman in a pool hall.[3] The cases were more popularly known as the "Big Dan's" rape trial.

Nevertheless, the opportunity to televise legal proceedings is very controversial. While some argue that it gives the public a chance to see what really happens in the courtroom, others maintain that the coverage presented is at least as distorted as the fictional dramas. As is usually the case in such controversies, the truth lies somewhere in between.

The ban on cameras in the courtroom can be traced almost directly to the kidnapping and murder of Charles Lindbergh's son in March 1932. The trial of Bruno Hauptmann, the man accused of the crime, has come to be a symbol of press misconduct in trial coverage.[4] Among the counters to responsible jurisprudence: a newsreel camera was run without the judge's knowledge or permission; unauthorized still pictures were taken; and throughout the proceeding, rumors were printed that distorted and sensationalized the trial. Overshadowing all of this was the sheer volume of the press coverage. The number of reporters covering the case and the space devoted to it by the media created the impression that the trial was no longer a legal proceeding but, rather, a public circus.[5]

Despite the fact that the photographers and newsreel crews were only one small component of the press coverage in that case, subsequent outrage seemed to focus on them. In 1937, the American Bar Association adopted Canon 35 of its Canons of Judicial Ethics:

> Proceedings in court should be conducted with fitting dignity and decorum. The taking of photographs in the courtroom, during sessions of the court or recesses between sessions, and the broadcasting of court proceedings, degrade the court and create misconceptions with respect thereto in the mind of the public and should not be permitted.[6]

In 1963, Canon 35 was amended to include a prohibition against television cameras. In 1972, the Canons of Judicial Ethics were replaced by the Code of Judicial Conduct, but the substance of Canon 35 was retained in a new Canon 3A(7).[7]

The Canons of Judicial Ethics were not binding on the courts, but many states did pass laws embodying the substance of Canon 35; others, including Texas, did not and continued to allow at least some camera coverage of legal proceedings. This practice was challenged in several cases, finally reaching the Supreme Court of the United States in *Estes v. State of Texas*.[8]

Billy Sol Estes had been tried for and convicted of embezzlement, fraud, and theft. Despite his objections, the court had allowed selected television camera coverage of both the pretrial hearing and the trial:

> Indeed, at least 12 camera men were engaged in the courtroom throughout the hearing taking motion and still pictures and televising the proceedings. Cables and wires were snaked across the courtroom floor, three microphones were on the judge's bench and others were beamed at the jury box and the counsel table. It is conceded that the activities of the television crews and news photographers led to considerable disruption of the hearings.[9]

Estes appealed his conviction on the grounds that televising the trial had deprived him of his rights to due process of law.

By the narrowest of margins, 5–4, the Supreme Court agreed with Estes. Justice Clark, who wrote the opinion of the Court, focused on several aspects of television coverage. His first concern was the impact that coverage would have on the jury. Clark felt that jurors who knew that their neighbors would be watching them on television would be more likely to be swayed by public opinion regarding the guilt of the accused. Further, jurors would be able to watch selected portions of the trial, complete with broadcasters' commentaries, unless special precautions were taken to prevent it. This could serve to prejudice the jurors.

Justice Clark was also concerned with the possibility that a mistrial or successful appeal would necessitate a new trial. At this point, the vast majority of potential jurors would have already been exposed to portions of the original trial.

Television's impact on jurors was not the only question:

> The impact upon a witness of the knowledge that he is being viewed by a vast audience is simply incalculable. Some may be demoralized and frightened, some cocky and given to overstatement; memories may falter, as with anyone speaking publicly, and accuracy of statement may be severely undermined.[10]

Justice Clark also worried about the reaction of judges to television coverage. He believed that both the presence of cameras and the necessity of monitoring their effect on a trial would distract the judge from his primary task—ensuring a fair trial for the defendant. This would especially be a problem in states where judges are elected.[11]

Justice Clark's final concern was the impact on the defendant:

> [Television's] presence is a form of mental—if not physical—harassment, resembling a police line-up or a third degree. The inevitable close-ups of his gestures and expressions during the ordeal of his trial might well transgress his personal sensibilities, his dignity, and his ability to concentrate on the proceedings before him—sometimes the difference between life and death—dispassionately, freely and without the distraction of wide public surveillance.[12]

If the other four justices who agreed with Justice Clark's decision had also agreed with his reasoning, that might well have been the end of cameras in the courtroom. However, Justice Harlan, in his opinion, left the door open for further experiments:

> The day may come, when television will have become so commonplace an affair in the daily life of the average person as to dissipate all reasonable likelihood that its use in courtrooms may disparage the judicial process.[13]

Perhaps relying on Justice Harlan's opinion, a few states continued to experiment with cameras in the courtroom. As television technology improved, the number of states allowing cameras in the courtroom grew. In 1977, Florida joined the ranks of these states, and it was the Florida program that led the Supreme Court to reexamine its position on this issue.

The case, *Chandler v. Florida*,[14] involved two Miami policemen who were convicted of burglary. They appealed their convictions on the grounds that the televising of selected portions of their trial deprived them of the right to a fair trial. Their position was that the decision in *Estes* banned such coverage.

The Supreme Court, in an opinion authored by Chief Justice Burger, disagreed. Noting that improved technology had eliminated the need for the bright lights and heavy cables that had been present in the *Estes* case, and that Florida had safeguards built into its program to protect those witnesses who might be especially sensitive to the presence of cameras, they upheld the convictions.[15]

Despite the jubilation of some members of the press, the decision was not a complete victory for cameras in the courtroom. What the Court said was that states had a *right* to allow cameras in the courtroom. It did not say that they were *required* to allow them in. Although the majority of states now allow cameras to enter courtrooms under at least some circumstances, some do not. Meanwhile, cameras are not allowed in any federal court under any circumstance.

Why is there still such strong resistance to permitting cameras to be present in courtrooms? As Chief Justice Burger pointed out in *Chandler*, improved television technology has eliminated many of the early problems. Indeed, based on surveys conducted during the initial Florida experiments with television coverage, the Florida Supreme Court concluded:

> Physical disturbance was so minimal as not to be an arguable factor. Technological advancements have so reduced size, noise, and light levels of the electronic equipment available that cameras can be employed in courtrooms unobtrusively.
>
> A related issue is whether the very presence of electronic media in the courtroom detracts from the decorum of the proceeding. The attitudes of all participants surveyed clearly indicate that there is no such discernible effect.[16]

Given this new unobtrusiveness, what are the current arguments against allowing cameras in the courtroom? Many are similar to those voiced by Justice Clark twenty years ago. Opponents of cameras in the courtroom still believe that jurors will be intimidated and prejudiced, that trial participants will act differently in front of a camera, and that defendants will be subject to greater harassment and intimidation by the media. Other concerns are that broadcasters will cover only cases involving sex or violence and that coverage will sensationalize certain trials, turning them into media events.

To what extent are these fears justified? Although little research has been done in this area, the findings of one study are indeed interesting. This study, conducted by Professor Dalton Lancaster, compared two separate trials for the same crime: the murder by the two defendants of a wealthy, eccentric woman (just the type of trial that camera opponents claim would be sensationalized by broadcasters). One of the trials was televised; the other was not.[17]

Professor Lancaster's study produced several pertinent findings. One was that television coverage of the two trials did not differ significantly in terms of the time devoted to it.[18] Banning cameras only reduces visual coverage; it in no way prohibits reporters—print or broadcast—from covering trials. Their stories can be just as long, just as detailed. Although television is indeed a visual medium, sketches and footage shot outside the courtroom—beyond the reach of the ban—usually suffice.

This, in fact, illustrates the biggest problem—other than lack of research—in resolving the controversy over cameras in the courtroom. Any negative effect of press coverage ends up being blamed on the presence of television coverage. This was true in the *Hauptmann* case, and it is true today. If there are 200 reporters and one television camera present, all complaints will center on the one camera. A perfect illustration of this was a special edition of ABC's "Nightline," devoted to the issue of cameras in the courtroom. In support of her argument against permitting cameras in the courtroom, one of the panelists, Ginny Foat, claimed that she was denied bail while awaiting trial on homicide charges (she was later found not guilty) because the judge was intimidated by the "hundreds of reporters and cameras." In response to a question from Ted Koppel, she clarified the situation: there were many reporters and "a camera."[19]

Indeed, the press is quite capable of sensationalizing stories and turning them into media events, even when cameras are not allowed in the courtroom. While cameras are more likely to be used in cases involving sex, violence, public figures, or the media, those same cases are also more likely to make the front pages of newspapers. Recently, a federal judge refused to allow cameras to be present during General Westmoreland's libel suit against CBS.[20] (General Westmoreland alleged that the 1982 CBS documentary, "The Uncounted Enemy: A Vietnam Deception," libeled him, and he sued for $120 million.) This has not prevented extensive print and broadcast coverage of the case.

The *Westmoreland* case illustrates another basic fallacy in the idea that cameras are predominantly responsible for sensationalizing trials. Cameras cannot be present at a trial until it starts. This seems obvious, but the point is that coverage of a trial starts much earlier. In a criminal case, press coverage starts as soon as the crime is discovered. By the time the actual trial starts, much more coverage has taken place than is likely to occur during the trial. The status of the trial as a media event has long since been established.

Similarly, distortion is not just a cameras-in-the-courtroom issue. In *Estes*, Justice Clark was concerned that jurors would be able to watch selected portions of the trial, accompanied by broadcasters' commentaries. But how does this differ from reading a newspaper account of the trial summarizing the highlights of the previous day's testimony and commenting on it? In either case, the juror will be exposed to someone else's opinion of what the important testimony was and why. Furthermore, keeping the camera out of the courtroom will not prevent the broadcaster from recounting testimony and commenting on it.

A very famous—or infamous—example of this was the 1954 Dr. Sam Sheppard case. In *State v. Sheppard*,[21] Dr. Sheppard was accused of murdering his wealthy, socialite wife. He claimed that an unidentified intruder had committed the crime. His original conviction was eventually overturned by the Supreme Court of the United States as a direct result of the press conduct before and during the trial. In his opinion, Justice Clark recounted some the more egregious examples of that conduct:

> Much of the material printed or broadcast during the trial was never heard from the witness stand, such as the charges that Sheppard had purposely impeded the murder investigation and must be guilty since he hired a prominent criminal lawyer; that Sheppard was a perjurer; that he had sexual relations with numerous women; that his slain wife had characterized him as a "Jekyll-Hyde"; that he was a "bare-faced liar" because of his testimony as to police treatment; and, finally, that a woman convict claimed Sheppard to be the father of her illegitimate child. As the trial progressed, the newspapers summarized and interpreted the evidence, devoting particular attention to the material that incriminated Sheppard, and often drew unwarranted inferences from testimony. At one point, a front-page picture of Mrs. Sheppard's blood-stained pillow was published after being "doctored" to show more clearly an alleged imprint of a surgical instrument.[22]

Believe it or not, these are only a few examples of what went on before and during the trial. While this was an extreme case, it does illustrate how distortion and sensationalism cannot be prevented by banning cameras from the courtroom and how responsible press coverage is a separate and distinct issue.

Why, then, is it so difficult to separate the question of television coverage from the more general issue of press responsibility? The answer lies in the public's perception of television as an entertainment medium. Even though the majority of people in this country depend on television as their primary source of news, it is still viewed as less serious than newspapers. This perception carries all the way to the Supreme Court, where Chief Justice Warren Burger has stated on more than one occasion that cameras will not be allowed in the Supreme Court as long as he has any say in the matter.

Is the perception accurate? Will television turn trials into the modern-day equivalent of the Roman Circus? Are broadcast journalists less responsible than print journalists? As the Hauptmann and Sheppard trials illustrate, the answer to these questions is *no*. The limited evidence available suggests that, given the opportunity, broadcast journalists prove just as responsible as others. The Florida Supreme Court cited with approval the conduct of the television stations during the Florida television coverage experiment.[23]

Advocates of allowing cameras in the courtroom go even further and argue that the use of cameras will reduce distortion. Which, they ask, is more accurate—a picture of a witness giving testimony or a description of how he or she appeared? Isn't it better for viewers to draw their own conclusions about how nervous, evasive, uncomfortable, or credible the witness seemed than merely to be given a journalist's conclusion on that subject?

What about Justice Clark's other concerns? Does the presence of cameras cause witnesses, judges, attorneys, and jurors to behave differently than they would in their absence? Can cameras affect the outcome of a trial? If so, this is a powerful argument for their exclusion.

Certainly, Justice Clark was correct in suggesting that, for most people, appearing on camera is a new experience. Of course, for most witnesses and jurors, just entering a courtroom is a new experience. Very few have any idea what to expect, since they have never observed a trial, much less participated in one. What expectations they have are most likely to be based on "Perry Mason" or other television shows. If cameras were allowed in courtrooms more often, people would have more accurate expectations.

As it is, many witnesses and jurors are very nervous, regardless of whether cameras are present. For witnesses, there is the knowledge that, because of the adversarial nature of our system, one of the attorneys present is going to do everything possible to discredit their testimony. For jurors, there is the knowledge that, ultimately, the fate of the parties will rest in their hands.

Logic dictates that the greater the importance of the trial, the greater the pressure on the participants. Press coverage certainly exacerbates this pressure, just as packed courtrooms do. In 1982, when Claus von Bulow was tried for attempting to murder his wealthy, socialite wife in *State v. von Bulow*,[24] there were long lines of people trying to gain admittance to the trial. Certainly, this had to increase the anxiety of the jurors and witnesses. In the context of all these other factors, can the presence of a camera really have that much effect?

Again, because of a lack of research on the subject, there is no clear answer. However, Professor Lancaster's study does provide one interesting note. Surveys of the jurors indicated that it was the presence of the television reporters, not the cameras, that caught the attention of trial participants and signaled to them that they were involved in an "important" trial.[25] This suggests that the effect of the cameras themselves has been overemphasized and that banning them does little to improve witness or juror performance.

Admittedly, trials are not a new experience for most attorneys and judges. But cameras don't have to be either. The only reason they are now is that they have been banned in most courts. To argue that they must continue to be banned because people aren't used to them begs the question. The transition might be difficult, but not impossible.

Another allegation is that judges and attorneys will "perform" differently in front of television cameras. One judge recently suggested that attorneys will start leaping over tables while on camera.[26] The assumption seems to be that everybody on television is an actor and that putting attorneys on television will turn them into actors also. In truth, any good trial attorney is an actor, and his or her audience consists of the judge and jury. Since this is the audience that decides the fate of the attorney's client, it would prove foolhardy to ignore them for the sake of a television audience.

The one situation in which that might be a serious temptation would be when a judge or attorney is running for an elected office. Under those circumstances, the television audience might be considered more important, with the client's fate being sacrificed to political ambition. But if an attorney or even a judge is likely to be diverted in this fashion, then it is logical to assume that he or she will perform his or her duties with an eye to the election, even in the absence of cameras. The press will still be there to report on the events of the trial, including the actions of all participants. In the *Sheppard* case, Justice Clark noted pointedly that "the trial began two weeks before a hotly contested election at which both Chief Prosecutor Mahon and Judge Blythin were candidates for judgeships."[27]

Yet even if the risks of allowing cameras in the courtroom are both overstated and highly speculative, there is no reason to take such risks unless there are substantial benefits to be gained. Do cameras in the courtroom really aid the flow of information to the public? If so, what value does this information have?

It should be clear that they can be used to increase the flow of information. Even a complete transcript fails to communicate many details about a legal proceeding. The witnesses' tone of voice, their facial expressions, and their delivery are all items of valuable information that can best be conveyed through television.

Such information has great educational potential. Videotapes of trials can be used to educate law students or to improve the skills of lawyers. For example, the Practicing Law Institute has used videotapes of the Carol Burnett libel suit against the *National Enquirer*[28] to produce an instructional program on libel.[29] (Ms. Burnett sued the *National Enquirer* for a story that claimed she caused a drunken scene in a restaurant. The jury awarded her almost $2 million in damages, although a California Appeals Court later reduced the award.)

More important, however, is the educational value to the general public. No longer would they have to rely on secondhand accounts of trials for their information. Instead, they would have the opportunity to see for themselves. Similarly, their knowledge of our legal system could be drawn from real as opposed to fictional examples.

The educational potential is supported by Professor Lancaster's study. His surveys showed that the public claimed to learn more about the criminal justice system and the trial when televised coverage was permitted. At the same time, the majority of those surveyed did not believe that allowing cameras in the courtroom would jeopardize the defendant's right to a fair trial.

However, further research is necessary. In the meantime, both judges and legislators are being forced to make decisions based on unsupported assertions and gut feelings. This explains why there is little or no consistency in these decisions.

Perhaps the best way to illuminate the issues is to examine a specific case. The "Big Dan's" rape trial (*Commonwealth v. Corderio et al.*) is probably the most notorious trial of the last few years.[30] It attracted nationwide media coverage, and most of the trial was televised live by the Cable News Network (CNN). Controversy over the media coverage was itself a national story. Furthermore, as a rape case, it raised especially sensitive issues regarding the presence of cameras in the courtroom.

The case began when a young woman alleged that she had been raped by several men on the pool table of Big Dan's, a New Bedford, Massachusetts, bar. Her further claim that, during the rape, other patrons of the bar stood around and cheered the rapists on attracted immediate national attention.

Gang rapes always draw media attention. The suggestion that the bystanders not only refused to assist the woman but actively encouraged the rapists could only make the case more newsworthy. An additional controversy emerged when it was revealed that all of the defendants charged in the case were of Portuguese descent. Some members of the large Portuguese community in New Bedford claimed that prejudice against the Portuguese community was behind the charges and that, as a result, the defendants would be unable to get a fair trial.

Quickly, the case became a symbol for various groups. Some women's groups felt that acquittals in the case would encourage further violence against women. Meanwhile, some members of the Portuguese community felt that convictions would perpetuate prejudice against them. Both sides held demonstrations and marches. Every development received extensive media attention.

Against this backdrop of intense media scrutiny, Judge William Young decided to allow both photographic and broadcast coverage of the trials. (There were actually two separate trials, one for four of the defendants and one for the remaining two. To minimize the risk of one case influencing the other, Judge Young ran the two trials concurrently, one in the morning and one in the afternoon.) He did, however, set up certain limitations, the most important of which was the banning of photographs of the alleged victim. Judge Young also retained complete discretion as to when the camera would be turned on or off. Many people immediately protested Judge Young's decision, while others applauded it.

In addition to the usual concerns about television coverage, several special issues were raised. The additional trauma that televising the trial would cause the alleged victim was of great concern. So was the possible effect on other rape victims. It was obvious from pretrial statements that a major defense tactic was going to be to put the victim herself on trial. Claiming that she was a willing participant in whatever took place, the defense was going to make her character and morals a central issue in the case. Many feared that seeing on television what she would be put through would discourage other rape victims from testifying, thus making it even more difficult to convict rapists in other cases.

In response, others argued that only by televising the trial could the public learn to appreciate what a rape victim is subjected to. This, in turn, might change public attitudes toward rape and toward laws that allow this tactic of putting the victim on trial. It would also prepare other rape victims for what they might face. Some went so far as to argue that concealing the alleged victim's identity was partially responsible for the negative societal attitude toward rape victims. Citing a recent study conducted in California, they contended that concealing the name contributes to the idea that there is a stigma attached to having been raped.[31]

One of the controversies surrounding the trial was a direct result of this continuous, live coverage. There had been an agreement among the trial participants not to call the alleged victim by name, so as not to have her identified to the radio and television audiences (remember, no pictures of her were allowed). This worked well until one of the attorneys slipped and addressed her by name. Since the CNN coverage was live, everybody who was watching heard it.

Here was a case of one of television's biggest advantages, its immediacy, being turned against it. And yet, while it aroused great controversy at the time, it is not very relevant to the basic issue. In the first place, a small tape delay, 5 to 10 seconds, could be instituted in any trial broadcast. If something unexpected were to occur, the telecast could be stopped before the audience saw what happened.

Second, it was not the law that prohibited the press from disclosing the alleged victim's identity. The Supreme Court has clearly stated, in a case involving a rape victim's identity, that the court cannot prohibit the press from publishing anything that is part of the public record.[32] Instead, most news media withheld her name of their own volition. As Phil Balboni, news director of WCVB-TV in Boston, observed: "For a rape, the woman is an innocent victim, and we have to assume the woman in the New Bedford case is an innocent victim unless proven otherwise. The *responsible* thing is to withhold the name." (emphasis added).[33]

Again, the issue seems to be one of responsible press behavior, not of whether to allow cameras in the courtroom. If the press wants to conceal the victim's identity, allowing cameras inside won't prevent them from doing so. Conversely, if the press wants to disclose her identity, banning the cameras won't stop them. Of course, as previously noted, there is some question regarding what constitutes responsible press behavior in this situation, but it is still an entirely separate issue from the cameras question.

As the trial progressed, there was an unusual level of interest in the coverage. While it may not have been surprising for a local radio station to find sufficient demand to run live coverage of the entire trial, it certainly was unexpected that Cable News Network would find the same level of demand across the country. Although CNN originally intended only to offer brief excerpts of the trial, it ended up televising everything.

Some cited this as evidence of the need to ban cameras from the courtroom.

They saw it as pandering to the morbid curiosity of the masses at the expense of the participants in this trial. Certainly, there was an element of sensationalism, but the issue is much more complex. In the first place, this was a media event long before the trial even started. The nature of the crime, as well as the degree to which the community became involved in the case, guaranteed widespread media attention.

Also, the novelty of this television coverage accounted for much of the interest. How many viewers had ever witnessed a real as opposed to a fictional rape trial? This was a completely new experience for most viewers. Its impact was greatly increased by the fact that it was not only real, but live. If coverage like this became commonplace, however, would the same level of interest exist?

The trials ended with some of the defendants being convicted and others being acquitted. Although this is far from conclusive evidence, it does suggest that the television coverage did not have any overwhelming impact on the outcome. It is also significant to note that Judge Young, throughout both trials, never once found it necessary to order the cameras turned off. He would have done so if there had been even a question in his mind that the cameras were causing any harm. A more difficult test for cameras in the courtroom could hardly be imagined. That a case of this complexity and controversy could be televised without serious negative consequences serves as a strong argument for opening courtroom doors to cameras.

Another recent case that illustrates the questionable logic of an outright ban on cameras involved Judge Alcee Hastings. who was to be tried on charges of corruption in *Judicial Conference of the U.S. v. Hastings*.[34] His trial was scheduled for federal court, where, as previously noted, cameras are not allowed under any circumstances. Judge Hastings, because of his position, should have been especially sensitive to any dangers inherent in allowing cameras into the courtroom; yet he challenged the rule and asked that his trial be televised. According to Judge Hastings, he was sure the evidence would demonstrate his innocence and clear his name, but the damage the allegations had done to his reputation could only be repaired by exposing the public to that evidence through television. The court found his arguments persuasive but, lacking the authority to change the rule, was unable to grant his request.

Appellate courts present a very different question. Many of the arguments against allowing cameras in trial courts are not applicable to appellate courts. Most important, there are no witnesses or juries to be influenced by the cameras. The only parties present are the judge(s) or justice(s) and the attorneys. As previously discussed, they should be less susceptible to any of the effects cameras are supposed to have. In addition, as you progress to the higher levels of the legal system, you should find more experienced and better qualified personnel—again less susceptible to the presence of cameras.

Another major difference is the subject matter of appellate proceedings, where the focus is on legal questions, not factual issues. They do not lend themselves to the theatrics that some fear will result from television coverage. Moreover, appellate proceedings are unlikely ever to draw the media attention that some trials do. Dry, unemotional legal arguments couched in the technical jargon of the law are unlikely to draw large audiences and are thus unlikely to get extensive television coverage.

On the other hand, allowing such coverage would result in extensive educational benefits. Currently, many law schools videotape their students during mock appellate arguments. How much more could the law students learn by studying tapes of actual appellate arguments? Similarly, lawyers could study their own arguments to improve their work.

The ultimate irony of the cameras-in-the-courtroom controversy is that no cameras can be present during Supreme Court proceedings. Chief Justice Burger, who wrote the opinion in *Chandler* allowing states to permit television coverage, is the one most adamantly opposed to allowing them in "his" courtroom. Yet it is hard to believe that he and the other Supreme Court justices really expect to be influenced by the presence of cameras.

Historians and legal scholars would undoubtedly find value in tapes of major cases. It is a tragedy that no visual record exists of the Supreme Court arguments in cases like *Roe v. Wade*[35] (the 1973 abortion case) or *University of California Regents v. Bakke*[36] (the 1978 reverse discrimination case).

Whether to allow television coverage of legal proceedings is not an easy decision. The difficulty in separating this question from the more general issue of responsible press coverage of these proceedings makes it an even tougher question, as does the lack of research on the issue. Nevertheless, the limited research and experience available strongly suggest that an absolute prohibition of cameras in the courtroom cannot be justified.

There are strong educational benefits to be gained from allowing television coverage, whereas most of the perceived harm is purely speculative. While irresponsible use of the cameras could cause serious damage in certain situations, the same damage could be caused by an irresponsible press, even without the cameras. Further, much of this feared harm could be controlled by means less drastic than an absolute prohibition.

Justifiable limitations might include restricting access to a single camera, with the feed available to everyone. The camera could even be installed by the court to guarantee that it be as unobtrusive as possible. Judges could always retain the right, as Judge Young did, to order the camera turned on or off at their discretion, even though such action would raise the specter of a judge doing so to protect his own image rather than in the cause of justice.

In addition, judges could be required to exclude cameras in those situations where harm could actually be demonstrated or where other societal interests could be shown to outweigh the benefits of permitting the cameras. For example, cameras might have a serious effect on a minor called to testify.

There is no denying that allowing cameras in the courtroom will provide both education and entertainment. The same could be said, however, of the decision embodied in the First Amendment to allow the press to function largely independent of government control. There will always be excesses and irresponsible press conduct, but the harm caused by them is outweighed by the benefits resulting from a more informed public.

# Part III
# Explaining Events, Diagnosing Situations

# 10

# Intellectual Foundations of Reagan's Soviet Policy: The Threadbare Emperor

*Walter C. Clemens, Jr.*

W hy did President Reagan's foreign policies—at least in his first term—fall so far short of their goals, especially toward the USSR?[1] As with the policies of other recent administrations, a variety of factors were at work: bureaucratic infighting, the pressures and cycles of domestic policies, conflicting priorities, and ambitions exceeding resources. Unlike most recent presidents, Reagan was blessed by a relative absence of bad luck. But his policies, particularly in foreign affairs, were undercut by a problem the magnitude of which was unprecedented, at least since 1945: ignorance. Mr. Reagan's conception of the other superpower rested upon very shaky intellectual foundations. It lacked the necessary and critical foundations needed to craft and pursue a wise policy likely to protect and enhance U.S. interests.

An enlightened policy toward the other superpower requires that the U.S. government possess a realistic and farsighted vision of its objectives and capabilities to pursue them. U.S. policymakers must also have a profound understanding of Soviet goals and the resources—military, economic, political, and other—available to the Kremlin. Not only must American analysts have comprehensive information on all vital subjects relating to the USSR, but they must be able to interpret the raw data with objectivity, circumspection, logic, historical perspective, and sensitivity. Decision makers must then construct policies that take into account the range of uncertainties, the lasting interests of the United States and its allies, and the likely effects of these policies on the Kremlin and other important actors in world affairs. They must overcome the tendency among rivals to see their relationship in zero-sum terms and look instead for possible "win-win" solutions to mutual advantage. To formulate and hold to such policies requires not only wisdom but domestic consensus, with bipartisan support.

The writings of Richard Pipes, the senior Soviet specialist on the National Security Council in 1981–1982, generate just such a zero-sum conception of U.S.–Soviet relations. Essays which he published in the 1970s before joining the Reagan team are reviewed in some detail in this chapter. The same strident themes emerge in essays written by Mr. Pipes after he departed Washington and in his book, *Survival Is Not Enough*. In this book, as in his previous works, Pipes suggests that the West should push the Bear into a corner, even though it may bite. Pipes concurs with some Polish dissidents who affirm that the Kremlin leaders wish to keep power by any means, and that, in their present crisis, "even war can be considered an acceptable price for this aim." Despite this risk, Pipes advocates a coordinated Western strategy designed to aggravate the "internal pressures which the [Soviet] system itself generates." Rejecting any effort to use sanctions and incentives to shape Soviet behavior, Pipes recommends policies designed to alter the core problem, the Soviet system itself. He postulates that Communism will subvert itself if the West neutralizes its military threat and withholds those political and economic concessions which enable the Soviet elite to maintain the status quo.[2]

If the President or his Soviet counterparts cling to a zero-sum conception of the U.S.–Soviet relationship, the second four years of his tenure will probably be as acrid as the first. Still, as the Soviets say, "life itself" may pull both superpowers to perceive and act upon shared interests in arms limitation, trade, scientific exchange and other fields. There were signs toward the end of Reagan's first term that he wished an improvement in U.S.–Soviet relations and that the Kremlin, after walking out of most arms talks in late 1983, wanted to resume a dialogue with Washington. Mr. Reagan no doubt retained his visceral dislike of the Soviet system and his somewhat primitive understanding of its operations and of modern weaponry. But he could also sense that the U.S. public wanted him to make some progress on arms limitation as well as on improving the U.S. image as a superpower. Perhaps he wished also to enter the history books as a peacemaker and not just as a cold or hot warrior. Perhaps, also, the experiences gained in trying to apply a dogmatic ideology to practical problems were pushing Mr. Reagan toward a more centrist position. As Henry Grunwald has noted, the first Reagan "Administration started out by confronting the world with a hard-line, aggressive and Manichean set of policies, or pronouncements, that in nearly every instance gave way to compromise and at least outward accommodation." Whether this trend continued would depend upon which aspects of Reagan's personality and which set of advisers dominated his second term. Would it be "the stubbornly hard-line or the flexible President, the 'ideologues' [such as Mr. Pipes] or the 'pragmatists' among his counselors?"[3]

Even with experience and knowledge, policymakers may misread events. They may overreact or underreact to Soviet words and deeds. They may draft enlightened policies but be shot down in an election year. Still, the sine qua non of successful policies is knowledge. A policy rooted in ignorance of Soviet realities or a highly skewed reading of them opens the way to bias, wishful thinking, fear, greed, and other such factors that obstruct the construction and implementation of effective policies.

In the decades since the 1917 Bolshevik Revolution, the United States has often pursued policies based on faulty knowledge of Soviet power. Sometimes, Washington has underestimated Soviet capabilities—in the 1920s, for example, the lasting power of Bolshevik rule, and after World War II, the speed with which the Kremlin could test and produce nuclear weapons. Since Sputnik I in 1957, however, Washington has frequently overestimated Soviet military and technological prowess, underestimating the weight of economic and bureaucratic inertia.

Washington has also leaned toward interpretations of Soviet intentions that emphasize Moscow's global ambitions and aggressiveness, downgrading the pragmatic, often defensive considerations that have played an important role in military actions along the Soviet periphery, from East Germany in 1953 to Afghanistan in 1979.

Holding an often exaggerated image of Soviet power and global ambitions, U.S. policies have tended to devote more resources to building a military response than are justified by the Soviet threat.[4] Paradoxically, these very policies have deepened Moscow's determination not to be outpaced militarily by the West and thus have contributed to a Soviet arms buildup to which Washington feels it must respond, perpetuating a vicious cycle.

"An evil empire." This notion sums up the basic picture of the USSR held by President Reagan and most of his key advisers who shaped the underlying thrusts of his policies to the Soviet Union in the early 1980s. As Mr. Reagan expressed his view in the 1980 campaign, "the Soviet Union underlies all the unrest that is going on"; but for the USSR, he noted, "there wouldn't be any hot spots in the world."[5]

This image corresponds to what Alexander Dallin and Gail W. Lapidus have termed the "essentialist" model of the Soviet Union: Because of its Russian heritage, its Communist doctrine, its totalitarian system—or all three—the USSR is an empire of evil. It will not change except by revolution from within or heavy pressure from without. Negotiations with such an adversary are futile.[6]

Earlier White House administrations viewed the USSR through the lens of a "mechanistic" or an "interaction" model. George F. Kennan, for example, emphasized the mechanisms of geopolitics and the balance of power as he drafted a rationale for the containment policies espoused by the Truman administration.[7] Still other presidents and their advisers were sensitive to the interactive ways in which the two superpowers could move toward war or toward a web of overlapping mutual interests. Henry Kissinger, under Presidents Nixon and Ford, articulated this view, as did Cyrus Vance and Marshall D. Shulman in the Carter State Department.

Most American presidents in this century had acquired significant life experiences abroad and/or had read deeply of world history before their election. True, they chose advisers who tended to support and legitimate their views rather than to challenge them; still, their conceptions of foreign affairs could usually be defended on the basis of considerable knowledge. Mr. Reagan's notion of the world, in contrast, took shape in the vortex of his careers in acting and later in

California politics. His immediate predecessor in the Oval Office, Jimmy Carter, also lacked experience in Washington, but he had already learned a great deal about external relations from his membership on the Trilateral Commission while he was still governor of Georgia. He also had a penchant for reading and learning, unlike Mr. Reagan, who is known more for his appreciation of the persuasive anecdote than of the grand theory.

"One kind of berry." This Russian adage helps explain why Mr. Reagan sought and found advisers on East–West relations who shared his essentialist image of the USSR, including, at the outset of his first term, Paul H. Nitze, Richard V. Allen, William R. Van Cleave, and Harvard professor Richard E. Pipes. Although the first three had long been concerned with the arms race,[8] and Allen had written on Communist ideology, Pipes was the only serious student of Russian and Soviet history close to the early Reagan White House.[9] Pipes helped in Reagan's 1980 campaign and then served some two years as the senior Soviet specialist on the National Security Council.

Pipes's influence on Reagan should not be overrated. The president's policies followed his own instincts, but Pipes helped to justify them. And he became a strong proponent of such policies as the attempt to block the Soviet gas pipeline to Western Europe. He contributed to the strategy of putting maximum political and economic pressure on the USSR to sharpen its internal strains and to thwart its expansion and influence abroad.[10] At times, his views became so militant that they were disavowed by the White House, to the partial relief of some Western European governments.[11] Pipes's influence was reduced also by his lack of experience in bureaucratic infighting. He later acknowledged that his two years in Washington had taught him a lot about the chemistry of political decision making.[12]

Pipes returned to Harvard in 1983, but many aspects of the essentialist image and the confrontationalist posture to which he had contributed remained firm in the belief system of the Reagan Administration. The arrival of new foreign policy principals such as George P. Shultz, Robert C. McFarlane, and others coincided, however, with the gradual shift toward accomodation noted in 1983–84. There were some grounds for thinking that more moderate mechanistic or interactive models of Soviet policy might be supplanting the more dogmatic images of earlier years.[13] Shultz, toward the end of 1984, seemed to be claiming arms control as his turf and persuaded the President to name Paul Nitze—himself committed now to balanced East–West accords—as his special adviser, a move that seemed to lower the influence of arms control critics and saboteurs within the U.S. Arms Control and Disarmament Agency, the State Department, and the Defense Department.[14] Mr. Pipes and others, in and out of office, did what they could to counter these trends. Pipes wrote about the Bulgarian connection with the attempted assassination of Pope John Paul II and promoted curbs on technology transfer to the USSR.[15] In *Commentary* and *Foreign Affairs* he published articles that reflected his larger thesis in *Survival Is Not Enough.*

Long a professor of history at Harvard, Pipes's scholarly reputation had been firmly established through his books on Russian history and the formation of the Soviet Union in the early 1920s.[16] In 1969, however, he began writing on current affairs, because he believed the Nixon-Kissinger detente policy lacked a basic familiarity "either with Russian history or Communist theory." Pipes's works soon attracted the attention of Senator Henry Jackson and others in Washington; in 1976, the then director of the CIA, George Bush, made Pipes chairman of the "Team B" experts, who concluded that the agency had been underestimating the Soviet threat.

Pipes continued to write on contemporary affairs during the Carter years. His 1977 essay in *Commentary*, "Why the Soviet Union Thinks It Could Fight and Win a Nuclear War," added academic dignity to the argument that the Kremlin might try to exploit the putative vulnerability of America's land-based missiles. This seminal essay did much to fuel anxieties about the Soviet threat, among Democrats as well as Republicans, as did the manifestos issued directly by the Committee on the Present Danger, on which Pipes also served. Regardless of their scholarly substance, these messages contributed to a public climate that looked for a hard-line leader to replace the vacillating Carter administration.

In the decade before Pipes joined the Reagan National Security Council, he wrote a number of other essays besides that in *Commentary*, which were collected and edited by him under the title *U.S.–Soviet Relations in the Era of Detente* and published in 1981, not long after the Reagan team took office. It is through these essays that we shall examine to assess the intellectual strength of Reagan's Soviet policies. This review will suggest that, to the extent Reagan's course has been inspired or sustained by Professor Pipes, it rests upon weak, sometimes shabby, intellectual foundations. The collected essays reveal an energetic, fertile, and broadly cultivated mind searching a thousand years of Russian history for insights into contemporary problems. But they also show a visceral dislike—not only for the USSR but for Russia; a strong tendency toward non sequiturs; and—most amazing for a professional historian—a propensity to confuse dates and causal sequences in Russian history. What surprises and even dismays Pipe's reader here is not the anti-Russian, anti-Soviet disposition of the author—or even his tendency to see "them" as black, "us" as white—but his almost cavalier disregard for factual accuracy and logical inference.

This review is mindful that men of good will and high intellect can look at the same set of facts and reach divergent conclusions, as did Cyrus Vance and Zbigniew Brzezinski, for example, in assessing Soviet support for Ethiopia against Somalia.[17] My review will not debate the *wisdom* of the policies advocated by Professor Pipes but will limit itself to a much narrower task: demonstrating that the interpretations of Soviet behavior offered by Pipes derive from a reading of history that abounds with factual errors, many of which may be explained by a deep anti-Russian as well as anti-Communist bias. Whatever policy recommendations the White House adopts, they should rest upon the most objective and reliable understanding possible of the historical record. Although I will not try to argue the merits of another approach to the USSR, this review commends the orientation taken in recent years by George F. Kennan and other members of the American Committee on East–West Accord.[18]

This review will commence with factual errors in Pipes's writings about Russia before the 1917 revolutions and proceed to his writings on more recent times, which illustrate how fragile are the reasons why he believes the "Soviet Union Thinks It Could Fight and Win a Nuclear War."

Commenting on Moscow's historic claim to be the "Third Rome," Pipes writes that Russians argued that the Greek Church betrayed the Orthodox faith by agreeing in the "1530s" to reunite with Rome (p. 3).[19] The accords Pipes refers to, however, took place a full century earlier![20]

Russia, says Pipes, "initiated" China's dismemberment in 1896 (p. 57), ignoring that Britain took Hong Kong in 1842 and that Japan seized Taiwan and other Chinese territories in 1895.

Pipes's anti-Soviet bias is at least as strong as his anti-Russian leaning: "Had Russia escaped [the Bolshevik] revolution, the non-Westernized bulk of its population in all liklihood would have become Westernized" (p. 5)—though the traits that Pipes elsewhere ascribes to the Russian peasant, even after he moves to the city, are hardly ephemeral.

More egregious is Pipes's charge (p. 5) that Russia's "Westernized elite" disappeared after October 1917, a blanket statement refuted not only by the careers of the first three heads of the Foreign Commissariat (Trotsky, Chicherin, Litvinov) but also, I would say, by Comintern leaders such as Zinoviev and Radek. Indeed, was Lenin himself not a Westernized leader? Beyond politics, many figures in the arts and sciences continued to go back and forth to Europe through the 1920s and 1930s.

In agreeing to the Brest-Litovsk Treaty with Germany in 1918, Lenin, according to Pipes, sacrificed "doctrine" (p. 53). But it was land—not theory—that the Bolsheviks traded for a "breathing space," thereby implementing Lenin's doctrine of expediency.

While noting that Lenin too believed in *divide et impera,* Pipes writes that Khrushchev "inaugurated" Moscow's "peaceful coexistence" campaign in the mid-1950s (p. 73), though Trotsky used the term in 1917–1918, Chicherin endorsed it in 1918–1920, and Lenin affirmed the idea in 1922.[21]

Pipes believes that Moscow's 1971 decision to seek technology and capital assistance from the West was a major historical turning point (p. 78), apparently forgetting that Lenin attempted and partially succeeded with similar policies in the early 1920s.

Still, Pipes contends that Soviet military preparations in the 1930s, launched "when no other country was rearming," set off "the great arms race of the interwar period" (p. 205). In reality, Germany was rearming clandestinely in the

1920s (with Soviet aid) and openly after 1934. Nor was Japan idle, even before it invaded Manchuria in 1931. Stalin pushed for heavy industry after 1928 but did not accelerate arms production or build up regular forces of the Red Army until the mid-1930s, responding then to mounting tensions abroad.[22]

America's role, by contrast, is idealized by Pipes. The United States, he avers, became the leader of "the noncommunist majority of humanity" as a result of Stalin's bullying (p. 75). But the U.S. alliance system has never included more than half of the world's population. Judging by the resolutions of the nonaligned movement's periodic conferences, much of the Third World does not see the United States as its leader.

Pipes claims that American confusion is "sophistication." Thus, Stalin erred in interpreting Dean Acheson's "defense perimeter" statement of 1950 "to mean just what it said," because "overly sophisticated signals bewilder Russian leaders and can mislead them (pp. 38–39)."

Some of Pipes's inaccuracies here may stem from ideological blinders, others from haste or sloppiness. In one place, he writes that the U.S.–Soviet dialogue was "inaugurated" in 1959 at Camp David (p. *x*), while elsewhere he recalls the 1955 Geneva Summit (p. 31). Similarly, in his *Commentary* article, Pipes wrote that the United States nuclear monopoly remained unbroken until 1957 "when the Soviets launched the Sputnik" (p. 141)—itself unarmed—rather than when the Kremlin started flying long-range bombers in the mid-1950s or deploying ICBMs at the end of the decade. Still, in another place, he notes that the Kremlin demonstrated its Bison bombers to impress foreign observers in 1955 (p. 30).

Some errors seem due to naiveté or self-righteousness. Thus, Pipes says that alleged Western designs on the Congo in 1960 were a fabrication of Soviet propaganda (p. 35), though top U.S. leaders plotted how to kill Patrice Lumumba.[23]

Pipes seems to assume dogmatically that Communist rule has no future. Thus, internal economic reforms are excluded for the USSR, says Pipes, because the Czechoslovak experience in 1968 showed the Soviet Politburo "how quickly and irreversibly economic reform led to a breakdown of communist controls" (p. 77). Pipes seems unfamiliar with the fact that the popularity of the Communist party within Czechoslovakia rose steadily from January through August 1968 or that, more important, Hungary's New Course, begun in the mid-1960s, has made Kadar's regime for years the economic and political *Wunder* of COMECON and a model that many Soviet leaders would emulate.

Historians will also marvel at Pipes's assertion that "the 1960s saw a steady thaw that prepared the ground" for the U.S.–Soviet détente formalized under Nixon (p. *x*), and insupportable reading of the era when American planes pounded Moscow's "sister socialist state"; when U.S. and Soviet Middle Eastern clients reached for the jugular in 1967; and when Soviet tanks in Czechoslovakia derailed LBJ's trip to Moscow.

Perhaps the presidential adviser has just spread himself too thinly. He writes (p. 189) that Egypt's "defection" from the Soviet camp came *after* the 1973

Arab–Israeli war, apparently forgetting that Sadat expelled Soviet forces in 1972.[24] Looking for more illumination on this point, the reader may turn to "Egypt" in the index, where several cross references can be found, including one to an entry that proves nonexistent—"Soviet Union, and Egypt."

Pipes says that "the literature on the theory of Russian foreign policy is so meagre that it may be said not to exist at all. That Russians have felt no need to compile the record of their external relations or to investigate its principles is in itself a significant fact, illustrative of their general attitude toward the outside world" (p. 9). While there is some truth to this assertion as regards the tsarist period, it does not hold for most of the Soviet years. The Bolsheviks relished publishing the secret dealings of the tsarist regime and its allies, not just the World War I understandings but previous records, such as the preparations for the Hague Disarmament Conferences (in *Krasnyi arkhiv*). Moreover, from the start of their regime the Soviets have published foreign affairs annuals; multivolume histories of Soviet foreign relations; monographs on problems such as disarmament and foreign trade; documentary records of international conferences; and, with a somewhat greater lag, the year-by-year *Documents of Soviet Foreign Policy (DSVP)*. Pipes's charge against Russian or Soviet historiography may simply reveal his own unfamiliarity with the literature.

Intracampus strife at Harvard may also contribute to this polemic. Pipes accuses Henry Kissinger of stating the obvious long after the fact in "prophetic" tones (p. 144). But in 1974, Pipes called on Washington to include China and Japan with Western Europe in formulating a coordinated policy to prevent future Russian encroachments in Europe and Asia—some two years *after* Nixon (said to be ignorant of communism and the like) had clinked glasses with Zhou Enlai in Beijing's Great Hall (p. 60). Adding to the confusion, Pipes denounces an alleged "Nixon Doctrine," which he claims was based on hopes of a growing "web of interests" between the two superpowers (p. 49). The main feature of the Nixon doctrine—American unwillingness to send troops to fight other people's wars—becomes lost in this diatribe against a man who, according to Pipes, did not understand that Communist leaders "have a material interest" in preserving and expanding their system (p. 50)—quite a charge to lay against one who debated Khrushchev in 1959 and negotiated with Brezhnev in 1972, 1973, and 1974.

Americans, says Pipes, have produced "no strategist of international repute" but for Admiral Mahan (p. 137); they have no general staff and grant no higher degrees in "military science" as the Soviets do—an indication, he says, of Moscow's more serious approach to military doctrine. These assertions can be argued, but they beg for the naming of a Soviet strategist taken more seriously "internationally" than Herman Kahn, Bernard Brodie, Albert Wohlstetter, or Robert S. McNamara and subsequent secretaries of defense. Pipes may reply that these are civilians—not professional military men. True, but this is the precise weakness of his argument: The writings of Soviet uniformed military leaders (*a fortiori* the many political commissars whom Pipes quotes) are not so well integrated in the Kremlin's grand strategy as the strategic ideas of the Rand Corporation, the Hudson Institute, or M.I.T. in the formation of U.S. policy. Thus, a major contributor to the Pentagon's publication, *Soviet Military Power* (1981) has a Ph.D. from the University of Pittsburgh, where he did dynamic analyses of U.S. and Soviet forces after simulated first strikes by both sides. Does the fact that his degree is not in "military science" diminish the value of his training to the Pentagon or enhance it?

The Soviet system of military academies is no more elaborate than that of the United States, which takes Army officers from West Point or ROTC to Fort Leavenworth, to Carlisle Barracks, to the National Defense University. Does the fact that civilians—for example, from the Foreign Service and the CIA—train with would-be majors and generals weaken or enhance America's capacity for "combined operations"? If the Kremlin's most famous living strategist is Admiral Gorshkov, what is he but an update of Admiral Mahan—many generations later? As for Soviet strategists playing some kind of independent role, as suggested by Pipes, I recall a conversation with a Moscow Institute researcher in 1969 in which I suggested some divergencies in the writings of Lt. Colonel Larionov on space weapons and statements by N.S. Khrushchev. The researcher smiled knowingly: "The Colonel is a very small man; the former First Secretary, a very big man."

Pipes argues that "the United States is accustomed to waging wars of its own choosing and on its own terms" (p. 138)—an idea that would seem strange to those surprised at Pearl Harbor or the Fiftieth Parallel, or to those who felt they fought with one hand tied in Vietnam. Russia's determination never again to be surprised as in 1941 is emphasized (p. 159); America's Pearl Harbor complex is ignored.

America's battle deaths since 1775 are "estimated" at 650,000, says Pipes, while Russia's exceeded 20 million in World War II; and the USSR could lose 30 million of its present population and be no worse off than in 1945 (pp. 166–167). Granted that U.S. war casualties have been much lower than the Soviet Union's, U.S. battle deaths in the twentieth century alone have exceeded 600,000, while Northern losses in the Civil War surpassed 360,000.[25] Adding Southern battle deaths and U.S. losses in other wars since 1775, total U.S. battle deaths since Lexington and Concord could reach almost twice the number suggested by Pipes.

Granted that the USSR has suffered enormous losses in war and other disasters (political and natural) since 1917, has this fact made the Soviets more or less prone to war? Most visitors to the USSR are struck by the anxieties that many Soviet citizens express regarding any more bloodshed. Americans, who have suffered less, strike many observers as less fearful of war than the Soviet public. The possibility of this opposite interpretation gets no attention from Pipes.

Instead, he argues that Americans' commercial tradition disposes them to look for compromise instead of solution by force. Russia, of course, has its own commercial tradition, extending from the Varengians and Novgorod to the "second economy" of today's USSR. Accepting that free enterprise is many times healthier in the United States than in Soviet Russia, the fact remains that the White House has used force much more often than the Kremlin in conducting its foreign policies since 1945[26] and that U.S. battle deaths since then have reached almost 100,000, while Soviet losses, mostly in Afghanistan, have probably been little more than one-tenth that number from 1945 to the early 1980s.

"They" versus "us"—the same Manichaeanism in Pipes that he discerns in others. There, Karl von Clausewitz; here, commerce. Buried in the United States, Clausewitz, according to Pipes, "seems to be alive and prospering in the Soviet Union" (p. 136). To support this view, Pipes cites several Soviet military writers, even though their function, as he says elsewhere, is to "indoctrinate." He hedges on whether Soviet military doctrine is basically hidden or accessible.

Citing mainly Soviet military writings, such as those translated by Leon Gouré, and by Harriet and William Scott, while deriding the declarations of Soviet representatives to Pugwash conferences as being for "export" only, Pipes ignores major statements on nuclear war by top party leaders and bodies such as the Central Committee and Congresses. In consequence, he misses Khrushchev's emphasis on nuclear weapons that led him to create the Strategic Rocket Forces in 1960 and to initiate a one-third cut in regular forces, hoping, somewhat like Eisenhower, to curtail defense spending through greater reliance on atomic arms—a goal attributed by Pipes only to the White House.

Pipes's 1977 article, "Why the Soviet Union Thinks It Could Fight and Win a Nuclear War," still reverberates in Washington, evoking fears that the Kremlin may exploit the alleged vulnerability of America's Minuteman missiles. Unlike the dominant view in the United States, Pipes argues that "the strategic doctrine adopted by the USSR over the past two decades calls for . . . not deterrence but victory, not sufficiency of weapons but superiority, not retaliation but offensive action." Its "five related elements" are "(1) preemption (first strike), (2) quantitative superiority in arms, (3) counterforce targeting, (4) combined arms-operations, and (5) defense" (pp. 158-159).

The 1977 article begins with the assertion that in the "real world of strategic nuclear weapons," the Soviets "possess a considerable larger arsenal than we" (p. 136). U.S. estimates then and later, however, credited the United States at that time with more than 9,000 strategic nuclear warheads, against less than 5,000 for the USSR.[27] If Pipes meant *delivery vehicles*, an area in which Russia led and now leads, he should have said so, for *warheads* cause destruction—not unloaded rockets or planes. Surely Pipes knows this distinction, but he does not make it. Here, as elsewhere, he uses ambiguous language in ways that maximize the Russian-Soviet proclivity to violence and capacity for war. If challenged,

Pipes could reply: "I was talking about strategic missiles—not warheads." Silent on this distinction, however, he suggests that the United States sat still while Moscow overtook the United States in strategic arms. His one-sided imagery overlooks the qualitative and quantitative improvements in U.S. warheads and delivery systems (for example, the transitions from Polaris to TRIDENT II), even though the number of U.S. ICBMs has been stable since the early 1960s. He takes no account of Soviet apprehension of U.S. technological leadership.

Pipes claims that there is a basic difference between U.S. and Soviet military doctrine: "We consider nuclear war unfeasible and suicidal for both [sides], and our chief adversary views it as feasible and winnable for himself" (p. 168). When Pipes adds certain qualifications, however, this dichotomy melts away. First, as Pipes makes clear, he agrees that the Soviets accept the *fact* of deterrence (note 19, p. 169); it is just that they see mutual deterrence as "undesirable and transient"—a view heard also among U.S. strategists. Second, "the actual, operative differences between the two doctrines may not be quite as sharp as they appear in the public literature: . . . our deterrence doctrine leaves room for some limited offensive action, just as the Russians include elements of deterrence in their 'war-fighting' and 'war-winning' doctrine. Admittedly, too, a country's military doctrine never reveals how it would behave under actual combat conditions" (p. 167).

Pipes also notes that Marshal Sokolovskii's edited treatise, *Military Strategy,* "the only Soviet strategic manual publicly available," was published *fifteen* years before his 1977 article,[28] and that the Soviet "Officer's Library," of which twelve volumes had already been translated into English, like the "flood of [other] military works" published in the USSR, "has as its purpose indoctrination"—to encourage readers and to impress on them "the principles of Soviet tactics and the art of operations." Since Soviet military literature is written in Aesopian code, one must labor diligently to discover "nuggets of precious information on Soviet perceptions and intentions" (p. 151). Having discounted his available sources of information in this manner, it may not be so astounding that Pipes draws inferences about Kremlin thinking from the writings of a "pro-Soviet" Englishman and some anti-Soviet Americans, as we shall see.

More important, Pipes misses Khrushchev's downgrading of "everything Vladimir Il'ich said" in the nuclear era; the publication in the early 1960s of Leniniana suggesting that Il'ich himself foresaw the day when technology would make war obsolete as an instrument of policy; and the 1963 Central Committee declaration to Beijing that "the atomic bomb does not adhere to the class principle—it destroys everybody within the range of its devastating force."[29]

The Kremlin does not accept the theory of mutual deterrence, says Pipes:

> After all, this theory, pushed to its logical conclusion, means that a country can rely for its security on a finite number of nuclear warheads and on an appropri-

ate quantity of delivery vehicles; so that, apart perhaps from some small mobile forces needed for local actions, large and costly traditional military establishments can be disbanded. (p. 154)

But this very premise lay at the core of Soviet proposals for General and Complete Disarmament, 1959–1962, qualified in 1962–1963 by Gromyko's endorsement of a limited nuclear umbrella. Khrushchev even talked in 1960 of shifting regular Soviet forces to a territorial-cadre militia, as in the 1920s and early 1930s.[30]

Although the Kremlin in recent years has not said much about eliminating large military establishments, it has signed two SALT accords setting ceilings on U.S. and Soviet strategic delivery vehicles and, in the second case, on warheads. Most important, the USSR has agreed to severe limitations on ABM defenses, writing off all practical hope of defending its population, industries, or remaining military targets from a U.S. strike, first or second.

Though Pipes contends we cannot assume that Soviet doctrine mirrors American doctrine, he suggests that Soviet thinking probably conforms with the views of certain Western writers. Thus:

> Not being privy to the internal discussions of the Soviet military, we can do no better than consult the writings of an eminent British scientist, P.M.S. Blackett, noted for his pro-Soviet sympathies, whose remarkable book *Fear, War, and the Bomb*, published in 1948–49, indicated with great prescience the lines which Soviet strategic thinking were [*sic*] subsequently to take. (p. 162)

These lines, according to Pipes, were that even thousands of atomic bombs would not produce decisive results in a U.S.–Soviet war. Pipes then cites Sokolovskii on the limited effect that U.S. and British strategic bombing had on Germany's war machine, apparently ignorant of the fact that a survey headed by his soon-to-be-colleague Paul Nitze had reached the same conclusion well before Sokolovskii.[31]

Pipes also says that Soviet strategists probably reject the mutual-deterrence theory on several technical grounds like those advanced by such U.S. writers as Wohlstetter, Kahn, and Nitze (p. 157)—for example, the possiblity of a technological breakthrough that makes one side's deterrent more vulnerable than the other's. But if leading American strategists are the only *published* sources for such thinking, should not their views be given as much weight in Washington as the *supposed* views of some unknown Soviet strategists in Moscow?

Pipes contends that Soviet targeting is counterforce, whereas American targeting is countervalue. But U.S. defense secretaries have talked repeatedly of adopting a preemptive counterforce posture from 1962 to the present. Although Washington has wanted for over twenty years to have the capacity to destroy a large fraction of Soviet citizens and industry in a retaliatory blow, it has trained many—probably most—of its nuclear warheads on military targets, from silos to bridges.[32] Judging by the selective targeting doctrine developed under President Carter and the protracted war doctrine that emerged under President Reagan, Clausewitz has been as much alive in Washington as in Moscow—or more so.

The main footnote references supporting Pipes's attribution to the Kremlin of a preemptive strategy are the studies of Soviet doctrine in the late 1950s by Herbert Dinerstein and Raymond Garthoff (both of whom have modified their views on contemporary Soviet policies significantly since the works cited by Pipes).

A corollary of the preemptive strategy holds that armed forces must always be in a state of high combat readiness, says Pipes, as if this explains Moscow's large conventional forces. He seems not to know that Soviet strategic forces have generally been kept at a far lower level of readiness than their U.S. counterparts and require longer to prepare for launching; that U.S. and Soviet readiness procedures for conventional military units are similar; or that some U.S. worldwide alerts (as in 1960 and 1973) were unfocused and probably needlessly provocative.[33]

Russia's preemptive doctrine, says Pipes, has probably been strengthened also by the success of Israel's 1967 preemptive strike and the unhappy consequences of Israel's more passive defense in 1973 (p. 160). But surely these lessons have been taken in by Western planners as well as Soviet.

How prone is the Soviet leadership toward bold moves such as preemption? Pipes emphasizes the Russian-Soviet tradition of large military expenditures and large standing armies to suggest an aggressive, militaristic power quite disposed to use all means, even nuclear arms, to promote its aims (pp. 198–199, 208). He ignores the historical record, underscored by most Sovietologists, that the Soviet government has usually behaved cautiously in foreign affairs, initiating military actions only against weak neighbors, and believing history to work on its side. There is little evidence to suggest, at least since Stalin, that Soviet leaders have been indifferent to battlefield casualties.

Nor is there any foundation for Pipes's assertion that "the formulation of Soviet military strategy in the nuclear age was turned over to the military who are in complete control of the Ministry of Defense" (p. 155). Unless the "strategy" in question serves mainly for *agitprop* or deals with the narrow technical problems usually known as tactics, the Politburo would relinquish its hold on grand military and political strategy only when shrimps learn to whistle.

As with certain other trends, Pipes says very little about the usual subordination of the Soviet military to party chieftains. Since Khrushchev, the Politburo has allocated resources to the military so as to keep most branches of the services content; his regime may even have responded positively to pressures from a Schumpeterian warrior class wishing to expand its overseas role regardless of costs and gains. But there is no evidence that the top Soviet party leaders permit their marshals any more leeway in formulation or execution of grand strategy than their U.S. counterparts.[34] My analysis of the slogans carried across Red Square on May 1 and November 7 in the past decade (1975–84)reveals no more than one or two slogans on each occasion praising the Soviet military—from a total of some fifty to seventy dealing with economic and political priorities within the country and with a variety of foreign affairs objectives.

Pipes says that a Russian *muzhik* mentality dominates the thinking of the Soviet elite as well as the Russian masses, fusing with Marxism to create a respect for cunning and an awe of naked power (p. 147). Apart, perhaps, from Khrushchev, one would be hard-pressed to think of other top Soviet leaders as Russian peasants. The man who ruled while Pipes penned his essays of the 1970s—Leonid I. Brezhnev—worked as a surveyor, as a metallurgist, and as a party organizer, and risked his career in bold ventures in agriculture and outer space before taking on the position of General Secretary, whence he quickly mastered many nuances of foreign policy. Still, Pipes suggests that the Soviet leaders have soaked up the peasant mentality, which holds, *"Bei Russkogo, chasy sdelaet"*—"Beat a Russian and he'll make you a watch" (p. 72).

The Reagan team dealt with the Kremlin along these lines through most of 1980–1983. As Secretary of State Haig noted in May l982, a balance of firmness and flexibility is usually needed to deal effectively with any adversary. But zero-sum gamesmanship was the leitmotif of most Reagan gestures toward the USSR, at least until 1984.

What does it matter that a Harvard professor has come and gone, helping to rationalize the half-baked ideas of another president? Pipes has contributed to a wide array of pseudoscientific propositions underlying President Reagan's "security" and "defense" policies. Some of the basic axioms are these:

1. The USSR is responsible for most if not all of the unrest in today's world.
2. The USSR wrested strategic supremacy from the United States in the 1970s, due in part to American laxity.
3. Strategic supremacy is a meaningful concept and a useful instrument. Once attained, it can be employed against other states, even those armed with nuclear weapons.
4. The United States can and should regain strategic supremacy—not just in offensive but in defense weaponry.
5. An effective strategic defense is attainable. If attained, it need not undermine strategic stability. Indeed, it could enhance it.

Operating from these large premises, the Reagan administration showed little interest in arms control for almost two years; it then offered a conciliatory posture to the Kremlin in 1984, after the Soviets had pulled out of most negotiating forums, in part because they felt that Reagan did not want mutually advantageous arms control agreements.

Reagan followed, at times, a classic "approach-avoidance" syndrome: He offered to negotiate with Moscow while accusing the Kremlin in the same speech of violating existing arms accords. Accusations of this kind are extremely serious and should be made only after conclusive evidence is at hand. Any uncertainties or doubts should be discussed privately before resorting to public diplomacy. The Reagan administration, however, rushed publicly to judgment, even with thinly supported charges about Soviet use of chemical warfare in Afghanistan and Southeast Asia (where "yellow rain" may be a natural phenomenon rather than manmade).[35]

The White House inaugurated deployment of Pershing II and ground-launched cruise missiles in Europe without detailed consideration of the Soviet claim that its SS-20 missiles amounted only to a modernization of obsolete systems, and without attention to the extremely destabilizing consequences of a new arms race in cruise missiles.[36]

Repeating arguments from the 1970s about the putative vulnerability of the U.S. land-based missile force to a Soviet first strike, the Reagan administration sought to deploy the MX missile. In the 1980s, no less than in the 1970s, the MX would undermine strategic stability, because its large, accurate, and multiple warheads could be used as a first-strike, counterforce weapon against the USSR. If U.S. land-based weapons are truly vulnerable, the appropriate response is to make them mobile, to hide them, or to put them elsewhere (for example, at sea). Instead, the Reagan Pentagon opted to site them in existing silos, the same ones already deemed vulnerable to a Soviet attack. This would create the worst of possible worlds: an American weapons system with a counterforce capability alarming to Soviet planners, based in a mode that would tempt Washington to "use 'em or lose 'em" to a Soviet attack. This logic, pursued to its conclusion, could provoke the Kremlin to shoot before the Americans could preempt. The MX, especially if deployed in soft silos, could thus heighten the incentives on both sides to strike first. Sensing these contradictions, many Republicans as well as Democratic lawmakers sought in 1984 to thwart any deployment of the MX.

Capping these other follies, the president called for a strategic defense initiative ("Star Wars") that is probably beyond the reach of foreseeable technology in this century, doing so in ways that could give us another worst of possible worlds. The initiative will be costly, even if it fails; it raises probably unrealizable hopes among some Americans; it strengthens fears of U.S. isolationism in Western Europe; it drives the Soviets to emulate or surpass U.S. defense efforts and plans to militarize outer space; and it denigrates the most important arms restraint of our era, the antiballistic missile limitations of 1972–1974.[37]

These policies have not served well the interests of the U.S. people or those of others who are vitally dependent upon peaceful relations between the superpowers. But for Reagan, as for the Spanish King Philip II, "no experience of the failure of his policy could shake his belief in its essential excellence."[38] "Doublespeak" can immediately convert failure to victory. As one of Reagan's more sophistic savants put it, the president's anti-Soviet rhetoric and arms buildup have been good for arms control. "The fact that the negotiations are indefinitely suspended is just part of the changing weather."[39] While it is arguable that arms control agreements are not attainable without comparable forces on both sides, I believe that rough parity already existed at the outset of Mr. Reagan's first term and that the time and opportunity lost during four years of anti-Soviet rhetoric and lavish military buildup have been unnecessary and probably even counterproductive to the best interests of U.S. security. The uncorking of the cruise missile genie during these four years, for example, will make future arms agreements extremely difficult to monitor. The advance toward anti-satellite weapons may make our surveillance systems more vulnerable. As the leader in these technologies, the United States decides by its actions whether or not they are restrained or unleashed. Even if "Reagan II" yields some U.S.–Soviet accords on arms control, I doubt that they will be an improvement on those that probably could have been reached in the early 1980s.

It is difficult to recall a president's policies—from supply-side economics to the feasibility of a strategic defense—in which the chasm between mind set and reality stretched wider. It is disturbing that U.S. policies can be shaped by anything short of the best possible intellectual mastery of the complex problems with which they must deal. Particularly in relations with the other superpower, prejudice and passion should be minimized. Dogmatism, machismo, personal profit, revenge—all such motives should be kept far away from the confrontation between thermonuclear giants. Neither America nor the rest of humanity can afford any policy that is not based on facts, logic, and wisdom.

Having risen to the pinnacle of power and reflecting some deep impulses of the American electorate, it is hardly surprising that Reagan would accept and welcome advisers such as Pipes. The inability of Mr. Reagan and his staff to discriminate in matters far from their expertise would be expected. What is more disturbing is that members of the American Historical Association and editors of *Encounter* and of *Commentary* could let pass such factual errors and sloppy reasoning as are evidenced in Pipes's writing. If major segments of the intellectual establishment are so undiscerning, could we expect more from the "California Mafia" in the White House?

The Reagan policies and the beliefs that underlie them are not a pure aberration. United States policies toward Soviet Russia since 1917 have often reflected a curious mixture of hatred, fear, self-doubt, self-confidence, wishful thinking, self-deception, and ignorance. Usually, these policies have resulted in a "hard line" toward the Kremlin, one that seemed to confirm Lenin's forecast that long-term cohabitation of the capitalist and socialist systems would be impossible. Instead of helping the Soviets emerge from their own paranoia, Washington often helped confirm them in the correctness of their hard line.

For brief periods, the United States has moved toward the opposite extreme, as when Franklin D. Roosevelt hoped that he could persuade "Uncle Joe" to alter his basic orientation in world affairs. There were also a few moments in the 1950s, 1960s, and 1970s when other American presidents exaggerated the ease with which momentary détente could be transformed into a more lasting entente.

Why has it been so difficult to find and pursue a golden blend of firmness and flexibility in dealing with the USSR? The complex (and somewhat ambiguous) recommendations of George F. Kennan in 1946–1947 were distorted and overmilitarized in the late 1940s and early 1950s, just as the subtle and balanced programs advocated by Vance and Shulman were distorted under Jimmy Carter, who veered first toward utopian idealism and then, after he was chastened by Afghanistan, toward a militaristic orientation that was continued and intensified by Reagan. Even the Kissinger blend of firmness and flexibility, which netted some meaningful accords with Moscow in the 1970s, proved unacceptably soft to many Republicans and some Democrats.

Why does the American public so readily accept paranoid depictions of the Soviet Union, its power and its machinations? Why, given the long record of economic failure in most Communist countries and continued U.S. leadership in the world marketplace and technological-scientific arena, do Americans so readily accept pronouncements from the White House about Soviet military superiority and the momentum of world communism? Why do they accept this bad news— even when it is usually false?

To answer these questions fully would take us well beyond the immediate impact of any presidential advisers, most of whom are virtually unknown to the public. We would have to explore the religious and ethical foundations of American ideology, with its tendency toward self-righteousness and Manichaean dualities; the insecurities and isolation borne of North America's geography and its complex historical relations with Europe; the tendency of Americans to depend on technological fixes in dealing with the threats of two world wars and the ongoing cold war; and the important roles played by refugees from Nazism and from Soviet totalitarianism in shaping the professional study of the USSR in this country.

We would have to face up to de Tocqueville's questions about the capacity of a democracy to forge a wise foreign policy, given that most of the voters do not care or know much about foreign affairs. What they do know comes mainly from high school texts, newspaper editorials, and speeches by contenders for public office. None of these views can lightly defy prevailing fashion. None can readily risk being charged with being a dupe of Soviet propaganda and *dezinformatsiia*.

Specialists such as Pipes, writing in *Commentary,* can exploit and bring out the worst in this network of information and value formation. Such articles help condition the world views of intellectuals who are not specialists on the USSR, but who are content to protect their flank with a wall of anti-Sovietism as they pursue their own visions (liberal, conservative, or other) of what is good for America and the rest of humanity. A certain consensus results, one that eventually filters to the writers of newspaper editorials and textbooks. To sell their products, these writers know that it is better to exaggerate than to minimize the dangers of Soviet communism.

It may be that the essentialist world view can be justified by others' accounts of Russian behavior.[40] Perhaps the USSR leadership is as aggressive as Professor Pipes suggests, but his own writings since the 1970s prove very little, except the deterioration of his own scholarship. The mainstream of U.S. specialists on the Soviet Union do not see the other superpower as a monolith inexorably bent on external aggression or internal repression. Most experts see the Kremlin, at least since Khrushchev, as pragmatic, fatigued, and hungry for quiet on its Western front, more interested in East–West trade than in confrontation or conquest.[41] The tragedy is that, goaded and/or justified by the professor's nostrums, the Reagan team has unnecessarily added to U.S. arsenals, inflated defense spending, and added to budgetary deficits, minimizing prospects to enhance security by negotiation rather than by confrontation. Operating on premises like those articulated by Professor Pipes, resting on foundations more emotional than factual, the West may continue to miss opportunities to cultivate peace and collaboration on its Eastern front to cope with the North–South and environmental problems that threaten humanity much more than the tenets of Marxism-Leninism.[42]

Unless the United States is able to improve the intellectual and other foundations of its policies toward the other superpower, it is likely to persist in what Barbara Tuchman calls the "wooden-headedness" that refuses to benefit from experience and so marches to folly, contrary to self-interest. As she points out, governments often assess situations "in terms of fixed notions while ignoring or rejecting any contrary signs." They often act according to wish instead of allowing themselves to be "deflected by facts." Emotionalism and religious mania often contribute to this condition.[43] Essays and advice like those proffered by Professor Pipes contribute to rather than ameliorate these manias.

The dilemmas are complex and difficult to manage. The truth, as most professional Sovietologists would concede, is that the Soviet regime is powerful; that its behavior toward its own people as well as toward foreigners has been cruel; and that prudence requires a powerful alliance headed by the United States to contain and, if possible, gradually to ameliorate Soviet ambitions. At the same time, it is important not to exaggerate Soviet power or expansionism. Americans must also understand that U.S. power, U.S. ambitions, and U.S. aggressiveness disturb many governments, including some non-Communist, even anti-Soviet regimes. American self-righteousness and exaggerated images of Soviet aggressiveness simply make it more difficult to reach understandings—with our friends and our foes—that could enhance U.S. interests.

# 11

# Marketing Communications Roles in Public Crisis Management; The EDB Dilemma

*Robert Montgomery*

American manufacturers and suppliers of goods and services must often walk a thin line marking the boundaries of what the consumer wants to acquire and what is feasible, safe, and economically profitable to offer. Crystalline, sparkling water may not be the "best" water. Sleek, chromed automobiles may not be the "safest" automobiles. Cigarettes must be marked with warnings about their use; seat belts must be installed in cars; proprietary drugs must be labeled with statements about possible effects of their use; and food products must be packaged with their contents clearly listed and identified—all required by federal law.

Sometimes this legislation comes after much study, being the product of research, investigation, and laboratory findings. Often, officialdom acts in a greater hurry, responding to discoveries of potentially harmful situations with action to shut off the dangers thought to be inherent. In such cases, the industries involved must also respond with haste, lest their positions in the marketplace be damaged. Whether it is product identification or company reputation, loss of consumer acceptance can tell considerably—possible fatally—on the performance of the supplier. At the same time, every firm dedicated to long life and respectability in the marketplace is concerned with the well-being of its customers. Whatever chance leads the firm into a situation that demands auditing by external forces, the response must be geared toward correction and modification to meet the standards that have been arbitrated. Above all, the firm must be prepared with strategies, developed long before the crisis emerges, that will open the lines of communication between the firm and its markets so that understanding will continue to exist.

This case study is about the EDB dilemma, which hit the grain-food producers of America early in 1984. It shows how the creative efforts of those most seriously affected were brought to bear on the situation, by quick and effective response and with virtually no loss of market position. At the same time, product compensation was made to reduce or eliminate the inadvertent dangers that had been presented to the consumers by the use of technologically advanced chemical controls of food impurities. All materials presented here have been taken from published documents and do not represent either pro or con influences on the part of the subject industries.

Marketing of goods and services in a free, barter-and-trade economy is guided by what are now well-defined parameters. In all areas of the marketing mix, practitioners know with significant certainty what their roles are, how they contribute to the distribution of products, and to what limits they can go in their particular activity. Like their counterparts in such worlds as science and education and human behavior, marketing professionals have been documenting methods and techniques used in their own sector and studying the data for indicators that will present greater efficiencies in the conduct of business. Following World War II, impetus was given to this work by the availability of millions of pieces of information about market demographics, generated by the input of personnel characteristics data derived from the military testing programs. Marketers grasped the opportunity and used that accumulation of statistical data to provide a base of material for sharpening the aim of their approach to prospective customers, whose identities were now more clearly defined.

This is the second of the two "building blocks" that must be developed before the strategies of budget, media selection, and message creativity can be entertained. First, of course, is the need to *position* the product within the marketplace—"positioning" being what prospective customers believe the product will do for them to protect or enhance their self-image.

From the earliest times, when humans began trading their surpluses of production for the excesses of production offered by their neighbors—thereby creating "a market"—they had not been precise in their trading. They approached whoever was nearby, shouting "goods for sale, goods for sale."

But in the post World War II era, the "graphics" of marketing began to appear—demographics, psychographics, and geographics. As mentioned earlier, it was the production of a monumental mass of demographic and psychographic data, reaped from military testing programs, that gave this activity validity. Now, with honed accuracy, marketers began choosing from among the crowd the particular persons who bore the characteristics to make them realistic candidates for trading.

Most people involved in the business of trade will agree that until that time, the introduction of targeting procedures was the most important factor in the development of the posture of the free economy. Now, the presence of sophisticated computer technologies has put us in a logarithmic time period, with marketing statistical data collapsing from days, weeks, and months into seconds and minutes.

What all of this means is that, today, marketers have at their command the information and the equipment for reducing that information to workable codes, unlike anything known before. Now, marketers are able to construct models that will enable them to locate their audience precisely and to deliver to it the message that will most strongly affect that audience. They have the ability to create a message made of the symbols most easily recognized by their target and to choose from an amazing number of media those that will deliver the message with efficiency and surety.

There are limitations, however, to the effect marketers can have on their audiences. Their communications—which have for long years been called "advertising" but which are now more frequently being called "marketing communications"—can do only four things: tell the prospective customers what the product is, where to get it, how much it costs, and what it will do for them (The last item was referred to earlier. "What it will do for them" is one of two acts: *protect* or *enhance* customers' self-images.) Beyond those four influences, marketing communicators have no other power to stimulate a desired action. This is an important point to remember as we study the subject of this chapter.

In addition to accepting the foregoing limitations of marketing communications, we must also recognize the fact that, as communicators, we are only answering a need or a want or a desire expressed by the prospective customer. We cannot generate those factors. They must be present, either consciously or subconsciously, individually or in combination, for our communications to work. Nevertheless, marketing communications can, without any doubt, have enormous power. But that power derives from the skill with which the communicators construct their messages and the detailed attention they give to the examination of available media before making their selection of the best carriers.

This, then, is the base upon which we stand as we study how to effectively apply practical communications to marketing problem solving. Also, in this introduction to the case, we must keep in mind that advertising is not always geared to be a direct influence on the movement of the potential customers. In many programs, that influence is indirect; that is, initial momentum is generated by building confidence, respect, and desirability in the attitude of the customers toward their supplier. A firm frequently presents itself to its target as "a good company to do business with." As L.L.L. Golden says in his book, *Only By Public Consent:* "The basis of the public's acceptance of an institution is its performance . . . the acts of the institution as a whole."[1] So marketers know full well that it is not only product and price that moves the consumer; *how* a firm goes about its business is also an important consideration.

This introduction leads to our consideration of what marketing communications can do to project a positive influence at a time when a firm is undergoing close and perhaps negative scrutiny. And, for that study, we shall investigate what the American food industry did during the most recent of its possible marketing embarrassments—the EDB (ethylene dibromide) situation.

Early in 1984, America's packaged foods industry came under attack as a result of the Federal Food and Drug Administration's findings that EDB was present in grain-based products. It is important to note here that we shall not be concerned with the "right" or "wrong" of the situation. We are, instead, using this case to show how organizations, through the use of critical communications, can maintain their position in the marketplace, assuming that their social responsibilities have been met or that corrections are being made to remedy possibly harmful actions.

EDB (ethylene dibromide) is a colorless, nonflammable liquid, used from the 1940s through February 1984 as a pesticide to protect citrus trees and other crops from parasitic worms. In addition, it was used to protect stored grain, and the machinery used to mill grain, from insect infestation.[2]

In July 1983, scientists assigned to the State of Florida Health Department reported having discovered traces of EDB in two water wells and subsequently banned the use of EDB in eight counties in the state's citrus belt. In December 1983, Florida's Agriculture Department issued stop-sale orders for several grain-based products in which EDB had been detected, and the governor of the state asked that the U.S. Environmental Protection Agency (EPA) set standards for EDB levels in food for human consumption.

In February 1984, William Ruckelshaus, administrator of the EPA, issued orders prohibiting the further use of EDB on grain and in grain-milling processes. At the same time, the EPA issued national safety guidelines of 900 parts per billion (ppb) in raw grain, 150 ppb in intermediate products such as flour and mixes, and 30 ppb in ready-to-eat grain products such as cereals. It should be pointed out here that at this time—February 1984—the EPA stressed that the agency did not view EDB as a health emergency.

Nevertheless, the situation came to the public's attention when news items began to appear, spelling out the scenario. Late in February, the *Orlando Sentinel* reported on the effect of the ban but approached it from the standpoint of the economic impact on the agricultural industry, claiming that Florida farmers were "stuck with thousands of dollars' worth of EDB because of differences in the state and federal bans on the pesticide."[3] But we now see that dollar losses in the "thousands" were a most conservative estimate. As the problem grew, the value of unused chemical products in inventory for the control of infestation soon rose to millions of dollars. Earlier in February, however, the *Boston Globe* had released a front-page, lead story headlined "State Finds EDB in Food Products" and subheaded "Emergency Meeting Monday." The story said that "Massachusetts public health officials [had] found the cancer-causing pesticide EDB in dozens of cake mixes, flours and other grain products and [were] urging consumers to return products containing the chemical to the place of purchase." The article went on to say: "Unless the federal government acts first, state officials [would] meet . . . to decide whether any products should be ordered off the market." Compounding the effect of this news item, the *Globe* listed by brand name or manufacturer the sources of EDB-affected products.[4] At the same time, or within a few days, other newspapers were picking up the same storyline as their markets were affected by the situation.

The problem heated up for the suppliers. On February 6—three days after the EPA action—the Commonwealth of Massachusetts Department of Public Health, without public hearings, adopted emergency regulations on EDB, calling for interim standards of 10 ppb in consumable foods through March 6, and 1 ppb thereafter. There began the rapid development of public awareness, based on the frightening news. Negative attitudes were manifested by the suspicions directed at the food products under investigation and the manufacturers and suppliers as well.

Two problems, therefore, were exposed to the marketers: (1) determining whether, in fact, their firms were in a position of fault and, if so, participating in corrective actions; and (2) setting out a policy to reduce the impact of negative reporting on their target audience.

In the meantime, the need for immediacy in seeking the answers to those questions was magnified by the flood of news stories covering the EDB situation from all angles. The Albany, New York, *Times Union* headlined in its February 26 edition: "EDB: EPA points to long-term threat as it clears off grocery shelves."[5] That same day, the *New York Times* reported that six Northeastern states "set maximum permissible levels of the chemical in food three times as stringent as those adopted ... by the Federal Environmental Protection Agency."[6] And *Time* magazine said in its February 27 issue: "Trouble at the Grocery Store—EDB recalls leave food manufacturers fretful and watchful."[7]

But the news wasn't all bad. Jim Auchmutey, a staff writer for the *Atlanta Journal*, said in his column: "Hazards of EDB are exaggerated, compared to natural carcinogens." He went on to point out that even peanut butter "harbors a much more powerful cancer-producing agent."[8] And Dr. Bruce Ames, chairman of the Department of Biochemistry at the University of California, Berkeley, was quoted as saying:

> Humans are ingesting, and have always ingested large amounts of many natural chemicals that might cause cancer. It is among these chemicals, not the traces of EDB allowed in our diets, where most scientists believe we will find the main environmental causes to the common human cancers.[9]

Marketing communicators know full well that the public is quick to react to fear-founded stimuli. Of all the basic emotional appeals presented by marketing messages—love, hate, safety, security, and others—fear has been shown to be consistently among the top motivators of buying or nonbuying action. Therefore, it takes strong advertising countermeasures to offset the serious negative forces that can be generated by such casual sources as uninformed comment and rumor, especially when the possibility of physical harm might befall those near and dear to the listener. In addition, we have a phenomenon present in today's consumer-oriented economy that puts buyers in the role of antagonist to American industry, willing to believe, and even support, accusations of misconduct.

There developed, then, a classic case of marketing communicators facing the dilemma of maintaining the true status of their company vis-à-vis the claims against it, disseminated widely by the mass media. Once the issue is determined, what steps must they take to minimize the resulting effect? In their daily operations, they are directly concerned with the movement of product into the marketplace through the channels of distribution. Their messages, the advertising for their firms, are concerned with product "sell." Although they may be involved in institutional advertising as well, their primary concern is moving product. Although the EDB situation had a great deal of effect on the images of the companies involved, which might well have been harmful in the long term, the most critical immediate aspect involved product rejection by the market. This by no means minimizes image-factor consequences—the possibility of considerable losses in investment opportunities and effects on employee and community relations and the conduct of business with government agencies. The vast amount of EDB-related product in the distribution chain was directly affected, however, and it was necessary for the marketing communicators to determine, using every resource available to them, exactly what their stance would be.

To show how reactive efforts can be martialed in such cases, we go to the records of a giant in the field, Procter & Gamble (P&G), the Cincinnati, Ohio, conglomerate with hundreds of product lines. Then we shall go to the organization representing every major and smaller food manufacturer and food processor in the country, the Grocery Manufacturers of America, Inc.

In the July 1984 issue of their marketing publication *Moonbeams,* P&G said:

> Misinformation and confusion about EDB residues in grain-based products has spread nationwide. Consumers from California to Massachusetts were bewildered and needlessly concerned about the safety of Duncan Hines baking mixes as well as products from General Mills, Quaker Oats, Pillsbury and other national and regional food manufacturers.[10]

Perhaps the most logical next step might have been for P&G marketing to have heeded the advice of William S. Sachs, who says that "regardless of how the task is approached, promoting the corporation as a way of building attitudes towards its many products implies a 'trickle down' philosophy. Its underlying assumption is that corporate images become associated with company products in consumers' minds."[11]

As we saw earlier, Florida's actions in banning the use of EDB and ordering out of the marketplace those products associated with the chemical, brought widespread media attention and concern about the safety of grain-based food products, and the focus quickly began to spread to other states.

As soon as the safety of P&G products was questioned, a task force led by Group Vice-President Gerry Dirvin was set up to coordinate the company's actions. A group of P&G scientists quickly convened to review all available information about EDB. "We were confident that our products were totally safe and represented no threat to consumers," said Gil Cloyd, director of P&G's Human and Environmental Safety Division. "But leading experts in the field were also consulted to confirm our assessments."

Despite the scientific evidence, however, public debate around EDB seemed to quickly lose all "rational perspective," according to Cloyd. He claimed that there are many naturally occurring animal carcinogens in our food supply, and that alarming the public about EDB levels in cake mixes was no more warranted than telling people to throw away their black pepper or never to eat celery or mushrooms—all of which, he says, contain trace amounts of natural animal carcinogens. This position reflects that of newspaper columnist Jim Auchmutey, quoted earlier. Gerry Dirvin added: "Although we knew public concerns about EDB were largely unjustified, our primary goal was to remove our products from the controversy and to minimize the disruption to P&G's business."[12] In review, the first part of his statement represents the company image point of view; the second part involves the movement of product in the marketplace.

At this stage, P&G marketing people brought other departments into the trenches. Employees in the Food Purchase Division worked over the Christmas holiday to identify suppliers who could sell to P&G flour with the lowest levels of EDB residue. The company had to locate, test, and buy millions of bushels of wheat directly—something P&G had not done before. And every silo of grain had to be sampled for EDB levels.

Once the wheat was purchased, systems had to be established to ensure that the P&G-owned wheat was not exposed to EDB residues as it moved from the grain terminals into rail cars and trucks and to the mills for processing into flour.

EDB also became a controlling factor for the five P&G plants that produce Duncan Hines mixes. "Manufacturing people spent a lot of time early in the controversy trying to isolate shipments of flour by EDB levels," explained David Mack, division manager in Food Manufacturing. An analysis of P&G's entire Duncan Hines manufacturing system was initiated to collect data and learn what controls could be established to minimize EDB levels in finished products. Daily coordination among those plants, located across the country from Port Ivory, New York, to Sacramento, California, as well as with the Purchases and Product Development divisions, was critical, according to Mack.

By early 1984, supplies of wheat and flour for the Duncan Hines business had been secured with very little or no EDB, and consumers could be reassured that Duncan Hines products being shipped were virtually free of the chemical.

While many segments of P&G personnel worked to meet the immediate business crisis posed by EDB, others focused their efforts outside the company. Across the country, decisions were being made on a state-by-state basis by public officials, with very little data on the actual residues of EDB in grain-based products. It soon became apparent that national tolerance standards for EDB were needed to provide for a consistent, coherent approach to dealing with the issue. Thus, P&G became a force within the Grocery Manufacturers of America, Inc. (GMA), an association of food processors and manufacturers based in Washington, D.C.

As a result, on February 3, the EPA announced recommended guidelines on EDB residue levels. Steps were also taken that would lead to an orderly phase-out of EDB from the food supply over several years.

Meanwhile, the GMA was also taking positive communications action. In addition to the scientific inputs from Procter & Gamble, information poured in from other member firms and contributing organizations, large and small.

Recognizing the association's commitment to public health and safety, Sherwin Gardner, vice-president of the Science and Technology Department of the GMA, pledged the member companies to assist federal and state agencies in their study of the risks associated with the use of EDB; to eliminate EDB from food products as quickly as possible; and to continually test and update data on the levels of EDB in raw grain and intermediate and finished grain products.

Through all of this, we must keep in mind that at no time did the manufacturers intend to manipulate the minds of the market. Their principal concern was to bring agreement between themselves and those prospects whom they had qualified as potential customers.

For more than a decade, suppliers to the American marketplace have, for the most part, been operating under a philosophical umbrella called "marketing orientation." To illustrate this point, let us consider refrigerators. It is well accepted by the engineers in the home appliance industry that it is realistically possible to build consumer food-keepers that would last a lifetime, that would provide outstanding preservative characteristics, that would supply enormous quantities of ice cubes, and that would freeze and keep meats and vegetables and dairy products for much longer periods of time than equipment presently offered can do. Yet none of this is available to consumers, simply because they do not want these features. Instead, they ask for style; decorative looks; fringe niceties, such as door-dispensed ice water and cubes; and pretty little shelves that serve no practical function, such as butter-storers and canned juice dispensers. Above all they do not want to pay the price of a lifetime refrigerator, even though, in the long run, it would be more economical to do so. This refusal is based on their knowing that five or six years from now, they will once again be remodeling their kitchens, and the old units will no longer fit the decor. The same can be said for carpeting, TV sets, draperies, shoes and socks, and automobiles. Whatever the product, the consumer says, "This is what I want. Build it for me." Some call it "consumer orientation"; some, "consumer demand." But the certainty is that, in virtually all industries today, the end user—whether retail or industrial—dictates to the manufacturer the conditions of the product. Price, delivery, color, weight, predicted service life, and other characteristics are the result of consumer demand rather than supplier offering. This is a well-accepted fact, known to today's marketers. Although the economic phenomenon of supply-and-demand equilibrium certainly enters the equation, major suppliers, especially in consumer marketing, pay close attention to the condition of consumer demand. To do less is to play into the hands of competition. With this in mind, we can understand the positive action that was taken by the producers of grain and grain-based foodstuffs. A spokesman for one of the companies involved in the EDB situation told a convention audience that open and direct communication with consumer customers is the only acceptable course of action in times such as these. He pointed out that for most people of the world, wheat is basic to the diet of humans. Consumed as baked goods, like bread and rolls, or as processed food, like cake mixes and cereals, grain is primary in the daily menu of American households. He told his audience:

> For us to fail to transmit our concerns—even though we were innocent of oversight—would have been both unforgiveable and stupid. Public safety has to come first in the minds of food suppliers, as it should and always will. Stupid, because we, as marketing professionals, know very well the dangers incumbent in the loss, even for a short period of time, of confidence in our products.

He went on to say that millions of dollars had been spent over many years to build acceptance of his company's products, and that to jeopardize this through inactivity or a willingness to compromise its position in the marketplace would be foolhardy. "Worse," he went on, "would be to believe that we could hoodwink our consumers, which would be an outrageous malfeasance of the practice of marketing communications."[13]

Consumers were not silent during the EDB crisis. Soon after the initial announcements by state and national government agencies, listing preventive measures that were being introduced, articles and letters to editors began appearing in newspapers across the country, indicating a thrust of negativitism toward the grain-based products that would also have to be counteracted by the marketing communicators representing the companies under scrutiny. A cover story dated March 18 in the *Boston Globe Magazine* was headlined: "How the government failed to protect us from pesticides." In this case, the finger was pointed at the federal government, saying that "the Reagan Administration failed to control EDB." The article, while calling for strict regulatory controls on chemicals used in the production of foodstuffs, didn't let the manufacturers off the hook. "Supporters of pesticides are visible and powerful," the story declared. "The network of advocates includes researchers at land-grant colleges, officials in state and federal departments of agriculture, county extension agents, and the industry that manufactures pesticides."[14] While it is interesting that the foregoing list did not include food processors, it was they who would bear the brunt of consumer reaction to the piece. Ever since the appearance of Rachel Carson's 1962 best-seller, *Silent Spring,* there has been significantly greater consumer awareness and, therefore, intelligence about contamination and pollution and infestation than ever before. Sometimes that scrutiny is in a media format hard to counter. Ilene Barth's op-ed piece in the February 20 edition of the *Boston Globe*—"What's a mother to do?"—is a creative expression in print. She wrote: "It was 7 a.m., one Wednesday morning, and the mother of two was preparing to poison her family." She went on to say that she asked her daughter what the little girl wanted for breakfast, and when told "oatmeal," wondered "whether the oats had been doused with ethylene dibromide, EDB." Then, she went on to say, "I try to make sure that what my loved ones eat won't kill them."[15] On the same date, a letter to the editor of the *Globe* denounced the chemical, saying that "the parent of a child with birth defects . . . might want to look at EDB a little more closely."[16]

However, not all the commentators were detractors. Dr. Gordon W. Gribbel, professor of chemistry at Dartmouth College, writes: " . . . a well-done T-bone steak and the smoke from one cigarette can easily contain 100 ppb of PAH . . . at least as carcinogenic as EDB."[17] And the *Schenectady* New York *Gazette* editorialized on February 27: "The five northeastern states that have just agreed on a . . . set of guidelines may be taking [the EDB dilemma] just a bit too seriously."[18]

It was this mixture of responses—positive, negative, and many in between— that became the focus of attention on the part of the communicators for the grain organizations. Some firms took a strong advertising position. Shop Rite Supermakets, from their Consumer Affairs Department in Elizabeth, New Jersey, commented in a paid advertisement: "But it must be stressed that the risks from EDB seem to be quite slight, and keep dwindling. We hope the worst of its exposure is over."[19]

Other organizations bided their time. Some, through their advertising agencies, had advertisements "plated" and ready to run in print media and tapes ready to roll on television. In every case, the messages were centered on *fact,* not rumor—the facts being that manufacturers had rushed every possible force into the breach of correction and that millions of dollars' worth of product had been taken off retail shelves and destroyed. In addition, many major producers, such as Procter & Gamble, had begun immediately to fill the distribution pipeline with grain-based foodstuffs of unquestionable purity.

While awaiting adjustments in public mood, marketing communicators in the food industry were watching for support mechanisms from other sources. For example, Senator Edward Burke, chairman of the Congressional Joint Committee on Health Care, urged "that [we do not undertake] unintentionally, some sort of witch hunt in the name of public health unless . . . other data submitted clearly establishes that it is in the best interest of the citizens." And he continued: "We ought to be very careful before we proceed to a standard which may not be scientifically justified, which may be difficult to implement and to enforce."[20]

Senator Burke was but one of a host of spokesmen who came to the defense of the food industry. Editors, commentators, and spokesmen from the biological and chemical laboratories repeated their assurances that the issue may have been grossly overinflated.

And overinflated it proved to be, as an analysis of the case now shows so clearly. Nevertheless, the communicators were ready with their tools. From the standpoint of marketing economics, the disaster was both imminent and probable of reaching a conclusion that could have spelled millions of dollars of waste-loss to the firms and to consumers affected by shortage-escalated prices. The command to the advertising professionals was to analyze the situation in full detail; to determine the position of their firms within the daily framework of developments; and to prepare to deliver to their target audiences the messages that would clearly assess the companies' positions and show what corrective measures were being taken.

This is, of course, the ideal to which marketing communicators aspire in virtually all areas of consumer and business-to-business advertising. The harmonious relationship that exists between buyer and supplier depends almost entirely upon open communications. Product price and delivery and performance are all characteristics of consumer need fulfillment, but all are affected by the message delivered from the producer. If that message is found wanting at the critical moment when the purchasers, at any level, are seeking information to support their selection, the relationship is certainly strained—if not, indeed, ended. And the "wanting" can be truth or fact or acceptance of an act of mischance. For this, only the marketing communicators can be responsible.

# 12

# Video Invasion:
# Afghanistan, 1979–1983

*Anne Rawley Saldich*

T elevision news has improved considerably since the Vietnam war. That conclusion emerges clearly from this study of ABC's, CBS's, and NBC's nightly reports about the Soviet invasion of Afghanistan. The analysis in this chapter begins with the border crossing in December 1979 and ends four years later, although the struggle continues. All information here, except for my interpretation and conclusions, came directly from the TV screen. Confining my research to what viewers saw will allow readers to appreciate the quality of the coverage. Some of it was superficial, and there were times when one wished for a thousand intelligent words instead of action shots. Nonetheless, these networks did a creditable job of putting events in their social and political context.

Events in Afghanistan forced innovation onto the networks because U.S. journalists were expelled a month after the invasion. Facts were hard to get or to verify, and it was even harder to produce meaningful visuals. One had to be imaginative to produce a good program. Television turned to international cooperation, clever strategies, tenacity, and daring clandestine photography. The practice of labeling visuals as to their source became a trend instead of an occasional sortie into professional work habits. In the mythic and myth-making world of the electronic press, that was a great stride forward—toward integrity. Viewers have a right to know who is telling them what and why. Only then can they decide how the news is biased—and it is *always* biased. Balanced reporting may be called "objective," but that ill-founded belief is subscribed to only by the naive.

There were flaws, of course. Visuals often dominated without adding quality to content. This weakness was overcome to some degree by micro-and minidocumentaries, presented within the programs, thereby reaching the largest TV news audience. Synthesis and interpretation were frequently missing. That is worrisome; however, it reflects the way people see the editorial function. Some think reporters should be limited to facts that "speak for themselves." Others, myself included, think facts never "speak for themselves." They believe it is more professional to interpret information, because viewers should be told where facts end and analysis begins, with conclusions labeled as such. If they conflict, so much the better.

As we go to press, the Soviet Union is intensifying its domination of Afghanistan and its abuse of human rights. Resistance fighters continue their struggle for freedom.

## Background

This analysis is based on 13.3 hours of uninterrupted nightly news, limited to Afghanistan and related events. It was compiled onto a series of video cassettes by the Television News Archive (TNA) at Vanderbilt University from master recordings of complete news programs.[1] Although the networks did other programs about Afghanistan, this case study is confined to an analysis of the nightly news as it was received and taped off the air in Nashville, Tennessee, by the TNA. There is one salient reason for such a narrow focus. A significant majority of people in the U.S. use TV's evening news as their primary, or only, source of public affairs information. Equally important, they believe what they see because most of us are raised on the myth that "seeing is believing."

The reporting environment in Afghanistan was one of tension and tight controls by the Russian and Afghan governments. U.S. camera crews and reporters were primarily in Kabul, Afghanistan's capitol. Prior to their expulsion, the constraints of censorship and technological problems were evident in most of the footage. Reports rarely originated from locations other than Kabul when the information was gathered inside Afghanistan. Much of the news content was supplied by the networks' facilities in the United States, by the United Nations, or by official U.S. sources, such as the Departments of State and Defense. During their stay in Afghanistan, it was no problem for the government to control journalists, regardless of nationality. Every form of transport had to be government-approved, and in many instances it was government-issued. That made it easy to keep television crews under surveillance.

Geographic constraints combined well with government control. In the northeast, there are the rugged Hindu Kush Mountains, among the highest in the world. A harsh climate and extremely severe landscapes are cruel enemies to all who are unprepared for dust storms, high winds in four seasons, freezing winters, torrid summers, desertlike expanse, awesome heights and thin air, swift-running rivers, and terrain that is impassable except on foot or with the help of animals. Mechanical transport is limited by the lack of roadways. Afghanistan is majestically elemental. Its economy is feudal, and its politics are tribal. Nationhood, a concept that Afghan tribes resist, is unwanted. Literacy is about 12 percent in a population that compares with Texas, a state whose size is also similar to Afghanistan. Westerners' necessities are wondrous luxuries to these "people of the wind," who are not plugged into our Information Age. Communication is accomplished today as it has been for centuries, by bellowing through great horns from one valley to the next. These realities were described beautifully by ABC.[2]

This is the environment from which Americans reported, firsthand, for a mere twenty-seven days, with the few exceptions to be discussed later.

Before analyzing the nightly news, let us get a feeling for some of the contemporary actors and events. In 1979, Afghanistan's Soviet-controlled President Amin was not sufficiently effective to suit the Kremlin. He was duly assassinated[3] and replaced by another puppet, Babrak Karmal.[4] The United States and the USSR were principal actors, with Russia being the protagonist because it took and kept the initiative. Despite several notices of the impending invasion, the U.S. response was limited to warnings.[5] Pakistan's initial role was as a base for Afghan "rebels" (also called "freedom fighters," "resistants," "insurgents," "guerrillas") and as an immense refugee camp for hundreds of thousands of homeless neighbors. Later, its role expanded, and Pakistan became one of several countries engaged in transshipping arms and munitions to fellow Moslems.

TV brought the political/economic issues into focus when CBS reported that the State Department would ask for a 10 percent increase in military aid for Saudi Arabia, Oman, Egypt, Israel, Tunisia, Somalia, Kenya, and Morocco.[6] This announcement was made only eighteen months after the invasion. In that way, the new Reagan administration hoped to anchor the U.S. "sphere of interest." CBS told its viewers that the president insisted the increases were needed to combat activities in South Yemen, Afghanistan, and Ethiopia, missiles aimed at the Persian Gulf, and the massing of Soviet troops on Iran's border.[7] ABC interviewed Egypt's President Anwar Sadat, "live." He candidly told the world that his government was aiding Afghan insurgents by opening its store of arms for purchase, by anyone, on behalf of the rebels. In the same report, viewers learned that the covert supply of arms was extensive, that it was coordinated by the CIA, and that it involved five nations: the United States, Egypt, Saudi Arabia, Pakistan, and the People's Republic of China. Reagan's administration maintained a discreet silence.[8]

Two other actors, powerful but invisible, transcended borders and peoples: the Moslem religion (Suni and Shiite) and Communist atheism. Tribal Afghanistan's history has been replete with internecine wars. Some were triggered by petty grievances or tribal assertiveness, and some took the form of antinationalism. However, the Russian invasion verified an old political principle: Nothing unites like an enemy from without, especially if it provides occasion for a holy war. Afghan rebels were fighting to protect fundamental values of religion and family.[9] With such motivation, no sacrifice was too great or unreasonable. That may explain why they fought, initially, with rocks and rifles against their most-feared enemy-weapon, the Russian helicopter "gunboat." Later, more sophisticated arms became available to them. Ideology was a prime mover for the Communists, also; they are true believers in a fervently proclaimed higher mission. Taking over other countries is an expression of Communism's global strategies.

Even before the invasion, there were many dissidents within the Soviet-controlled Afghan army. After 1979, spying and desertions increased markedly. Consequently, Russians did more of the fighting. Soviet forces increased from 30,000, initially, to an occupation army of 100,000 in February 1980.[10] At that time, one out of every fifteen people in Afghanistan was in the Russian military. Someone had a grand plan in mind.

When the Soviets invaded, Jimmy Carter was president of the United States, and he revised a foreign policy called "linkage." Basically, it juxtaposes events so that there are tradeoffs: if you do this, we'll do that. Carter's protest was to withdraw from the 1980 Summer Olympics in Moscow. That was shrewd. Afghanistan was hardly well known. By linking the invasion to the Olympics, Carter focused American hearts and minds in no time at all. Other U.S. pressures included trade embargoes against the Soviet Union, notably on U.S. exports of wheat and high technology.

Were Carter's motives moral or economic? Was he moved to action by Persian Gulf oil and potential Communist expansion into our sphere of influence? This fundamental question was handled in a shallow way by the nightly news, although it could have been the vehicle for an excellent report. As for embargoes, the USSR did have serious wheat shortages that complemented American overproduction; and High technology, another Russian import, is a prime U.S. export. Again, network treatment was superficial. The history of embargoes would have been an excellent analytical tool. Unfortunately, the subject was not explored. Viewers did not learn from the nightly news that embargoes usually fail because there are so many ways to circumvent them.

Other world events that framed news coverage of Afghanistan were as follows. Americans were held hostage at our embassy in Iran. There was increasing speculation that the Persian Gulf was Russia's real target, which meant the risk of a wide war, if not of world war. Soviet troops massed on Iran's border. Polish rebellion was repressed by Soviet force. Russia was accused of chemical warfare in Afghanistan. The United States broke off SALT II discussions as another protest, which "chilled" U.S.–Soviet relations because the talks had been a means for informal communication during a dozen years. President Carter was routed out of office in 1980. Shortly thereafter, President Reagan ended the grain embargo. He also supplied military aid to Afghan "freedom fighters." During the four years covered by this analysis, he was "invited" to "rescue" the island of Grenada from "Communist infiltration." On that occasion, Reagan made history by censoring the press. For the first time, U.S. journalists were not permitted to accompany American troops into battle.

This background indicates that the world was functioning in a mode of classic power politics between 1979 and 1983: heightened nationalism, spheres of influence, and the balancing of power. For example, India's Indira Gandhi first blessed the invasion but soon recanted. [11] The nightly news reported this event without analysis. Why?

## Video's Version of the Invasion

Afghanistan is not a "livingroom war," as Vietnam was. Its brutal reality does not come with the nightly news, because it was, and still is, difficult to get relevant pictures. Between 1979 and 1983, "talking heads" were often used to summarize events in front of symbols that replaced action shots: a blue-and-white globe represented the UN; the steps of the State Department indicated that source as a scene of activity; five entwined circles were a frequent backdrop for the Olympic boycott; and flags of various countries and still photographs of principal personalities were commonly used to support an oral report about places and people. TV's voracious appetite for images was also fed by "voiceovers," running commentaries that tell about the action photos on-screen. Sometimes, old footage was used to report about Afghanistan, although the narrator was describing current events—and occasionally such footage was properly identified as "stock" photos.

Despite visual problems, network teams managed to produce micro-and minidocumentaries, running three to five or even twenty minutes. This was done by interconnecting related subjects. For example, footage about the invasion of Afghanistan was spliced back-to-back with the boycott of the Olympics, and that was given a time slot right next to economic news about the embargo and the hostages in Iran. As a result, we had something that looked like a small documentary on Central Asia, which was aired in the middle of the news, during peak viewing for public affairs.

Linking themes and events improves TV journalism, because several facets of the same event allow viewers to appreciate the complexity and fragility of international relations. One day nobody knew where Afghanistan was; a month later, that word was shorthand for a distant war that could become more than regional—It might lead to a nuclear holocaust. "Afghanistan" spilled with connotations: because of a Soviet invasion, half a world away, American values were reassessed by would-be Olympians, their coaches, fans, politicians, diplomats, people of every political persuasion.

What about oil? A Soviet push south, across Iran, would threaten vital Persian Gulf resources. President Carter decided that words were not enough. As soon as he moved to symbols—the boycott—he galvanized the nation. People began to have a fairly sophisticated understanding of international politics, not because they had a better grasp of "godless Communism" or Moslem "holy wars" but because even political illiterates understand sports. Athletics is part of the American tradition. "Just plain folks" were asking themselves deep questions and discussing them with others: Should we pour Olympic glory and hard currency into Moscow while Russia flagrantly violates values that are intrinsic to freedom? Boycotting the Olympics, persuading others to do the same, setting up alternative games, the social and political reasons for doing such things—all this was debated within the framework of sports. It was extremely well reported by TV, whose journalists let many people speak directly to the nation, on-camera, pro and con. In addition, efforts were made by each network to provide understanding of how the games had evolved and the nonathletic uses to which they had been put in the past. We will come to that again later.

The short documentaries within the nightly news were strikingly effective. They may be the reason why only American journalists were expelled from Afghanistan. The USSR had no sooner invaded than TV began hard-hitting reports that were given extensive aritime and well-rounded coverage. Thirteen minutes, half the "news hole," were assigned by NBC two weeks after the invasion.[12] (A "news hole" is the time allocated to news, as distinct from the time given over to advertising.) That minidocumentary explained Afghanistan's geography, the economic embargoes against Russia, the possible Olympic boycott, plans for selling arms to the rebels, and efforts to improve relations with China. The following night, another several minutes were devoted to fast-breaking events. There were reports from Kabul, from the Khyber Pass in northeastern Afghanistan, from the UN, from Peking, and from NBC's studio.[13] Other networks also committed long time periods to Afghanistan. ABC assigned eight minutes to the Moslem guerillas and provided background material that is essential to understanding the politics of the region.[14] During the first eight days of the new year (1980), CBS gave Afghanistan five, six, and seven minutes each night.[15] Almost always, reports about Afghanistan were among the first few time slots in the evening news. Almost always, coverage about U.S. hostages in Iran was before or after such reports, and information about the Olympic boycott or U.S. embargoes was linked onto that. In this way, the duration and multifaceted aspects of events affecting and being affected by Central Asia was significant in terms of a television presentation. (The term *Significant* needs a context. Historically, television news has an established reputation for superficiality, which is often due to overemphasis on action shots. Also, there is a tendency to emphasize negative events and to put them on the screen without a framework. The networks did not do this with the evening news about Afghanistan. In this respect, progress toward quality journalism was "significant.") These were not "firsts." Networks had juxtaposed related events before. However, toward 1983, the Afghanistan coverage developed another dimension. Minidocumentaries became a series, night after night, on important themes. That was a highly successful technique for adding depth and breadth to reports.

Perhaps it was tempting for editors to hesitate about programming "unpatriotic" material. If so, it was not evident. Reports were balanced, and even the rhetoric never became polemic. For example, one ABC series included a segment on espionage, which was reported as more pervasive in Russia than in the United States because America's CIA is subject to congressional review. If "my country, right or wrong" came into play, the network could have stopped there. Instead, it chose to say that the CIA had regained much of its anonymity under President Reagan. As an example of covert operations, it cited Afghanistan.[16] One may argue that that was going too far. But it was balanced reporting; a condition that added another perspective was made known to the public, though the White House surely could not have been pleased. ABC did not say that the CIA should not be insulated from the democratic process, but the fact that its covert status had increased was broadcast so that it could be openly discussed. It is necessary for journalists to provide several perspectives, because that is the real world—events are interconnected. News reports should help viewers realize that the planet Earth is a small place, so small that "Star Wars" is not just the name of a film—it's the name of a possibility.

"Balanced reporting" is relatively new to TV. The phrase came into fashion with Nixon, when the White House was frequently unhappy about its bad press, especially on television. The administration took an active role in rectifying that by insisting that the networks must report pro and con and that both sides of an issue were to be presented *within* a program, not simply as a correction on another occasion. This was particularly true if the news presented the administration in a less than flattering light. Although it is the Federal Communications Commission that controls renewal of broadcast licenses, the White House made it plain that renewal would not be so automatic as it had been in the past unless TV executives complied. The networks pleaded First Amendment privileges, and there ensued quite a complicated public debate about balanced reporting and freedom of the press. But the message was not missed. TV executives had their awareness raised, and self-examination set in even though the press did not cave in.

There were other impressive examples of balance, sometimes called "fairness." When ABC reported that Sweden *would* participate in the Moscow Olympics, the network could have stopped there. One might say it had cause to do so, for its journalists had been expelled from Afghanistan just twenty-one days earlier. That kind of bias could have been forgiven. If the temptation occurred to anyone at ABC, it was overruled. The ABC report went on to explain Sweden's powerful reason for staying in: Olympic games were held while the United States was at war with Indochina. The implication was clear: the games went on during that invasion; therefore, they should go on during this invasion.[17]

CBS gave us another example of balance, in a minidocumentary, the night before its journalists were expelled.[18] It was an excellent social-historical analysis of how the Olympics have been politicized since they were revived in 1896. At that time, France was intent upon using them to regain a sense of national glory, following its terrible humiliation during the Franco-Prussian War. In 1936, Adolph Hitler wanted them to be a showcase for white supremacy, but a famous black athlete, Jesse Owens, won the gold medal for track. Thirty-two years later in Mexico City (1968), Tom Smith and John Carlos made the Black Power salute (a raised, closed fist) from the victory stand. It was a political gesture that earned them suspension by the Olympic Committee. (Apparently, one of the Committee's functions is to keep alive the unfounded belief that sports and politics are separate, historically.) Munich's 1972 games are unforgettable. Eleven athletes were killed by Palestinian terrorists, but after a day's suspension the games continued. Even Israel voted to proceed. Four years later, thirty-two nations withdrew because New Zealand sent rugby teams to South Africa, whose apartheid policies are incompatible with democratic values. When Carter decided to boycott the Olympics, a famous sports columnist told the TV audience that he believed the president was right, that our participation would be a charade. CBS did not stop there. Its journalists continued to probe. American athletes who had been training to participate were broadcast live. Many were against withdrawal from Moscow; they thought the White House should not mix politics and athletics. Other would-be participants reluctantly endorsed Carter's policy. It was heart-wrenching to see these young people struggling with the complex values that underpin foreign policy as well as with their personal ethics.

When the Moscow Olympics were over, NBC reported that although thirty-five countries did not participate," the boycott did not ruin the games nor did it achieve its stated political objectives."[19] The narrator continued: Soviet forces were not withdrawn from Afghanistan, nor did the Russian people question the invasion. The United States paid the price of being a free society by showing its allies participating in something that we asked them not to do. Russia, a closed society, "eliminated" internal discord and international uncooperativeness by not reporting it in its government-censored media.

In brief, the networks achieved a degree of balance that even the Nixon administration would find hard to criticize. ABC, on the third anniversary of the invasion, went so far as to introduce a note of skepticism about its *own* news on Afghanistan as well as that from other media. They reminded viewers that reporting is unreliable.[20]

If facts are hard to get and difficult to verify, what obligation do journalists have with respect to using ambiguous news sources? And—a related question—how do they meet the American public's right to know? The networks had learned from their experience during the Indochina war, when visuals on American television screens were sometimes government-issue without being labeled as such. That was propaganda, not journalism. It could have become journalism if the visuals had been identified. Instead, editors often broadcast the footage as if their own news departments had produced it. That was misleading and dishonest.

Fortunately, Afghanistan seems to have been handled differently. In the 13.3 hours of news that I analyzed, there were a dozen instances in which material was labeled "file footage" or "White House photo." Or a narrator told the audience that the source was French, Dutch, British, or that it was purchased from a freelance photographer; that it was the cooperative effort of a network and the Afghanistan government; that it was given to a network by the rebels; and so forth. That additional input allowed viewers to make informed judgments about what they saw. It also added credibility to the news.

Accountability to the public was introduced to TV journalism when the Television News Archive at Vanderbilt University started taping the evening news off the air (1968). Network executives may protest that they always respected accountability to the public. Perhaps they did. However, there is a difference between a policy of respect and a policy of public access to the news after it has been broadcast, so that one may verify that the responsibility has been carried out. Certainly, networks believe the public has a right to know. That has been the clarion call of the American press since the Constitution's First Amendment was written to protect press freedom. But the networks had their own version of this: The public had a right to know between 6:00 P.M. and 6:30 P.M. while the news was broadcast. *When the nightly news* was finished, at 6:31 P.M., the public had no right to know if what they heard and saw was accurate. Networks did little to help the public *review* the news. Indeed, they made it difficult. The important point is that one minute after the news was over it was, effectively, impossible to gain access to what was broadcast. Whether the news was aired at 6:00 P.M. 5:30 P.M., or some other time, is irrelevant to this discussion.

Returning now, to the improved ways in which news about Afghanistan was gathered and broadcast, the networks became more flexible and imaginative. For example, eighteen months after ABC was forced out, it had a camera crew back in Afghanistan, with John Lawrence as principal reporter. His visuals showed Russian Mig attacks on civilians and resistance fighters undergoing military training. Using a voiceover while the camera photographed rebels, a narrator explained how the problem of disunity among tribes was related to their military inefficiency. In other words, the lack of cooperation is frequently rooted in social and political traditions. Also included was a brief segment showing the rebels fighting Soviet forces. The report ended with: "John Lawrence, London".[21] ABC could have been more explicit. Did that mean Lawrence worked for ABC but was a British national? Is that how he got into the country? Does it mean that Lawrence is a British freelancer and ABC borrowed or bought the footage? The source information was far from perfect, but it was progress over telling viewers nothing about how the news originated.

A year later, ABC again had footage from Afghanistan, this time of rebels attacking a Russian convoy. The visuals were identified as the work of a British amateur photographer.[22] Again, that was a flag flying in the right direction. The audience was not misled into believing that the Afghanistan government had rescinded its expulsion of ABC. On another evening, ABC identified footage as "old." Yet another time, viewers were told that the film shown had been given to ABC by one of the guerrilla groups and that it "purports to show" (notice the careful rhetoric) the execution of a captured Russian soldier and his Afghan ally. The narrator said that "the guerillas seemed to be taking directions from a cameraman. . . . Why guerillas would release film of their own atrocities is not clear but vengeance is a deep and dominant emotion among the Afghanistans while murder and terror are characteristic of both sides."[23] Balanced reporting, restrained rhetoric, identification of the film as having been given to ABC—all this took the report beyond propaganda into the realm of news. Overall, that is encouraging progress toward responsible journalism when it is judged within the historical context of how well TV used to identify sources.

CBS did an interesting broadcast on June 26, 1981. That evening's news dealt with reports of gas being used as a weapon by the USSR against the rebels. Viewers were told clearly that what they saw had been shot a month earlier in collaboration with the Afghanistan government. It was the result of CBS being invited by the Soviets to bring a film crew back into the country for a ten-day period. CBS told its audience that the terms of the arrangement included the network's agreement that its material would be blended with Soviet propaganda, which was spliced into the CBS report.

It may seem shocking that CBS agreed, but that is a problem of ethics. Our problem is the public's right to know how networks gather news, especially when it is not through traditional reporting techniques. Given the history of TV news, it is remarkable that CBS was explicit about how and why the footage was made. Its aplogia has a certain logic. Chemical warfare had become an increasingly important subject during the first six months of the invasion. There were mounting claims and apparent evidence that the Soviets used gas and "yellow rain." The information became public by word of mouth from refugees who found their way to Pakistan. Working with the government's film crew was CBS's passport to verify the rumors. The network took it. Paul Fitzgerald said, on camera, that he had no idea why he was selected by Afghanistan. He had been there before—perhaps the government wanted someone who could make comparisons. This he did. He and his camera reported that life seemed peaceful in Kabul and Jalalabad. (The entire country as a handful of cities. These were the two to which they were restricted.) There were few Russians in view. All seemed normal. But, said Fitzgerald, at night they could hear convoys rolling along at about 45 mph, and they did get brief, clandestine shots of Russian military transport. The camera team did not uncover hard evidence about chemical warfare, but they did confirm the continuing military presence of the Soviet Union.

On another occasion, CBS told its news audience that it had purchased exclusive rights to the footage that was being shown from a British reporter, Peter Gill, who had spent two weeks in Afghanistan during the preceding month.[24] That's quite good source information for the TV industry: We know that it was bought, not produced by CBS; that the reporter was British; and that material was at least two weeks old. That standard of documenting sources was repeated in October, when CBS identified visuals as the product of a French film crew, which had produced them between mid-June and mid-August.[25] They showed that modern military might, such as Russia's much-feared helicopter gunboats, was not always a guarantee of victory when rebels "know the turf." The same truism about guerrilla warfare was broadcast three months later.[26] That report was labeled as the product of a British cameraman who had been filming in Afghanistan "for the past two months." Clearly, the action shots were slightly aged. On the theme of chemical warfare, ABC's news showed Russian helicopters spraying something that was allegedly deadly chemicals. That footage was identified as the work of a Dutch journalist.[27] During the same report, the U.S. State Department was cited as having detailed evidence that the USSR was engaged in chemical warfare.

"Truth in packaging" is finding its way to the TV screen, so that consumers are getting a clearer look through their "window onto the world." For this giant step toward the public's right to know, it is the television archives that deserve credit, because we can now retrieve and analyse TV news.

Despite the networks' progress toward greater depth, breadth, and accuracy, there were some remarkably obvious missed opportunities. First, the history of boycotts and embargoes and their ineffectiveness, generally, could have been a useful piece of reporting for a nation like the United States, which was in anguish over not sending its athletes to the Moscow Olympics. One of the networks could have done a few minutes on the feelings and sources of patriotism that bind together a people as one within a nation's borders—on what it means to be a nation. Second, the networks came close but always just missed another opportunity: to document in depth the relevant subject of morality and politics. Traditionally, countries use morality to cloak political and economic policies. Perhaps more people would have understood the Olympic boycott if U.S. political and economic realities were discussed in tandem with the idea of a moral obligation to protest. Adding economic insight would have made the reporting more realistic. CBS had the perfect chance to do that on January 31, 1980, when it identified some footage as having been produced by the U.S. government. On-camera was a presidential advisor, Clark Clifford in India, who said that aid to Pakistan from the United States was a clear message to the USSR: if part of its plan is to move toward the Persian Gulf, "that means war." There had been a change in presidents about that time, and it seems there was also a change in policies. President Jimmy Carter's message was symbolic, moral. When he took office, Ronald Reagan's message was "war." The mix of morality (human rights), politics (change in administrations), and economics (Gulf oil) would have been a powerful teaching device for the networks. TV executives might not like the word *teach*, but teach they do. That's exactly what it means to communicate information. (The effectiveness of the commercial networks' role as teachers can be easily quantified by their advertising and its influence on viewers' purchasing habits.)

Another oversight was the subject of "buying" peace through the boycott. India was reported as endorsing the Russian invasion, but three weeks later Indira Gandhi recanted.[28] There is no way to measure the value of life itself, but the networks could have taken a swing at analyzing war versus peace, in terms of how much each costs when you do not factor in those who have died. Possibly it is less expensive to buy peace than to wage war? Isn't that what we were doing by increasing foreign aid, both military and economic?

The public should be told what reporters know about how the United States "persuades" (buys?) other countries' cooperation. Viewers should not have to make that deduction. It is part of the reporting process to present facts, interpret them, and draw conclusions. The networks should explain more about why the United States cultivated both China and Pakistan, traditionally mutual rivals, both of whom share borders with the USSR. (They became part of the CIA's freight train for the transshipment of arms to Afghanistan.)

In passing, it should be noted that all reporters on all the networks in this study were white, with one exception. On November 25, 1983, ABC's Max Robinson, who is black, reported about Afghanistan from the ABC studio. Yes, there were several women—all white, all blonde, all beautiful enough to be on the cover of any American glamour magazine. Whether or not "blondes have more fun" is debatable, but these blondes got good work.

Is there any significance to this? Yes. The airwaves belong to the American public—to women who are not blondes, to American Indians, to blacks, to Hispanics, to Mexican-Americans, to Orientals, to all peoples who are distinctively different and who comprise the diversity of this country. It is unfortunate that they were not used to report some of this news. Surely, somewhere in these United States one of them is an expert on Central Asia; maybe several speak the languages of Afghanistan and its neighbors. People do not have to be white-male or white-blonde-female to be good analysts. Intelligence makes itself known through any skin or hair color. Why don't TV news executives know this? Could it be because their upwardly mobile potential buyers of advertised products—in that other four minutes of the "half-hour" news—are white? Could it be because of racism at the top level of network news management? If the function of news is to reflect reality, than ABC, CBS, and NBC should take a hard look at their own television screens. Their choice of journalists definitely does not reflect any real-world-U.S.A. as it is now or has ever been since the birth of this nation.

## Conclusions

It would be difficult to fault ABC, CBS, or NBC for not covering political and social issues about Afghanistan between 1979 and 1983. Considering that this study is limited to the nightly news, it is remarkable how much air time was committed to precisely those subjects.

Perhaps it was a benefit when American journalists had to leave Afghanistan. That made things difficult, especially for TV reporters who found fewer "photo opportunities," as they say in the trade. It forced some creative thinking onto network executives and their staffs; they groped for imagery. What may be most important is that without easy access to "hot history," the networks reached into the past and presented powerful short documentaries about the effects of religion, politics, culture, geography, society, and values.

The networks should give their viewers *the rest of the news* through interpretations and conclusions that are identified as such. If news is to reach maturity, its managers will have to stop believing the big lie: "Facts speak for themselves." They do not; they never have; they never will. Conclusions are not the same as editorials, but maybe there is confusion about this. Conclusions are by-products of research. Editorials may be, also, but they are subjective, by definition. There is a place for news bulletins, for brief highlights of events. However, anything that is worth three minutes out of a twenty-six-minute news hole deserves an intelligent wrap-up. The networks need a new motto: "If it's worth reporting, it's worth interpreting."

# Appendix 12A: Database

The references for this study are untraditional. All sources were compiled videotapes on eight cassettes, equaling 13.3 hours of uninterrupted news about Afghanistan (no advertisements). The sources are limited to ABC's, CBS's and NBC's nightly news as it was taped off the air by the staff of the Television News Archive (TNA) at Vanderbilt University (419 21st Avenue, South; Nashville, TN 27240-0007).

The TNA may choose to erase these cassettes now that they have been returned. However, they can make the same material available at any time, because they keep the master tapes of complete news programs, including the commercials.

Readers who want access to the TNA's resources will find its *Television News Index and Abstracts* in most large libraries. It is similar to the *New York Times Index and Abstracts*. News segments are listed according to network, date, time, length, and reporter. A brief comment describes the segments' contents and the place from which the news originated. Instructions for information retrieval are in the front of each volume. The TNA began publishing the *Index* in 1968.

The eight tapes I used—labeled "For Anne Saldich" by the TNA—were made in the winter of 1984:

| Tape No. | Description of Contents | Duration (mins.) |
|:---:|:---:|:---:|
| 1 | ABC, 9/9/79—NBC, 8/12/79 | 120 |
| 2 | NBC, 9/19/79—NBC, 1/9/80 | 60 |
| 3 | ABC, 1/10/80—ABC, 8/28/80 | 120 |
| 4 | ABC, 9/18/80—CBS, 3/3/80 | 120 |
| 5 | CBS, 3/5/80—NBC, 1/30/80 | 120 |
| 6 | NBC, 2/4/80—ABC, 11/21/83 | 120 |
| 7 | ABC, 11/22/83—NBC, 12/28/81 | 120 |
| 8 | NBC, 3/10/82—NBC, 11/23/83 | 19 |

*Note:* The foregoing compiled tapes represent the vast majority, substantively and quantitatively, of ABC's, NBC's and CBS's evening news on the subject of Afghanistan between September 1979 and December 31, 1983.

What were the criteria for selecting segments from the *Index*? That is hard to answer accurately. Almost automatically, bulletins of thirty seconds and less were ruled out. If descriptions of news segments seemed to be exactly alike, *and* if they were under two minutes, they were ruled out as repetition. If the descriptions in the *Index* were similar but the durations were two to five minutes, those news items probably were compiled onto the tapes. Roughly, that is how selections were made. The result is a unique database.

# 13

# Is the Press Quietly Promoting Suicide and Other Forms of Death Chic?

*Loren Ghiglione*

In today's make-believe worlds, death and doom sell. Video arcade games such as "Destroyer," "Space Invaders," and "Berzerk" deliver large doses of death. Ad campaigns by Prudential Insurance Company of America and other firms reflect, as the *Wall Street Journal* reports, "increased media attention to death, 'near-death experiences' and what one news magazine calls a 'gloom boom.'"[1]

The movie industry churns out *The Towering Inferno, Death Race 2000, Rollerball,* and *Death Watch,* a film about a TV show of the same name that pays terminally ill people to record their last months.

Television, challenging film for the title of *the* medium of mayhem, this season tackles teenage suicide. Three made-for-TV movies—"Silence of the Heart," "Surviving," and "Hear Me Cry"—provide more than enough pop psychoanalysis. "What was life all about for them?" a teacher in "Hear Me Cry" asks about two high school friends who plotted to drive off a cliff together. "Performance, competition, pressure . . . a showbiz world under a nuclear cloud."

But what about real-world death—in particular, suicide—as portrayed in the press? Photos and news reports distort, too; indeed, as communications professor George Gerbner suggests, the distinction between dying on an entertainment medium and dying in the press is "increasingly hard to make."[2]

Perhaps, in one sense, press coverage of death is no worse than the public deserves. Journalism professor Jack Haskins, a student of the public's morbid curiosity about the "unpleasant, gruesome, death-dealing" side of life, says: "Reader interest in bad news averages about one-fourth to one-third higher than for all other kinds of news combined."[3]

The public buys death news. "Death sells best," says Patricia Ryan, managing editor of *People* magazine. *People's* three top-selling covers of all time were, in order, the death of John Lennon, the death of Grace Kelly, and the death of Karen Carpenter. Ryan recalls:

> The Grace Kelly cover we ran appeared four or five days after her death; it sold
> 92 percent of the draw. And we had run a cover on Grace Kelly five months

before. The photograph on the cover was from the same take and it sold 56 percent. So, death sells, believe me.[4]

The reader, says press critic Alexander Cockburn, "wants what he has always wanted in a free press: dramatic descriptions of other people being killed."[5] Cockburn theorizes that the reader finds comfort in others' misfortune, "starting at the simple level of relief that it is happening somewhere else to someone else."[6]

Reporters, editors, and news photographers insist, however, that they do not seek out death. Harold Blumenfeld, the retired executive newspicture editor of United Press International, argues typically:

> Neither newspaper editors nor staff photographers blow up airplanes, stage riots and demonstrations, set fire to nursing homes, hire people to pose as victims of accidents, turn snipers loose to shoot at innocent people, take hostages, or start declared and undeclared wars.[7]

But death's drama makes for a good story or a good photo. And, despite the disclaimers of newspaper people, they highly value articles and photos that capture the horror of violent, tragic death. An analysis, for instance, of the news photo winners in the Pulitzer and Pictures of the Year competitions over almost four decades shows that 54 percent were tragedy/violence photographs. Lil Junas writes:

> Trends in the selection of tragedy/violence photographs as prize winners shows an increase in later years. For example, since 1963, every news winner in the Pulitzer Prize competition was of tragedy/violence with the exception of 1975's which was of firemen recuperating on a curb (tragedy-related), with the charred remains of a building in the background.[8]

And when press people choose the best of the best—in such collections as *Moments: The Pulitzer Prize Photographs*[9] and *Moments in Time: 50 Years of Associated Press News Photos*[10]—the images most honored (and given the most space) capture the very second of a violent death: a Japanese student plunging a foot-long sword into a "pro-communist" politician, Vietnam's national police chief shooting a suspected Vietcong in the head, citizens of Bangladesh bayoneting four East Pakistanis suspected of collaborating, a Vietnamese Buddhist monk setting himself afire, a woman falling from a Boston fire escape, a New York man leaping from a bridge.

Such images of death provoke criticism and criticism of the criticism. Wallace Stevens wrote: "Most modern reproducers of life, including the camera, really repudiate it. We gulp down evil, choke at good."[11] But Nora Ephron argues that such pictures "deserve to be printed because they are great pictures, breathtaking pictures of something that happened. That they disturb readers is exactly as it should be."[12]

However, are the images of death presented by the press in both words and photos really mere reflections of "something that happened"? Or does the press warp the public's perception of death? Does it emphasize certain forms of death through front-page or feature treatment and censor others? Does it fall victim to institutional conventions, faddishness, professional elitism, and racism?

Consider the following examples:

I. *Feature stories about suicide victims inevitably focus on (1) an outstanding student, (2) a gifted athlete, (3) a media celebrity, or, at the very least, (4) an overachiever in business, politics, or crime. Invariably, the subject of the feature is young, white, affluent, and bright.*

Reporters like their suicides to be brilliant—for example, Emily Ann Fisher, "a brilliant, deeply troubled"[13] Harvard Phi Beta Kappa who was a reporter/intern at the *Washington Post;* James Dallas Egbert 3d, a "brilliant"[14] computer student who had entered Michigan State University at the age of 16; Paul Leahy, one of the "most brilliant students"[15] at Conestoga High School, Berwyn, Pennsylvania; Eddie Seidel, Jr., "a sometimes brilliant boy"[16] from St. Paul who jumped 200 feet to his death. If they're not brilliant, they should at least be "a perfect all-round student"[17] or "all-American."[18]

If the person who commits suicide can't be extraordinarily bright or all-something, great achievement is an acceptable substitute. Jennifer Amdur was an "exceptional"[19] top-ten teenage tennis player who, at 18, shot herself to death; race horse veterinarian Dr. Janice Runkle was "at the top of her profession at the age of 28";[20] jockey Tony Ricci was "one of the best . . . around these parts";[21] Danny Lee Thomas was the "most valuable player"[22] in professional baseball's Eastern League; Philip Zeltner was a former "teacher of the year"[23] at the University of South Carolina; Rosemary Russell was a $75,000-a-year California businesswoman with a "life many people would have envied";[24] Alan Saxon was president of $360 million-a-year Bullion Reserve of North America;[25] Brenda Benet, 36, was "a soap-opera star" with "a bright future";[26] and Freddie Prinze was a 22-year-old overnight success on television.[27]

The feature treatment of criminals who are murdered parallels that of people who commit suicide. The *New York Times* gives page-one space to the life and death of Barry S. Weinbaum, 22, a former "outstanding" Bennington College student and cocaine dealer.[28] The *Washington Post* features Cindy Herbig, 21, an honors high school student who had won a scholarship to Radcliffe. Herbig, stabbed outside her Washington, D.C., apartment, died a street-walking prostitute.[29]

Newspaper editors and reporters—generally white, well-educated, and comparatively affluent—can generate great sympathy for white, well-educated, and affluent suicide victims and criminals, however reprehensible their behavior. Thus, Eric M. Breindel, a 27-year-old junkie caught dealing in heroin, was portrayed in a front-page Sunday *Washington Post* story as a magna cum laude graduate of Harvard (and Harvard Law School), a "golden youth" whose life and $40,000-a-year Capitol Hill career had been tragically ruined.[30]

Three days later, *Post* columnist William Raspberry wrote a column that questioned the paper's sympathetic treatment of Breindel. Acknowledging the ostensible reason—"the lost promise of this brilliant young man"—Raspberry wrote:

> What happened, I suspect, is that reporter Ronald Kessler, like a lot of *Post* readers who saw his piece, can identify with . . . Breindel. If he had chosen journalism rather than the law and economics, he might well have worked in *The Post* newsroom. Breindel's was one of those but-for-the-grace-of-God stories that can evoke the sympathy of the similarly situated. My guess is that few low-income blacks read that story and came away saddened over lost potential. In fact, I've talked to a fair number of middle-class blacks who wonder what all the hoopla was about.[31]

Raspberry's complaint was not really about racism or the sympathetic treatment Breindel received. The columnist argued, instead, for a newsroom staff economically and culturally representative of America: "A lot of the people we write about, not just the brilliant ones who find themselves in predicaments, could be written about with a little more human understanding and sympathy."[32]

The suicide rate among the elderly, for example, is higher than that among the young. And a recent report predicts that, as Glenn Collins of the *New York Times* writes, "a growing suicide rate among the elderly will accompany future cuts in financing for social services."[33] But the elderly who commit suicide rarely receive sympathetic feature coverage.

Teenage suicides, partly because of a 300 percent increase over the past twenty years, grab most of the headlines. Only certain groups of teenage suicides, however, receive detailed feature coverage—those in the affluent, white suburbs. CBS produced two teenage suicide segments—one for "Magazine" and the other for "30 Minutes"—about "San Mateo, a wealthy suburb of San Francisco" where "the suicide rate is the highest in the country."[34] The *Wall Street Journal* devoted a front-page feature to teenage suicides that "point up the dangers of growing up rich."[35] This time it was the rich suburbs just north of Chicago that were being credited with having "one of the nation's highest youth-suicide tolls." Blaine Harden, a *Washington Post* reporter, wrote a similar account of Chicago's North Shore "suicide belt." The *Boston Globe* headlined it: "Young, wealthy . . . and mixed up."[36]

The *New York Times* featured "an affluent Houston suburban high school"[37] where six suicides occurred in two and a half months; it also reported heavily on the Westchester area, struck by "a rash of teen-age suicides."[38] *USA Today* focused on Plano, a Dallas suburb of upwardly mobile families, which "has agonizingly reeled from seven teen-age suicides."[39]

Poor teenagers are overlooked, though suicides are no less frequent among them than among the wealthy. As Dr. Calvin Frederick of the National Institute of Mental Health explains, suicide is "a very democratic phenomenon."[40] The high suicide-attempt rate among runaways—"to an overwhelming extent, black or Hispanic,"[41] according to one New York study—suggests that they also deserve greater coverage. But they, too, are overlooked. "When a well-off teenager takes his life," Jane E. Brody of the *New York Times* acknowledges, "the death gets more publicity, in part because people view the act as especially tragic and unexplainable."[42]

II. *Newspaper features in recent years have bordered on presenting suicide and death as positive experiences—what Nora Sayre perceptively calls "trashing the self as an act of heroism."*[43]

The press, reflecting society's changing values, projects suicide positively in at least three ways. First, killing oneself—even helping someone kill himself—translates into a Romeo-and-Juliet act of love or a supreme expression of friendship. Second, suicide at its most shocking—a photo of a mental patient leaping twenty stories to his death—has a beauty that, ironically, attracts as much as it repels. Third, the romanticizing of suicide—the vision of death as a place of profound peace free from life's hassles and nightmares—pervades news reports of "rational suicide," the right-to-die movement, near-death experiences, "good dying," and other examples of death chic.

As for suicide as the ultimate expression of friendship, one only has to remember Kenny Wright, 24, the former star end on the Ledyard (Connecticut) High Colonels, voted in his senior year to the All-Eastern Connecticut Conference team. Turned into a partial quadriplegic by some innocent rough-housing at a weekend picnic, he became depressed and began talking of suicide. Only two friends continued to come by Wright's home—Brian Taylor, who had known him since they were nine, and Billy King.

On September 29, 1980, a football Saturday, King and Taylor drove Wright to a nearby woods. Then they pushed him in his wheelchair into the woods and left him alone with his 12-gauge shotgun. King and Taylor had sawed eight inches off the shotgun so that Wright could aim it at his heart and still pull the trigger. He didn't miss.

After first pleading innocent, Taylor and King changed their plea to second-degree manslaughter; in return, the prosecutor agreed not to recommend a prison sentence. Connecticut law makes it a felony, punishable by up to ten years in prison, to "intentionally aid another person to commit suicide other than by force, duress or deception." News reports of the suicide treated Taylor and King sympathetically.[44] A *Boston Globe* editorial, "The injured athlete's friends," argued the altruism of their actions.[45]

At about the same time, the press began reporting at length on the activities of prosuicide groups. A British organization, the Society for the Right to Die with

Dignity, otherwise called Exit, announced that it was going to publish a "how to" book on suicide. Exit and other euthanasia groups also talked about changing the law to make it legal for a patient to enlist the help of a doctor or a friend to end his life.

Doctors, lawyers, and journalists began describing in the press how they had assisted others to commit suicide. In *Good Life, Good Death: A Doctor's Case for Euthanasia*, Dr. Christiaan Barnard advocated "suicide parlors," where "an easy death is administered under pleasant circumstances."[46] In the United States, Derek Humphry formed Hemlock, "a society supporting active voluntary euthanasia for the terminally ill," which also planned a book on "people's planned death, the successful and the not-so-successful."[47] Humphry said "rational suicide" was the ultimate civil liberty. But Dr. John D. Arras, philosopher-in-residence at Montefiore Medical Center in the Bronx, worried about "the popularization of suicide. It's one thing to stake out the abstract right to die, another thing to parade this before depressed people who may take advantage of it."[48]

Even the newspaper images and reports of suicide that are the most difficult to stomach carry an ambiguous message. Suicide requires strength, courage, and determination. It's active, not passive. It's as positive as it is negative.

Whenever the press gets a chance, it transmits one of two macho images of suicide. A man jumps from a bridge or a building to his death. A man puts a gun to his head. Although people also overdose on pills, fill their garages with carbon monoxide, or turn on the gas, those images—associated with a steroetypically female suicide—are rarely presented by newspapers. A *Boston Globe* feature, "The mystery behind suicide," is illustrated with a drawing of a man about to jump from a building.[49] A *New York Times* feature, "Young Suicides," includes a photo of a young man contemplating a leap.[50] A *Newsweek* report, "Teen-Age Suicide," leads with a photo of a 19-year-old Georgia man being restrained from jumping off a water tower.[51]

The unstated message of such macho images was expressed by John Mattarazzo, a New Yorker who committed suicide by shooting himself in the head. He told a reporter beforehand that he wanted to "die like a man." Mattarazzo, the reporter concluded, "wanted to do the one thing in his life worthy of being a man, and that was commit suicide."[52]

Today's romanticized, trendy images of death—"rational suicide," "good dying," the near-death experience—make death sound better than life.[53] Near-death experiences, as reported in the *Boston Globe* over the past eighteen months, provide an example. On May 2, 1983, the Sci-Tech section of the *Globe* published a long front-page feature entitled "Brush with death changes life." The article oozed enthusiasm. The photo illustrating the story was accompanied by an upbeat quote: "I could see the pain and agony on my face down there in the bed. I felt very happy, very secure." The story claimed that survivors "nearly always utterly and permanently lose their fear of death."[54] Citing Dr. Kenneth Ring, president of the International Association for Near-Death Studies, the

*Globe* described the major aftereffect as "a dramatic shift of values away from materialism and toward greater spirituality."[55]

The *Globe* then led its Living section with a feature on near-death experiences; the caption under a photo of Dr. Ring proclaimed: "An NDE (near death experience) increases your desire to live . . . it removes the fear of death."[56] On October 8, 1984, the *Globe's* Living section excerpted the first of five installments from Ring's book, *Heading Toward Omega:* "Near death experience: Researchers probe meaning of phenomenon shared by millions."[57] Hurry, don't be the only one on your block to miss the fun!

Dr. Elisabeth Kubler-Ross and other positive thanatologists want to demystify death and make it as pleasant as the near-death experiences of the living. On his death bed, Tolstoy said, "I don't understand what I'm supposed to do." Dr. Kubler-Ross answers, "Rejoice in dying." The press dutifully reports her "joy" at sharing the experience of death with a family.[58] "Every goodbye is a hello," she concludes cheerfully.[59]

But Kubler-Ross is no match for the advocates of "rational suicide." They are the P.T. Barnums of positive death. Such death exhibitionists as Jo Roman successfully massage the media to make sure the whole world understands that life's biggest thrill is death.

Roman, a 62-year-old artist who had been planning her death for years, had a cameraman videotape nineteen hours of conversations on her right to kill herself (excerpts became "Choosing Suicide," a one-hour public television documentary). She completed a 205-page book, *Exit House,* about a thanatopia, a "gentle" suicide center where people could kill themselves or have others kill them if they wished. She wrote farewell letters to dozens of friends and prepared a statement and obituary notice for her literary agent to deliver to the *New York Times.*

She could not have been disappointed by the front-page coverage she received from the *Times:* "Artist Ends Her Life After Ritual Citing 'Self-Termination' Right." Her prepared statement was quoted sympathetically and unquestioningly. She said "that life can be transformed into art"; a person should "take command of making life's final brushstroke."[60]

"Also I am averse to demeaning myself," she wrote, "by closeting an act which I believe deserves respect."[61]

A medical examiner, based on an autopsy, concluded that Roman may have exaggerated the danger to her of the cancer in her lymph nodes. But the advocates of suicide's appropriateness were given the last word. The *Times* quoted Roman's husband as saying that she was terminally ill: "Not a single doctor gave us the slightest hope of curing her . . . the life expectancy they came up with was three to five years."[62] And Roman herself was quoted as saying she wanted to save herself, her family, and her friends from the "ravages" of cancer.

The *Times* article described Roman's final hours of working on her "life sculpture," a pine box in the shape and size of a coffin filled with personal me-

mentos. The piece ended with a final congratulatory salute to Roman. Her husband, while acknowledging the loss, spoke in press agent prose about Roman's champagne-and-Seconal suicide:

> I'm glad she brought it off—as she did every other project she ever touched . . . she wanted to die at home, while she was still clear, leaving nothing unfinished and with time to say goodbyes—and she wanted her death to be a personal statement.[63]

The straight news report conveyed little of Roman's weirdness. A sister before her had died; so as a child, Roman was not let out of her parents' sight, except at funerals where she, in her words, "played a game with corpses."[64]

She searched for a way to leave her life, repeatedly changing her name—from Mary to Mary Joanne to Mary Jo to Jo. "Each new name was a new identity, a push toward a new future, a severance from an unwanted past."[65] After her first of three husbands died, she gave her two children away.

She was overcome by "relentless wishes to be dead."[66] Always, there was the desire to die. Irrationality, not rationality, ruled. To satisfy her parents, she had to be as good as her sister. And that meant being as dead as her sister. The death wish predated any thought about rational suicide.

The *Times* account and "Choosing Suicide," the public television documentary, conveyed none of the irrationality and perhaps too little of Roman's fixation with leading a painless life. "I don't want to have a day of pain," she said. "I don't want to have a minute of pain."[67] Forget the old-fashioned notion that life is a battle—a battle worth fighting.

There is but one truly serious philosophical problem," Camus wrote, "and that is suicide." Today, more than ever, the press needs to think about how it will respond to that problem.

Journalists need to determine their personal role. Christine Wolff, a court reporter for the *Bradenton* (Florida) *Herald*, was returning to her office when she spotted a house painter about to leap from a bridge. A trade magazine reported: "Wolff tossed reporter's notebook and objectivity aside and grabbed the man instead; a struggle ensued but she never let go."[68] Wolff was surprised later by some critics who said she shouldn't have tried to save the man. Wolff recalls: "They said he was an adult and he had a right to do what he wanted."[69]

Reporters also need to assess how they will respond professionally to suicide. Elizabeth Bouvia, a 26-year-old arthritic quadriplegic, paralyzed by cerebral palsy since birth, asked doctors at Riverside (California) General Hospital to let her starve to death. A court said Bouvia could not require the hospital to let her starve. The hospital began force-feeding her. Bouvia rejected offers from sympathetic people who volunteered to let her die privately at their homes. After reporting Bouvia's circumstances, a *Newsweek* article, while convolutedly trying to avoid the appearance of editorializing, ended by editorializing: "By one not unreasonable conjecture, Bouvia, while not seeking publicity, may be asserting a deeply felt point: namely, a society that so reluctantly took responsibility for her life must now take some responsibility for her leaving it."[70]

Finally, and perhaps most importantly, the press must consider the human impact of its coverage. The National Coalition of Television Violence reported that sixteen persons killed themselves while imitating the Russian roulette scene from the movie *Deer Hunter*, which was widely shown on television.[71] Scholars argue that newspapers have a similar impact. David P. Phillips, a sociologist at the University of California at San Diego, contends that massive newspaper publicity triggers suicides and single-car and small-airplane accidents (often suicides in disguise).[72]

The notion of an account of one suicide causing another suicide—through suggestion or imitation— is at least 200 years old. In 1774, Johann Wolfgang von Goethe, inspired by a diplomat's suicide, wrote a novel, *The Sorrows of Young Werther*. Goethe did not discourage reports (since refuted) that an epidemic of suicides followed publication of his book. "My friends," he wrote, "thought that they must transform poetry into reality, imitate a novel like this in real life and, in any case, shoot themselves; and what occurred at first among a few took place later among the general public."[73] Officials in Italy, Leipzig, and Copenhagen were sufficiently worried that they banned *The Sorrows of Young Werther*.

In the nineteenth century, newspapers came under the same kind of attack. In the British Registrar-General's report for 1841, William Farr, a statistician, wrote: "A single paragraph may suggest suicide to twenty persons; some particular, chance, but apt expression, seizes the imagination, and the disposition to repeat the act, in a moment of morbid excitement, proves irresistible."[74] Farr suggested that newspapers restrain themselves: "Why should cases of suicide be recorded at length in the public papers, any more than cases of fever?"[75]

By the beginning of the twentieth century, the notion that newspaper reports of suicide triggered other people to kill themselves became the center of sociological and philosophical debate. French social theorist Gabriel Torde propounded his "laws of imitation"—that accounts of suicides in newspapers could stimulate other people to kill themselves. French sociologist Emile Durkheim dismissed that theory. In his classic study, *Suicide*, he wrote that suggestion does not affect the national rates of suicide: "Imitation is not an original factor of suicide."[76]

But that didn't prevent American doctors, sociologists, journalism professors, and editors—as they saw the U.S. suicide rate rise 60 percent between 1900 and 1908—from describing the new mass-circulation metropolitan papers, because of their suicide reporting, as "accessories to crime." The accusors' proof, however, wasn't statistical or scientific, only impressionistic and anecdotal.

After newspaper accounts of a young Georgia banker's suicide by swallowing bichloride of mercury, Leon Nelson Flint, a journalism professor, reported:

It was noticeable in the weeks that followed his death that numerous stories of bichloride of mercury poisoning appeared under date lines from widely separated parts of the country. Many of those were suicides, and the natural conclusion was that the Georgia affair had worked as a suggestion to morbid persons.[77]

Henry B. Hemenway, a doctor from Evanston, Illinois, focused on the aftermath of front-page reports in Chicago papers about "a spectacular suicide by jumping from a high place in Chicago." In a paper read to the 1911 convention of the American Academy of Medicine, Dr. Hemenway concluded: "Several similar attempts were made within a few days."[78]

Even newspapers pointed an accusing finger at themselves. The *Baltimore American* reported the suicide of May Fackler of York, Pennsylvania, who inhaled illuminating gas: "The reading of the many suicides that have occurred in this county recently is believed to have temporarily unbalanced Miss Fackler's mind and caused her to commit suicide."[79]

The *Cleveland Plain-Dealer* described a "wave of tragedy" in September 1910 during which "eight die by their own hands . . . within two weeks."[80] The paper concluded that the "deluge" of suicides "is probably due in part to suggestion, the news of one suicide leading to another."[81]

When the *New York World* published a series in 1911 about suicide, the *New York Times,* not missing a chance to jab a competitor, charged that the *World's* articles had been "followed by an unprecedented number of suicides."[82] Edward Bunnell Phelps, who attempted in 1911 to statistically validate the *Times* charge, failed. Another half-century would pass before social scientists would undertake serious statistical studies of newspapers' impact.

In 1967, Dr. Jerome A. Motto, a psychiatrist, examined newspaper blackouts of 25 to 135 days in seven cities between 1949 and 1965. He hoped to learn whether the general unavailability of reports about people killing themselves would reduce the cities' suicides. But Motto's data showed "no significant change in six of the seven cities" and an increase in suicides—the opposite of what might be expected—in the seventh.[83]

Then Dr. Motto conducted a more detailed study of the 268-day newspaper blackout in Detroit between November 17, 1967, and August 10, 1968—"the longest complete suspension of publication in a major metropolitan area in newspaper history."[84] Data for the blackout period were compared to those for the same 268-day period in each of the previous four years and then for the same period in the year following the blackout. The overall suicide rate during the blackout, Dr. Motto acknowledged, was inconclusive ("within the range of prior fluctuation").[85] When he looked at the data for young men and young women during the blackout, he discovered conflicting patterns. The rate of suicide in the males under 35 increased 25 percent over the mean of the previous four years. The rate of under-35 females dropped 60 percent from the mean of the previous four years.

Dr. Motto chose to emphasize the "statistically significant" drop in female suicides during the blackout. He concluded:

> Fuel is added to the growing concern that news media are generating increasingly destructive expression in young people by not only portraying, but subtly glorifying various forums of destructive behavior. A systematic effort is called for to eliminate emphasis in the press on the sensational details of suicidal behavior.[86]

Sol Blumenthal and Dr. Lawrence Bergner, two researchers at the New York City Department of Health, Health Services Administration, attempted to replicate Dr. Motto's study, applying it to the 140-day strike at three of New York's six dailies (30 percent of the city's total daily circulation) in 1966. They found no significant change in male and female suicide rates during the strike. It was interesting, however, that the suicide rates for younger women, 15 to 24 years and 25 to 34 years, "were the lowest in the six years studied,"[87] echoing Dr. Motto's Detroit results.

Statistical evidence that some might judge more persuasive was to come from sociologist David P. Phillips, whose studies between 1974 and 1979 approached the question of newspapers' impact very differently. Phillips was fascinated by statistics compiled by Robert E. Litman, chief psychiatrist at the Los Angeles Suicide Prevention Center, following the 1962 suicide of Marilyn Monroe, which was front-page news in many papers. Immediately after the suicide, the suicide prevention center was flooded with calls. The suicide rate in Los Angeles increased about 50 percent for three weeks (though for the next three weeks, the suicide rate dropped about 50 percent).

Phillips decided to examine systematically the suicide level after dozens of publicized suicides. He studied thirty-five suicides (treated, because of their timing, as thirty-three deaths to ensure statistical significance). All of the suicides made page one of the *New York Times* (between 1947 and 1968). Phillips compared the national suicide rate the month after each of the front-page suicides to the rate for the same month in the previous and subsequent years. Suicides increased after twenty-six of the front-page stories and decreased after seven of them. Phillips called the pattern of increases the Werther effect—after Goethe's suicidal hero—and blamed the increases on "newspaper publicity and suggestion."[88]

The average increase was small—only 2.51 percent nationally—after the *Times* front-page stories. But front-page stories in the *New York Daily News,* with double the circulation of the *Times,* were followed by a 3.27 percent average increase. The largest increase followed Marilyn Monroe's death—12 percent for the month; Phillips counted 303 "excess suicides" in the United States for the two months following her death. (Phillips also raised doubts about one conclusion that might have been drawn from Litman's study—that the publicity surrounding Monroe's suicide caused people on the brink of killing themselves to move up their suicides a month or two; he found no such pattern following a rise in suicide.)

Phillips carried his statistical studies two steps further, examining patterns of death that, at first glance, appeared unlikely to answer his earlier question about the press triggering suicides. First, he studied California motor vehicle fatalities following front-page suicide stories in the state's five largest papers (accounting for 41 percent of daily circulation). He found an increase of 9.12 percent in motor vehicle fatalities during the week following a suicide story. He concluded that suicide stories stimulate a wave of imitative suicides, some disguised as motor vehicle accidents.[89]

Phillips pointed to some correlations that couldn't help but concern newspaper editors: the "excess" fatalities occur mainly in the circulation areas of the papers reporting the suicides; suicide stories about young people tend to be followed by single-vehicle crashes involving young drivers, and, similarly, accounts of older suicides tend to be followed by single-vehicle crashes involving older drivers; and the more publicity given to a suicide—that is, the larger the total newspaper circulation—the greater the increase in motor vehicle fatalities.

Phillips also theorized that newspaper reports of murder-suicides "trigger" subsequent murder-suicides disguised as airplane accidents. He found a nationwide increase in multifatality crashes of small, noncommercial planes following eighteen heavily publicized murder-suicides that he studied in detail. The crashes, like the motor vehicle fatalities in his earlier study, peaked three days after the publicized deaths. "Some persons are prompted by newspaper stories to commit murder as well as suicide," Phillips concluded, "and noncommercial airplanes are sometimes used as instruments of murder and suicide."[90]

The scholars' statistical studies may be dismissed as so much numerical nonsense. Perhaps despondent people don't imitate the suicides they read about in newspapers. But certainly the press should think twice about the real message it sends to its readers. As Judie Smith, program director of the Suicide and Crisis Center in Dallas, says:

> Someone doesn't pick up a newspaper and commit suicide because they read about someone else who did. But if that person is already at risk of suicide, the media reports may inadvertently convey the message that it's okay to kill yourself, that suicide is an acceptable solution to your problems.[91]

At the beginning of the twentieth century—in the heyday of blood-guts-and-sperm journalism—reporters at mass-circulation papers chased suicides. Early photographers emulated the *New York American* whiz who persuaded a policeman to pose with a distraught mother while showing her the rope with which her 11-year-old son had hanged himself.

More than one cub reporter worked his way onto the staff of a newspaper by making up a good suicide story. Silas Bent recalled how, as a journalistic buck private, he was ordered by his city editor to extract a story from the family of a driver who had committed suicide by swallowing carbolic acid. "In a home like that," said the city editor, "there is always a good human interest story. Get it." Bent, with no stomach for interviewing the family, faked the story, writing about the father stifling screams of agony lest he wake his children. "The story made the front page," he concluded. "My place on the payroll was assured."[92]

The spicier the suicide article, the more it was appreciated by the editor. The era's headlines heralded: "Chain of Suicides Strangely Arise from Love Match"; "That Frightful Scream Haunted Me"; "The Desire for Life Decreasing"; "That Pathetic Mystery of Suicide on the Eve of Marriage—What Secret Hides Behind the Recurring Tragedies of Self-Destruction at the Brink of Nuptial Union, Even Where Every Known Promise Is for a Happy Future."[93] That kind of suicide reporting survives today in only the murder-and-muck tabloids. But the so-called respectable press should not rush to pat itself on its back.

This is the age, as death historian Philippe Aries reminds us, in which most people want death to occur quietly, invisibly, in a hospital or nursing home with no rites of passage.[94] It is not surprising that the public prefers its suicides to be reported quietly, if at all. And newspapers oblige. Most do not tell the truth about the cause of death in obituaries. A person who commits suicide, according to his obituary, died suddenly or after a short illness.

The greatest distortion, however, may not be on the obituary page. It may be in the feature story that coos sympathetically about the latest death fad, whether it be rational suicide or autoerotic death. Or in the editorial that scolds Dr. Barney Clark, the man with the first artificial heart, for fighting to stay alive.

Yes, committing suicide and going quietly are viable options. No, newspapers don't need to modishly applaud people who choose those options. The press needs to tell the truth about suicide, not celebrate it.

# Notes

## Chapter 1: Women, Myth, and the Media

\
1. Elizabeth Janeway, *Man's World, Woman's Place* (New York: Dell, 1971).
2. Theodore White, "New Powers, New Politics," *New York Times Magazine*, February 5, 1984, p. 25.
3. Julian Stanley and Camilla Benbow, cited in Caryl Rivers "Got Good Math Genes," *New York Times*, op. ed. page May 30, 1981.
4. Barbara Beckwith, "How Magazines Cover Difference Research," *Science for the People*, July/August 1984, pp. 20–21.
5. Jo Durden Smith and Diane de Simone, "The Sex Life of the Brain, *Playboy*, March 1982, p. 224
6. Jean Baker Miller, cited in Caryl Rivers, Grace Baruch, and Rosalind Barnett, *Beyond Sugar and Spice* (New York: Putnam, 1979), pp. 202–203.
7. Jon Beckwith, "An Historical Parallel," *Science for the People*, July/August 1984, p. 21.
8. *Education Digest*, cited in Beckwith, "How Magazines Cover Difference Research."
9. Dr. Karasek directed a multidisciplinary study in Sweden and the United States. For reports of the research, see *American Journal of Public Health*, July 1981, and *Social Science Medicine*, March 1982

## Chapter 2: The Baggage of Buzzwords

1. See Michael Brown, *Laying Waste: The Poisoning of America by Toxic Chemicals* (New York: Pantheon, 1980).
2. See Rachel Carson, *Silent Spring* (Boston: Houghton Mifflin, 1962).
3. Peter Grace, "Waste-Deep Spending," *New York Times*, September 27, 1984, p. A23; Fred Kaplan, "Two from Air Force Tell Senate Panel About Wasteful Practices," *Boston Globe*, September 20, 1984, p. 4.
4. "Major Bob's New Command," *Boston Globe*, April 6, 1984, p. 12.
5. *Boston Globe*, December 19, 1983, p. 63; December 16, 1983, p. 59.
6. "A Dangerous Telephone Disorder," "The Value in Heroin," "The Merger Mania," *New York Times*, July 20, 1984, p. A18.

7. *New Yorker,* August 30, 1982, p. 9; Judy Foreman, "A Collegiate Upstairs, Downstairs," *Boston Globe,* September 17, 1982; Jim Quinlan, "A New Work Ethic," *Boston Globe,* December 17, 1983, p. 9; *Brookline Citizen,* September 20, 1984, p. 37.

8. "Glossary: 'Waste,'" *Boston Globe,* August 9, 1982, p. 22; "Critics: Gains of '70s Lost," *Boston Globe,* December 12, 1982, p. 28; "A Wasteful Mortgage Lottery," *New York Times,* August 8, 1984, p. A22; J. Peter Grace, *War on Waste: President's Private Sector Survey on Cost Control* (New York: Macmillan, 1984).

9. William C. Redfield, "The Moral Value of Scientific Management," *Atlantic* 110(August 1912): 416–417.

10. Frederick Jackson Turner, *The Frontier in American History* (New York: Holt, 1920), pp. 1–39, 269–310.

11. Thorstein Veblen, *The Theory of the Leisure Class* (1899; reprinted New York: Penguin, 1979), pp. 160–168, 176, 115ff., 97–101, 139.

12. Stuart Chase, *The Tragedy of Waste* (New York: Macmillan, 1925), p. 277; Theodore Roosevelt, *The New Nationalism* (New York: Outlook, 1910), p. 49; Gifford Pinchot, *The Fight for Conservation* (New York: Doubleday, Page, 1910), p. 48; "Waste," *Atlantic* 115(April 1915): 574.

13. Henry J. Spooner, *Wealth from Waste* (1918; reprinted Easton, Pa.: Hive, 1974), pp. ix–xv.

14. Committee on Elimination of Waste in Industry of the Federated American Engineering Societies, *Waste in Industry* (New York: Macmillan, 1921), p. 3.

15. Edward E. Filene, *Successful Living in the Machine Age* (New York: Simon and Schuster, 1932), p. 31; "Novel Ways of Saving Your Time, Labor, and Money: Interview with M. Dewey," *American Magazine* 98(September 1924): 34.

16. See "To Help Us All by Cutting Out Waste," *Literary Digest* 85(May 2, 1925): 16–17.

17. Walter Lippmann, "More Brains—Less Sweat," *Everybody's,* 25(December 1911): 827–828.

18. Rudolf Cronau, *Our Wasteful Nation* (New York: Mitchell Kennerley, 1908), pp. 130–131.

19. See Henry James, *The American Scene* (1907; reprinted Bloomington: Indiana University Press, 1968), pp. 113, 158–159; Ezra Pound, *Literary Essays* (1918, 1920, 1935; reprinted New York: New Directions, 1968), pp. 214–215; William Carlos Williams, "Waste and Use," in *The Embodiment of Knowledge,* ed. Ron Loewinsohn (New York: New Directions, 1977), pp. 186–191; Upton Sinclair, *The Jungle* (1906; reprinted New York: New American Library, 1980), pp. 332–334; Robert Herrick, *Waste* (New York: Macmillan, 1924); Lewis Mumford, *Sticks and Stones* (New York: Norton, 1924), pp. 179, 204–205; T.S. Eliot, "The Waste Land" in *The Complete Poems and Plays, 1909–1950,* N.Y.: Harcourt, Brace and World, 1962) pp. 37–55.

20. Frederick Taylor; quoted in Horace Drury, *Scientific Management: A History and Criticism* (New York: Columbia University Press, 1915), p. 168. See also Frank B. Copley, *Frederick W. Taylor,* 2 vols. (New York: Harper, 1923); and Sudhir Kakar, *Frederick Taylor* (Cambridge, Mass.: MIT Press, 1970). See also Samuel Haber, *Efficiency and Uplift* (Chicago: University of Chicago Press, 1964), pp. 1–49.

21. William James, "The Energies of Men" (1907), in *Faith and Morals* (New York: New American Library, 1962), pp. 216–237.

22. Haber, *Efficiency and Uplift*, p. 62; Mildred Maddocks, "The Household Efficient," *Good Housekeeping* 67(September 1918): 57.

23. Haber, "The Politics of Efficiency," in *Efficiency and Uplift*, pp. 99–116.

24. See advertisements in *Literary Digest* 56(March 23, 1918): 81; *Scientific American* 116(January 6, 1917): 26; *Good Housekeeping* 66(March 1918): 59; *Literary Digest* 62(July 12, 1919): 88, 92, 111.

25. E.D. Schoonmaker, "The Moral Failure of Efficiency," *Century* 90(June 1915): 187–192; William C. Redfield, "The Moral Value of Scientific Management," *Atlantic* 110(August 1912): 411–417.

26. Ernest Poole, "Efficiency," *Delineator* 77(March 1911): 170–171.

27. A.L. Byard, "The Efficient Wife," *Woman's Home Companion* 50(January 1923): 30–32.

28. Laura H. Wild, "Training for Social Efficiency," *Education* 32(February 1911): 342–353.

29. See Mark Muro, "Work, School, Family at the Crossroads," *Boston Globe*, August 30, 1984, p. 20.

30. See Ben Bradlee, Jr., "A New Breed of Farmer," *Boston Globe*, February 9, 1983, p. 2.

31. See Robert Levey, "Bok: US Legal System 'Grossly Inequitable,'" *Boston Globe*, April 22, 1983, p. 1.

## Chapter 3: Visualizing Stereotypes

1. Walter Lippmann, *Public Opinion*. (New York: Harcourt, Brace, 1922).

2. Ibid., introduction, n.p.

3. Ibid., p. 15.

4. Ibid., p. 80.

5. Ibid., pp. 167–168.

6. Ibid., pp. 168–169.

7. Walter Lippmann, *A Preface to Politics* (New York: Mitchell Kennerley, 1913).

8. See Ronald Steel, *Walter Lippmann and the American Century* (New York: Vintage Books, 1980), pp. 47–48

9. Edward L. Bernays, *Crystallizing Public Opinion* (New York: Boni and Liveright, 1923); quotation from 1961 edition (New York: Liveright, 1961), p. 98.

10. Abbott Lawrence Lowell, *Public Opinion in War and Peace* (Cambridge, Mass.: Harvard University Press, 1923).

11. W. Brooke Graves, *Readings in Public Opinion* (New York: Appleton-Century, 1928), p. 3.

12. Lowell, *Public Opinion in War and Peace*, p. 91.

13. Walter Lippmann, *Liberty and the News* (New York: Harcourt, Brace and Howe, 1920), p. 10.

14. Ibid., pp. 19–20.

15. Lippmann, *Public Opinion*, p. 114.

16. Harry S. Ashmore, "Apostle of Excellence: The View from Afar," in Marquis Childs and James Reston, eds., *Walter Lippmann and His Times* (New York: Harcourt, Brace, 1959), pp. 161–162.

17. Lippmann, *Public Opinion.*

18. Ibid., p. 89.

19. Steel, *Walter Lippmann and the American Century,* p. 192.

20. Ibid., pp. 330–331.

21. See *Newsweek* magazine issues for 1980–1983.

22. See William B. Helmreich, "Stereotype Truth," *New York Times,* October 15, 1981.

23. See Gary Kriss, "Proud Polish Overcoming Stereotypes," *New York Times,* March 18, 1979.

24. See Norman Black, "Study Says Kids Shows Hurt Minorities," *Boston Globe,* July 14, 1982.

25. *Los Angeles Times,* March 31, 1982.

26. *New York Times,* October 12, 1981.

27. *New York Times,* January 27, 1981.

28. *Washington Post,* October 28, 1979.

29. *New York Times,* December 16, 1982.

30. Carol Stocker, "Published On the First Try," *Boston Globe,* February 11, 1983, p. 15.

31. "'Superteacher' in Chicago Under Fire From Parents and Press," *New York Times,* March 7, 1982.

32. Sheila Rush, "My Turn: Do We Have Freedom of Religion?" *Newsweek,* July 19, 1982.

33. See "Editorials, A Decade of 'Communion and Progress,'" *America,* April 25, 1981.

34. See "Anti-Stereotyping Policy Wins Praise," *Editor and Publisher,* December 27, 1980.

35. Robert Stam and Louise Spence, "Colonialism, Racism and Representation," *Screen,* (March-April 1983), pp. 2–20.

36. Ibid., p. 9.

37. Ibid., P. 17.

38. Karin Dovring, *Road of Propaganda: The Semantics of Biased Communication* (New York: Philosophical Library, 1959), p. 113.

39. Lippmann quoted in John Luskin, *Lippmann, Liberty and the Press* (University: University of Alabama Press, 1972), p. 156.

40. See Mobil Corporation advertisement, "1. The Myth of the Villainous Businessman, *Time,* August 29, 1983, p. 4.

41. See Mobil Corporation advertisement, "2. The Myth of the Informed Public," *Boston Globe,* August 29, 1983.

42. See Mobil Corporation advertisement, "3. The Myth of the Crusading Reporter," *New York Times,* September 1, 1983. Also, for particulars about distortions Mobil complains about relative to the energy situation in the United States, see Public Affairs, Mobil Corporation, *The Energy Crisis and the Media: Ten Case Histories* (New York: Mobil Oil Corporation, 1983).

43. Walter Lippmann, *The Good Society* (Boston: Little, Brown, 1937), p. 31.

44. Walter Lippmann, *Essays in the Public Philosophy* (Boston: Little, Brown, 1955), pp. 26–27.

45. *Fighting TV Stereotypes: An ACT Handbook* (Newtonville, Mass.: Action for Children's Television, 1983), fifth page.

46. Ralph E.Friar and Natasha A. Friar, *The Only Good Indian: The Hollywood Gospel* (New York: Drama Book Specialists, 1972).

47. William B. Helmreich, *The Things They Say Behind Your Back* (New York: Doubleday, 1982).

48. Leonard C. Archer, *Black Images in the American Theatre* (Brooklyn, N.Y.: Pageant-Poseidon, 1973).

49. Walter White, "Negro Leader Looks at TV Race Problem," *Printers' Ink,* August 24, 1951, p. 31.

50. William A. Henry III, "The Jeffersons: Black Like Nobody," *Channels,* March–April 1983, pp. 62, 64.

51. See Robert F. Berkhofer, Jr., *The White Man's Indian* (New York: Knopf, 1978).

52. Friar and Friar, *The Only Good Indian,* pp. 260–261, 166.

53. Helmreich, *The Things They Say Behind Your Back,* p. 244.

54. *Window Dressing on the Set: An Update* (Washington, D.C.: U.S. Commission on Civil Rights, January 1979), pp. 60–62.

55. Louis Nunez, "TV Image of Women: Distorted," *Chicago Tribune,* January 25, 1979, Sec. 3, p. 4.

56. "Jean Gaddy Wilson Offers Preliminary Look at Major Study . . . Women in News Media," *Media Report to Women,* March–April 1983, p. 4.

57. "Judge Upholds Award to TV Anchorwoman," *New York Times,* September 1, 1983. After award overturn, legal battles continued into 1985.

58. See a report of the study in W. O'Donnell and K. O'Donnell, "Update: Sex-role Messages in TV Commercials," in Matilda Butler and William Paisley, eds., *Women and the Mass Media* (New York: Human Sciences Press, 1980), p. 74.

59. See Robert M. Liebert, Joyce N. Sprafkin, and Emily S. Davidson, *The Early Window: Effects of Television on Children and Youth* (New York: Pergamon Press, 1982), p. 167.

60. "Television and Politics," *Television: The Management of Broadcast Advertising* July 1960, p. 47.

61. Jacques Ellul, *Propaganda* (New York: Vintage Books–Random House, 1973), p. 278.

62. Jean-Louis Servan-Schreiber, *The Power to Inform* (New York: McGraw-Hill, 1974), p. 213.

## Chapter 4: "Killed by Idle Gossip"

1. A. Blumenthal, "The Nature of Gossip," *Sociology and Social Research* 22(September–October 1937): 31–37.

2. See, for example, the following discussions: D. Handelman, "Gossip in Encounters: The Transmission of Information in a Bounded Social Setting," *Man* 8(June 1973):

210–227; M. Georgoudi and R.L. Rosnow, "The Emergence of Contextualism" *Journal of Communication*, in press.

3. R. Paine, "Lappish Decisions, Partnerships, Information Management. and Sanctions—A Nomadic Pastoral Adaptation," *Ethnology* 9(January 1970): 52–67.

4. M. Gluckman, "Gossip and Scandal," *Current Anthropology* 4(June 1963): 307–316.

5. M.H. Goodwin, "He-Said-She-Said: Formal Cultural Procedures for the Construction of a Gossip Dispute Activity," *American Ethnologist* 7(November 1980): 674–695.

6. U. Hannerz, "Gossip, Networks and Culture in a Black American Ghetto," *Ethnos* 32(1967): 35–60/

7. F.E. Lumley, *Means of Social Control* (New York: Century, 1925).

8. E.B. Almirol, "Chasing the Elusive Butterfly: Gossip and the Pursuit of Reputation," *Ethnicity* 8(1981): 293–304.

9. Lumley, *Means of Social Control.*

10. George Eliot, *Daniel Deronda*, in Anna L. Ward Ed., *A Dictionary of Quotations and Prose* (N.Y.: Thomas Y. Crowell & Co., 1889) P. 212.

11. Gluckman, "Gossip and Scandal."

12. A. Arno, "Fijian Gossip as Adjudication: A Communication Model of Informal Social Control," *Journal of Anthropological Research* 36(Fall 1980): 343–360.

13. Almirol, "Chasing the Elusive Butterfly."

14. R.B. Stirling, "Some Psychological Mechanisms Operative in Gossip," *Social Forces* 34(1956): 262–267.

15. Ibid.

16. R.L. Rosnow and G.A. Fine, *Rumor and Gossip: The Social Psychology of Hearsay* (New York: Elsevier, 1976).

17. H.W.S. Francis, "Of Gossip, Eavesdroppers, and Peeping Toms," *Journal of Medical Ethics* 8(1982): 134–143.

18. A. Rysman, "How the 'Gossip' Became a Woman," *Journal of Communication* 27(Winter 1977): 176–180.

19. L. Rosten, *The Joys of Yiddish* (New York: McGraw-Hill, 1968).

20. J. Levin and A. Arluke, "An Exploratory Analysis of Sex Differences in Gossip," *Sex Roles*, in press.

21. J.T. Adams, "Our Whispering Campaigns," *Harper's Monthly Magazine* 165(1932): 444–450.

22. N. Mailer, *Marilyn: A Biography* (New York: Grosset & Dunlap, 1973).

23. See, for example, M. Herskovitz, *Life in a Haitian Village* (New York: Knopf, 1937); J. Sabini and M. Silver, *Moralities of Everyday Life* (New York: Oxford University Press, 1982).

24. See also discussion by Handelman, "Gossip in Encounters."

25. Almirol, "Chasing the Elusive Butterfly."

26. Sabini and Silver, *Moralities of Everyday Life.*

27. O.E. Klapp, *Currents of Unrest: An Introduction to Collective Behavior* (New York: Holt, Rinehart & Winston, 1972), p. 221.

28. Ibid.

29. J. Szwed, "Gossip, Drinking, and Social Control: Consensus and Communication in a Newfoundland Parish," *Ethnology* 5(1966): 434–441.

30. G.A. Fine, "Social Components of Children's Gossip," *Journal of Communication* 27(Winter 1977): 181–185.

31. Goodwin, "He-Said-She-Said." See also M.H. Goodwin, "'Instigating': Story-telling as Social Process," *American Ethnologist* 9(November 1982): 799–819.

32. H.J.S. Taylor, "Teaching Your Pupils to Gossip," *English Language Teaching Journal* 31(April 1977): 222–226; H.J.S. Taylor, "Exploiting Classroom Incidents," in H. Moorwood, ed., *Modern English Teacher* (London: Longman, 1978).

33. J. Levin and A.J. Kimmel, "Gossip Columns: Media Small Talk," *Journal of Communication* 27(Winter 1977): 169–175.

34. Stirling, "Some Psychological Mechanisms Operative in Gossip."

35. S. Yerkowich, "Gossiping as a Way of Speaking," *Journal of Communication* 27(Winter 1977): 199–202.

36. I. Altman and D.A. Taylor, *Social Penetration: The Development of Interpersonal Relationships* New York: Holt, Rinehart & Winston, 1973).

37. J.M. Suls, "Gossip as Social Comparison," *Journal of Communication* 27(Winter 1977): 164–168.

38. Gluckman, "Gossip and Scandal."

39. R.P. Wolff, "Reflections on Literary Style and Social Theory: The Case of Karl Marx's *Capital*," Paper presented at Philosophy Colloquium, Bryn Mawr College, October 1, 1983.

40. Levin and Kemil, "Gossip Columns."

41. G. Eells, *Hedda and Louella* (New York: Warner, 1972), p. 177.

42. See, for example, review in *Newsweek*, May 24, 1976. Richard Stolley, managing editor of *People*, was quoted in *New York* magazine (May 3, 1976): "Gossip? We have expunged that word from our vocabulary. The term has held connotations of untruthfulness. If we're asked to describe what we are doing we prefer to call it 'personality journalism' or 'intimate reporting.'"

43. Rosnow and Fine, *Rumor and Gossip.*

44. T.S. Lebra, "An Alternative to Reciprocity," *American Anthropologist* 77(September 1975): 550–565.

45. Ibid.

46. Almirol, "Chasing the Elusive Butterfly."

47. H. Sutton and L.W. Porter, "A Study of the Grapevine in a Governmental Organization," *Personnel Psychology* 21(Summer 1968): 223–230.

48. Paine, "Lappish Decisions."

49. Szwed, "Gossip, Drinking, and Social Control."

50. J. Turow, "Talk Show Radio as Interpersonal Communication," *Journal of Broadcasting* 18(Spring 1974): 171–179.

51. Almirol, "Chasing the Elusive Butterfly."

52. Gluckman, "Gossip and Scandal."

53. S.E. Asch, "Effects of Group Pressure upon the Modification and Distortion of Judgments," in H. Guetzkow, ed., *Groups, Leadership, and Men* (Pittsburgh: Carnegie Press, 1951).

54. M. Sherif, *The Psychology of Social Norms* (New York: Harper & Row, 1936).

55. Blumenthal, "The Nature of Gossip."

56. Francis, "Of Gossips."

57. See "Kissinger Apologizes for Overheard Words on Nixon," *New York Times*, October 17, 1975, p. 3.

58. Francis, "Of Gossip."

59. F. Nightingale, *Notes on Nursing* (Glasgow: Blackie, 1974), pp. 70–71 (originally published 1859); cited in Francis, "Of Gossip."

60. H. Schuler, *Ethical Problems in Psychological Research* (New York: Academic Press, 1982).

61. See, for example, S. Bok, *Lying: Moral Choice in Public and Private Life* (New York: Pantheon, 1978); also, J.L. Esposito, E. Agard, and R.L. Rosnow, "Can Confidentiality of Data Pay Off?" *Personality and Individual Differences*, vol. 5, pp. 477–480, 1984.

63. R. Le Gallienne, "The Psychology of Gossip," *Munsey's Magazine*, October 1912, pp. 125–126.

64. Specific factors thought to be instrumental in generating false accusations include mistaken identifications, reliance on irrelevant circumstantial evidence, negligence due to general overzealousness, and prevarication with malicious intent. For discussion of the issue of the "falsely accused deviant," see L.W. Klemke and G.H. Tiedeman, "Toward an Understanding of False Accusation: The Pure Case of Deviant Labeling," *Deviant Behavior: An Interdisciplinary Journal* 2(1981): 261–285.

## Chapter 5: Warning Visions

1. Included in this category, for example would be films warning of the fearful errors that lynching can involve, such as Fritz Lang's *Fury* (USA, 1936) and William Wellmen's *The Oxbow Incident* (USA, 1943), or the gangster films that thrilled as well as warned audiences in the 1930s. There was surely a strong element of warning in such films as *Little Caesar* (USA, 1930) and *Public Enemy* (USA, 1931).

2. Roger Manvell and Heinrich Frankel, *The German Cinema* (London: J.M. Dent, 1971), p. 25.

3. The film derived from Wells' book, *The Shape of Things to Come* (1933), in which he attempted to forecast a future civilization based on the humane application of science to the universal welfare of mankind—always provided that a totally destructive war did not intervene to frustrate his positive hopes. The initial script by Wells, later to be much revised, was itself published by the Cresset Press (London, 1935). Originally, set and costume designs were invited from the architects Le Corbusier and Walter Gropius and the painter Fernand Léger, but their work proved impracticable. The sets were finally created by Alexander Korda's brother, Vincent, and the music, composed by Sir Arthur Bliss, was later issued on records as a suite.

4. Norman and Jeanne MacKenzie, *The Time Traveller* (London: Weidenfeld and Nicolson, 1973), pp. 390–391.

5. For fuller accounts of this film, see Karol Kulik, *Alexander Korda* (London: W.H. Allen, 1975); and Michael Korda, *Charmed Lives* (London: Penguin Books, 1980).

6. For Renoir's own views, see the introduction to the published script of the film, *The Rules of the Game (London: Lorrimar, 1970), pp. 5–14; and Jean Renoir, My Life and My Films* (London: Collins, 1974), pp. 169–173.

7. Britain was alone in Europe but, of course, was aided throughout by the countries of the British Commonwealth—notably, Canada, Australia, New Zealand, and India. They were all at great geographical distance from the mother country, however, and were soon embroiled, like Britain, in the Middle Eastern, North African, and Far Eastern theaters of war.

8. Roger Manvell, *Films and the Second World War* (New York: A.S. Barnes, 1974), p. 201.

9. These five-minute films for the theaters, made in both Britain and Canada, are splendidly illustrated by the ghoulish Canadian animated film made by Norman Mc-Laren, *Keep Your Mouth Shut* (1944).

10. Cavalcanti, Brazilian by origin, had come to Britain via France early in the 1930s to work with John Grierson on documentaries.

11. For this and the preceding quotation, see Roger Manvell, *Chaplin* (Boston: Little, Brown, 1974), p. 207. For the censorship issue, see Charlie Chaplin, *Autobiography* (London: Penguin Books, 1966), page 429 *et seq.*

12. A film of warning about blacklisting itself—*The Front* (USA, 1976), with Woody Allen—was to made much later, exposing these investigations and their destructive effects. Several of those involved in the making of this film had themselves been blacklisted.

13. The aspect of our subject covered in this paragraph has been more fully discussed in my article, "The Media in Film," in *Questioning Media Ethics,* ed. Bernard Rubin (New York: Praeger, 1978).

14. For a discussion and evaluation of this film, together with an interview with the director and the writer of the film (Ron Shelton), see the British Film Institute's *Monthly Film Bulletin,* January 1984.

15. See David Wilson's interesting analysis of this film in *Monthly Film Bulletin,* April 1969.

16. See John Pym's reviews in the *Monthly Film Bulletin* of *Man of Marble* (November 1979, p. 225), *Rough Treatment* (June 1981, p. 108), *Man of Iron* (November 1981, p. 218). Philip Strick reviews *Danton* (September, 1983, p. 242). See also Gustaw Moszcz's highly informed review of *Man of Iron* in *Sight and Sound,* the quarterly journal of the British Film Institute, London (Autumn 1981, p. 275), discussing the cuts in the film imposed by the Polish censorship and claiming that, nevertheless, the film remains Wajda's "masterpiece."

17. Rainer Boldt's *Due to an Act of God* (West Germany, 1983) shares this distinction with *The War Game* in having been banned for transmission on television, in this case by its TV sponsors, WDR SFB. It shows the drastically violent manner in which a community contaminated following an accident to a plutonium-waste transporter is treated by the authorities.

18. For recent accounts of the background to the production of the film and the controversy it has aroused, see the section on *The War Game* in Joseph A. Gomez, *Peter Watkins* (Boston: Twayne, 1979), pp. 45–66: and also *American Film,* October 1982, p. 64 *et seq.*

19. For insightful descriptions and analyses of *Dr. Strangelove,* see especially Alexander Walker, *Stanley Kubrick Directs* (London: Davis Poynter, 1972), p. 158 *et seq.*; and Norman Kagan, *The Cinema of Stanley Kubrick* (New York: Grove Press, 1972), pp. 111–144.

20. About a half-hour of this film was cut by the British distributors, Hemdale, following the failure of the film at U.S. box offices. A very informative list of these cuts and their content (covering most of the discussion between the president and his advisers on U.S. involvement in Vietnam) appears in *Monthly Film Bulletin,* January 1977, p. 136.

21. In September 1984, the BBC responded to ITV's transmission in 1983 of the American television film, "The Day After," by screening "Threads," a two-hour drama-documentary showing the situation that might obtain in Sheffield after a nuclear attack, and a documentary, "On the 8th Day," showing the world submerged in a lethal "nuclear winter."

## Chapter 6: George Orwell's *1984* and the Freedom of the Media

All quotations from George Orwell's *1984* are taken from the Signet Classic edition (New York: New American Library, 1981).

1. *1984*, p. 5.
2. *1984*, pp. 6–7.
3. Eugene Zamiatin, *We*, trans. Gregory Zilbourg (New York: Dutton, 1959), p. 34.
4. *1984*, p. 41.
5. *1984*, pp. 176–177.
6. *1984*, pp. 169–170.
7. *1984*, pp. 46–47.
8. *1984*, pp. 205, 210.
9. *New York Times Magazine*, January 30, 1983, p. 21.
10. Christopher Evans, *The Micromillenium* (New York: Viking Press, 1979), p. 229.
11. Oliver Goldsmith, "The Deserted Village", Lines 211 et. seq., in Charles Dudley Warner, ed., *Library of the World's Best Literature*, vol. 2 (Metuchen, N.J.: Mini-Print Corporation, 1972) selections 6525, 6526.
12. Robert Jastrow, *The Enchanted Loom* (New York: Simon and Schuster, 1981), p. 159.
13. *Time*, January 3, 1983, p. 24.
14. John Wicklein, *Electronic Nightmare* (New York: Viking Press, 1981).

## Chapter 7: A Spectrum of Press Watchers

1. *Wall Street Journal*, October 25, 1982.
2. Letter to the author, August 21, 1984.
3. *Freedom at Issue*, July–August 1984, p. 38.
4. *Freedom at Issue*, January–February 1984, p. 44, trans. Pamela Hadas.
5. Leonard R. Sussman, *Glossary for International Communications* (New York: Freedom House, 1983), unpaged. Copyright 1983 by the Media Institute, Washington, D.C. Reprinted with permission.
6. Mary A. Gardner, "The Inter American Press Association: A Brief History,"

*Journalism Quarterly* (Autumn 1965), unpaged reprint. Copyright 1965, Journalism Quarterly, University of Minnesota, Minneapolis. Reprinted with permission.

7. Lee Hills, "The Story of the IAPA," *Nieman Reports* 23(March 1969): 4, 5.

8. *IAPA News*, August 1984, p. 4. From the United States: newspapers—*Miami Herald, Miami News, Wichita* (Kansas) *Eagle-Beacon;* individuals—Morris S. Thompson of the Latin American Bureau of *Newsday;* Jackson Diel of the *Washington Post;* Sig Gissler of the *Milwaukee Journal;* and David Woo of the *Dallas Morning News.* From Latin America and the Caribbean: Leslie Pierre of the *Grenadian Voice; El Espectador* of Bogota; *Ultimas Noticias* of Quito, Ecuador; Hector Davalos of *Novedades,* Mexico City; and Romeo Guida Mastrangelo of Uruguay, for his work in *La Guia Financiera* of Montevideo.

9. Rosemary Righter, *IPI—The Undivided Word: A History of the International Press Institute* (Zurich: International Press Institute, 1976), p. 16.

10. Ibid., p. 19.

11. Ibid., p. 68.

12. Ibid., p. 109.

13. Ibid., p. 123.

14. Letter to the author, September 5, 1984.

15. Mark Fitzgerald, "A Fighter for Press Freedom" *Editor & Publisher*, August 4, 1984, p. 44.

16. "World Press Freedom Review," *IPI Report* 32(December 1983): 7.

17. See *The Observer*, May 1961.

18. *Amnesty International Handbook* (London: Amnesty International Publication, 1983), p. 5.

19. Ibid. Reprinted with permission.

20. Ibid., p. 36. Reprinted with permission.

21. *Amnesty International Report 1983* (London: Amnesty International Publications, 1983), p. 3. Reprinted with permission.

22. Information provided by Elaine English, Esq., director of the Freedom of Information Center, Reporters Committee for Freedom of the Press, undated.

23. Ibid.

24. "Pavel Litvinov and Index on Censorship," *Index on Censorship*, January 1975, reprint.

25. Sarah Woodhouse, *Your Life My Life: An Introduction to Human Rights and Responsibilities* (London: Writers and Scholars Educational Trust, 1980).

26. Jeremy Cunningham, *Human Rights and Wrongs: An Introduction to Human Rights* (London: Writers and Scholars Educational Trust, 1981).

27. *The Media Crisis: A Continuing Challenge* (Washington, D.C.: World Press Freedom Committee, 1982), p. 38. Reprinted with permission.

28. From "The World Press Freedom Committee Story," undated material.

29. See note 27.

30. From World Press Freedom Committee material, "World Press Freedom Committee Adds Nine New Assistance Projects," August 3, 1984.

31. From a Committee to Protect Journalists (CPJ) leaflet, undated.

32. Letter to the author, September 19, 1984.

33. From CPJ leaflet; see note 31.

34. From letter to the author; see note 32.

## Chapter 8: Irreplaceable Experiences

1. Allen L. Woll, *The Latin Image in American Film* (Los Angeles: UCLA Latin American Center, 1977); Arthur G. Pettit, *Images of the Mexican American in Fiction and Film* (College Station: Texas A & M Press, 1980); Thomas Cripps, *Slow Fade to Black: The Negro in American Film, 1900–1942* (New York: Oxford University Press, 1977); Donald Bogle, *Toms, Coons, Mulattoes, Mammies & Bucks* (New York: Viking Press, 1973); Randall M. Miller, ed. *The Kaleidoscopic Lens: How Hollywood Views Ethnic Groups* (New York: Jerome S. Ozer, 1980).

2. Julian Smith, *Looking Away: Hollywood and Vietnam* (New York: Scribners', 1975): Jeffrey Richards, *Visions of Yesterday* (London: Hopkinson & Blake, 1973); Folk Isaksson and Leif Furhammar, *Politics and Film* (London: Studio Vista, 1971); Jim Cook and Mike Lewington, eds. *Images of Alcoholism* (London: British Film Institute, 1979).

3. *United States v. Paramount Pictures*, 334 U.S. 131 (1948). See especially Michael Conant, *Antitrust in the Motion Picture Industry: Economic and Legal Analysis* (Berkeley and Los Angeles: University of California Press, 1960). In *Bigelow v. Balaban and Katz Corp.*, 199 F.2d 794 (1952), Judge Kerner stated: "We think that compulsory divestiture did not result in such immediate change in relationships between distributors and exhibitors as to require immediate relaxation of restraints in an industry whose members have been described as having 'shown a marked proclivity for unlawful conduct.'" As late as 1974, *Variety* reported that the initial chance for commercial success or failure of a motion picture rested in the hands of the twenty-four persons who booked the major theater circuits, which returned an estimated 70 percent of net rentals to the production companies. *Variety*, May 24, 1974, p. 6.

4. Hortense Powdermaker, *Hollywood, The Dream Factory* (Boston: Little, Brown, 1950), p. 10.

5. Ibid., pp. 19, 22, 26–27.

6. John Sayles, interview with author, January 23, 1981.

## Chapter 9: Cameras in the Courtroom

1. See Donald Gillmor and Jerome Barron, *Mass Communication Law*, (St. Paul: West, 1984).

2. *Commonwealth v. McClusky, Commonwealth v. Macauda, Commonwealth v. McLeod, Commonwealth v. Aiello, Commonwealth v. Nadworny*, Massachusetts Superior Court, 1983.

3. *Commonwealth v. Corderio, Commonwealth v. J. Medeiros, Commonwealth v. V. Medeiros, Commonwealth v. Raposo, Commonwealth v. Silvia, Commonwealth v. Vieira*, Massachusetts Superior Court, 1984.

4. *State v. Hauptmann*, 115 N.J.L. 412, 180 A. 809, *cert. denied*, 296 U.S. 649 (1935).

5. Kielbowicz, *The Story Behind the Adoption of the Ban on Courtroom Cameras*, 63 Judicature 14 (June–July 1979).

6. 62 A.B.A. Rep. 351–352 (1937).

7. See Gillmor and Barron, *supra* note 1 at 547.

8. 381 U.S. 532 (1965).
9. Id at 536.
10. Id at 547.
11. Id.
12. Id at 549.
13. Id at 595.
14. 449 U.S. 560, 571 (1980).
15. Id at 577–578.
16. *In re Petition of Post-Newsweek Stations, Florida, Inc.*, 370 So.2d 764, 775 (Fla. 1979).
17. Dalton Lancaster, "Cameras in the Courtroom: A Study of Two Trials" (Bloomington: Indiana University School of Journalism, Center for New Communications, 1984).
18. Id at 2.
19. "Viewpoint: Cameras, Courtrooms, Justice," Ted Koppel (host), ABC, 11:30 p.m., May 24, 1984.
20. *Westmoreland v. CBS, Inc.*, 1984.
21. 100 Ohio App. 345, 128 N.E.2d 471 (Ohio App., 1955).
22. *Sheppard v. Maxwell*, 384 U.S. 333, 356–357 (1966).
23. *Post-Newsweek, supra* note 16.
24. 447 R.I. 380 (1982).
25. Lancaster, *supra* note 17 at 2.
26. "Viewpoint," *supra* note 19.
27. *Sheppard v. Maxwell, supra* note 22 at 354.
28. *Burnett v. National Enquirer, Inc.*, 193 Cal. Rptr. 206, 144 Cal. App. 3d 991 (1983).
29. "Anatomy of a Libel Trial: Carol Burnett v. National Enquirer," Video cassette program, PLI, 1983.
30. *Corderio et al., supra* note 3.
31. Jonathan Kaufman, "Cable stations broadcast name of woman in Big Dan rape case," *Boston Globe*, February 24, 1984.
32. *Cox v. Cohn*, 420 U.S. 469 (1974).
33. See Kaufman, *supra* note 31.
34. No. Civ. A. 83-3850 (1984).
35. 410 U.S. 113 (1973).
36. 438 U.S. 265 (1978).

# Chapter 10: Intellectual Foundations of Reagan's Soviet Policy

1. Examples: Failure to stop West European support for and acceptance of the Soviet gas line; failure to weaken Soviet and Syrian influence in Middle Eastern affairs; failure to weaken martial law and Soviet influence in Poland; failure to weaken the Soviet presence in Afghanistan; failure to strengthen ideological or ethnic dissent within the USSR; failure to weaken Soviet strategic power. Reagan's greatest achievements in foreign

policy in his first term were the intervention in Grenada, a country with the same number of people as Lynn, Massachusetts,—at some cost to the Western alliance—the deployment of new theater weapons in Europe. Both "achievements," it may be argued, were misguided. If more modern weapons were wanted in Europe, for example, NATO should have sought systems less vulnerable to a possible Soviet first-strike than the Pershing II and ground-launched cruise missiles.

The victories of the anti-Soviet confrontationalists over the years have been decidedly Pyrrhic. Ostensibly hoping to allieviate the plight of Soviet Jews and other minorites, Richard N. Perle helped Senator Henry Jackson put through the Jackson–Charles A. Vanik amendment in 1974, linking economic concessions from the United States to explicit commitments by the Soviet regime to freer emigration. The result: Moscow charged the United States with abrogating its obligations; the flow of Jewish emigrants lessened; and the Kremlin lost incentives for restraint in the Third World. In 1979, Perle and Jackson helped prevent ratification of SALT II. Both Moscow and Washington have since continued to enlarge their arsenals, but each has said that it would adhere to the SALT restraints if the other did the same. In 1984, Mr. Perle, then assistant secretary of defense for international security policy, intensified his efforts to halt all technological transfers of direct or indirect benefit to Soviet military programs, though critics charged that his policies would harm the United States in the long run because of lost markets and ever-greater trade deficits. See the portrait by Clyde H. Farnsworth, "The Bureaucratic Maneuverers' Outmaneuverer," *New York Times*, May 3, 1984, p. B14. In Mr. Reagan's first term Mr. Perle outmaneuvered other bureaucratic rivals to persuade the president to endorse the controversial "zero option" in intermediate-range nuclear force talks. See Strobe Talbott, *Deadly Gambits: The Reagan Administration and the Stalemate in Nuclear Arms Control* (New York: Alfred A. Knopf, 1984). The resulting impasse helped justify deployment of the Pershing II and cruise missiles in Europe.

2. *Survival Is Not Enough* (New York: Simon and Schuster, 1984), pp. 12–14. For a critique of the scholarship in this work, see the author's review in *Worldview*, forthcoming in 1985.

3. "Foreign Policy under Reagan II," *Foreign Affairs*, LVIII, No. 2 (Winter 1984/85), pp. 220–239 at 220.

4. As Andrew Cockburn shows, Soviet weaknesses are much more visible to those inside the USSR than to outsiders who focus on numbers of missiles and tanks deployed. See his *The Threat: Inside the Soviet Military Machine* (New York: Vintage Books, 1984).

5. *Wall Street Journal*, June 3, 1980, cited in Alexander Dallin and Gail W. Lapidus, "Reagan and the Russians: United States Policy Toward the Soviet Union and Eastern Europe," in Kenneth A. Oye, Robert J. Lieber, and Donald Rothchild, eds., *Eagle Defiant: United States Foreign Policy in the 1980s* (Boston: Little, Brown, 1983), p. 210.

6. Ibid., pp. 206–207.

7. Kennan also endorsed parts of the "essentialist" model. His "Sources of Soviet Conduct" (*Foreign Affairs*, July 1947) argued that the Soviet dictatorship required an external bogey to justify its existence. Kennan's view in 1947 resembles in some respects that of Pipes in *Survival Is Not Enough* (1984), for both emphasized the consequences for Soviet external policy stemming from the internal imperatives of the regime. Since Stalin's death, however, the USSR and Kennan's views have evolved.

8. See William R. Van Cleave, "Implications of Success or Failure of SALT," in William R. Kintner and Robert L. Pfaltzgaff, Jr., eds., *SALT: Implications for Arms Control*

*in the 1970s* (Pittsburgh: University of Pittsburgh Press, 1973), pp. 330–331; and critique in Walter C. Clemens, Jr., *The Superpowers and Arms Control* (Lexington, Mass: Lexington Books, D.C. Heath, 1973), chapter 1.

9. There were, however, a number of old Soviet hands in the State Department including Walter J. Stoessel, a former ambassador to Moscow and to Bonn (who retired in 1982). For an essay reviewing the influence of other Soviet specialists remaining in Washington, see Leslie H. Gelb, "For Soviet Experts, a Fading Dream," *New York Times*, March 12, 1984, p. A14.

10. Some reports from Washington hold that Pipes was the principal author of National Security Decision Directive 75, calling for economic pressure and propaganda to alter the internal life of the USSR and urging the creation of instruments such as Project Democracy to confront and undermine the Soviet presence abroad.

11. *New York Times*, March 19 and March 20, 1981.

12. Ibid., August 9, 1982.

13. In September 1983, Jack F. Matlock, Jr., was appointed senior Soviet specialist on the staff of the National Security Council, with the additional title of Special Assistant to the President. Matlock had served three terms in the USSR and had been U.S. Ambassador to Czechoslovakia just before his appointment to the NSC. His appointment was expected to help moderate White House rhetoric on the USSR.

14. The term "saboteur" is not too strong. See Strobe Talbott, *Deadly Gambits: The Reagan Administration and the Stalemate in Nuclear Arms Control* (New York: Alfred A. Knopf, 1984). See, for example, p. 102.

15. *New York Times*, December 18, 1982, and August 21, 1983.

16. Pipes's major works include *Formation of the Soviet Union: Communism and Nationalism, 1917–1923* (1954; rev. ed., 1964); *Karamzin's Memoir on Ancient and Modern Russia* (1959); and two volumes on Peter Struve (1970 and 1980). Born in Poland in 1923, Pipes came to the United States in 1940; he received an A.B. from Cornell (1945) and a Ph.D. from Harvard (1950). He has taught at Harvard since 1950, becoming the Frank J. Baird, Jr., Professor of History in 1975. Two years later, he joined the executive committee of the Committee on the Present Danger.

17. Cyrus Vance, *Hard Choices* (New York: Simon and Schuster, 1983), p. 74; Zbigniew Brzezinski, *Power and Principle* (New York: Farrar, Straus & Giroux, 1983), pp. 178–179, 184–185, 189.

18. See, for example, the contributions by Kennan, Walter C. Clemens, Jr., and others in Burns H. Weston, ed., *Toward Nuclear Disarmament and Global Security* (Boulder, Colo.: Westview Press, 1984), chapters 6–8.

19. All page references in the text are to Richard E. Pipes, *U.S.–Soviet Relations in the Era of Detente* (Boulder, Colo.: Westview Press, 1981).

20. On the reconciliation meetings of the Eastern and Western churches at Florence, 1437–1439, see James H. Billington, *The Icon and the Axe* (New York: Vintage Books, 1970), pp. 70, 84, 659. The incorrect date given by Pipes also appears in the essay as published in *Encounter* 35(October 1970): 4. The paper was first presented at the American Historical Association meeting in Washington, December 1969. That an error of such dimensions could pass through several layers of reviewers is a commentary on the times.

21. Stalin also spoke of peaceful coexistence as the basis for Soviet relations with the West, but he did so, at least in the interwar years, from a position of relative Soviet weak-

ness. Khrushchev endorsed peaceful coexistence in the mid-1950s as the foundation of Soviet policy at a time of mutual deterrence. See Clemens, *The Superpowers and Arms Control*, pp. 41–42.

22. See Walter C. Clemens, Jr., "Soviet Disarmament Proposals and the Cadre-Territorial Army," *Orbis* (Winter 1964): 778–799, especially pp. 779, 796; N.M. Kiriaev, *Partiia bol'shevikov v bor"be za ukreplenie Sovetskoi Armii v gody mirnogo sotsialisticheskogo stroitel'stva, 1921–1940 gody* (Moscow: Izdatel'stvo "Pravda," 1951), p. 15; also Harriet Fast Scott and William F. Scott, *The Armed Forces of the Soviet Union*, 2nd ed. (Boulder, Colo.: Westview Press, 1981), pp. 16–17.

23. For this and similar cases, see Thomas Powers, *The Man Who Kept the Secrets: Richard Helms and the CIA* (New York: Pocket Books, 1979), pp. 152, 156, 164–185.

24. In March 1976, President Sadat abrogated the five-year-old Soviet–Egyptian Treaty of Friendship and Cooperation, but the 1972 break was sharp indeed. See, for example, Walter C. Clemens, Jr., "Behind Sadat's Eviction Order," *New Leader*, October 2, 1972, pp. 6–8.

25. *Historical Statistics of the United States* (Washington, D.C.: Bureau of the Census, U.S. Department of Commerce, 1975), Part II, p. 1140 and table 605.

26. For documentation, relying partly on two recent Brookings Institution studies of U.S. and Soviet use of force as a political instrument, see Walter C. Clemens, Jr., "The Superpowers and the Third World: Aborted Ideals and Wasted Assets," in *Sage International Yearbook of Foreign Studies: Vol. VII, Foreign Policy: USA/USSR*, eds. C.W. Kegley, Jr., and Pat McGowan (Beverly Hills, Calif.: Sage, 1982), pp. 117–118.

27. See, for example, *Department of Defense Annual Report, Fiscal Year 1979* by Harold Brown, p. 47. The ratio is given as 9,000 to 4,000 + at the beginning of 1978 and 9,000 to 4,500 at the end. A similar assessment for 1977 appears in *NATO and the Warsaw Pact: Force Comparisons* (Brussels: NATO, 1982), p. 28.

28. A second revised edition appeared shortly after the first, and a third revised edition was published in 1968.

29. See references in Walter C. Clemens, Jr., *The Arms Race and Sino-Soviet Relations* (Stanford, Calif.: Hoover Institution, 1968), pp. 3, 74–75, 226.

30. N.S. Khrushchev in *Pravda* and *Izvestiia*, January 15, 1960.

31. Paul Nitze worked on the U.S. Strategic Bombing Survey, 1944–1946, which analyzed the results of strategic bombing in Europe and Japan, completing its studies well before the Blackett book appeared. The survey may have understated the impact strategic bombing had on German's military-industrial machine. For an analysis, see Bernard Brodie, *Strategy in the Missile Age* (Princeton, N.J.: Princeton University Press, 1959), chapter 4.

32. See Milton Leitenberg, "Presidential Directive (P.D.) 59: United States Nuclear Weapon Targeting Policy," *Journal of Peace Research* 18(1981): 309–317.

33. See Joseph J. Kruzel, "Military Alerts and Diplomatic Signals," in Ellen Stern, ed., *The Limits of Military Intervention* (Beverly Hills, Calif.: Sage, 1977), pp. 83–99, especially pp. 87–89 and 96–97. A former Defense Department participant in SALT I deliberations, Kruzel based his article partly on interviews with senior government officials. The contrasts in the U.S. and Soviet approaches to "readiness" leads him to discuss possible reasons for the "more relaxed" Soviet approach.

In 1984 Pipes granted that Soviet forces are maintained at "low levels of alert," which he now attributed to the fact that the Kremlin does not fear a sudden attack from the West. See *Survival Is Not Enough*, p. 225.

34. Dimitri F. Ustinov, Soviet Minister of Defense, 1976–1984, despite his title of Marshal, came from the civilian side of the Soviet military-industrial complex, where he labored for more than two generations.

35. See Joan W. Nowicke and Matthew Meselson, "Yellow Rain: A Palynological Analysis," *Nature,* April 1984; and the letters by Peter S. Ashton and others on the origin of yellow rain in *Science* 222(28 October 1983): 366, 368. For a broader picture, see Philip M. Boffey, "Evidence Is Fading as U.S. Investigates Use of 'Yellow Rain,'" *New York Times,* May 15, 1984, pp. Al, B6.

36. See Raymond L. Garthoff, "The Soviet SS-20 Decision," *Survival* 25(May/June 1983): 110–119.

37. See McGeorge Bundy, George F. Kennan, Robert S. McNamara and Gerard Smith, "The President's Choice: Star Wars or Arms Control," *Foreign Affairs* LXIII, No. 2 (Winter 1984/84), pp. 264–278; for a partial justification of the President's Strategic Defense Initiative, see Kenneth L. Adelman, "Arms Control With and Without Agreements," ibid., pp. 240–263.

38. Many dissidents from the Soviet system, for example, warn Western liberals that they do not understand the evil nature of the Kremlin leadership and its totalitarian reach. Most of these persons have suffered enormous personal injury from the Soviet system, which helps to animate their cause; few of them possess a broad knowledge of East–West interactions.

39. *Encyclopedia Britannica,* 14th ed., anon., quoted in Barbara Tuchman, *The March of Folly* (New York: Knopf, 1984), p. 7.

40. W. Scott Thompson, "Good Reagan Rhetoric," *New York Times* February 10, 1984, p. A27. Thompson portrays himself as one "involved in, for lack of a better term, the intellectual apparatus of the Reagan campaign." He later served in the U.S. Information Agency, joining the American Security Council in early 1984.

41. See, for example, Kennan's contribution in Weston, *Toward Nuclear Disarmament,* pp. 283–290; Dallin and Lapidus, "Reagan and the Russians"; and the survey data and analytic models discussed in Clemens, *The Superpowers and Arms Control,* especially chapter 1 and appendix A.

42. On the dim prospect for greater inputs by Soviet specialists in U.S. policy formulation, see Lelie H. Gelb, "For Soviet Experts, a Fading Dream," *New York Times,* March 12, 1984, p. A14.

43. Tuchman, *The March of Folly,* pp. 7, 14.


# Chapter 11: Marketing Communications Roles in Public Crisis Management

1. L.L.L. Golden, *Only By Public Consent* (New York: Hawthorne Books, 1968), pp. 19–20.

2. "EDB: Science and Public Policy," a report by the Grocery Manufacturers of America, Inc., Washington, D.C., April 1984.

3. "Ban leaves farmers with EDB," *Orlando* (Florida) *Sentinel,* February 24, 1984.

4. "State finds EDB in food products," *Boston Globe,* February 2, 1984.

5. "EDB: EPA points to long-term threat as it clears off grocery shelves," *Times Union* (Albany, N.Y.) February 26, 1984.

6. See "The Region: States Stiffen the Standards on EDB in Food," *New York Times,* February 26, 1984.

7. "Trouble at the Grocery Store: EDB recalls leave food manufacturers fretful and watchful," *Time,* February 27, 1984, p. 75.

8. See Jim Auchmutey "Analysis: Hazards of EDB are exaggerated compared to natural carcinogens," *Atlanta Journal and Constitution,* February 19, 1984, p. 14-D.

9. Ibid.

10. "P&G People Meet The EDB Challenge," *G.O. Moonbeams* (a publication for the employees of the Procter & Gamble Company), Cincinnati, Ohio, July 1984.

11. William S. Sachs, *Advertising Management: Its Role in Marketing* (Tulsa: PennWell, 1984), p. 427.

12. Auchmutey, "Analysis."

13. From a speech by J.H. Kristoff at the convention of the Packaged Goods Distributors Association, Denver, March 1984.

14. Jonathan Lash and Katherine Gillman, "The politics of pesticides," *Boston Globe Magazine,* March 18, 1984, p. 11 and continuing.

15. Ilene Barth, "What's a mother to do?" *Boston Globe,* February 20, 1984.

16. Jeanne Kristaponis, letter to the editor of *Boston Globe,* February 20, 1984.

17. Dr. Gordon W. Gribble, letter to the editor of the *Boston Globe,* February 20, 1984.

18. Editorial, "EDB and Reality," *Schenectady Gazette,* February 27, 1984.

19. "Consumer Insights: EDB Update," an advertisement for Shop Rite Supermarkets, Consumer Affairs Department, Elizabeth, N.J., 1984.

20. From a speech given by Senator Edward Burke before the Congressional Joint Committee on Health Care, Washington, D.C., March 1984.

## Suggestions for Further Reading:

### Articles

The following five papers were prepared and presented as testimony at hearings before the Commonwealth of Massachusetts Department of Health in March 1984. Copies of the documents may be obtained from The Grocery Manufacturers of America, Inc., Washington, D.C.:

Peter M. Bonyata, Director of Quality Assurance, Quaker Oats Company: "Problems in Sampling and Measurement."

David Brown, PhD, Professor of Toxicology, Northeastern University: "Toxicology and Risk Assessment."

F.J. Francis, Director, Department of Food Science and Nutrition, University of Massachusetts: "Food Science and Nutrition."

Frederick A. Hegele, Director of Quality Assurance, General Mills, Inc.: "Industry Actions: Food Supply and Production."

Joseph J. Vitale, M.D., Director of Nutrition Education, Boston University School of Medicine: "Nutrition and Risk Assessment."

## Publications

Various issues of *Chemical Substances Control*, an advisory bulletin on industry practices, regulatory impact, and control techniques, Bureau of National Affairs, Washington, D.C.

Various issues of *Chemical Regulation Reporter*, a weekly publication of the Bureau of National Affairs, Washington, D.C.

Publications issued by the Department of Health and Human Services, Food and Drug Administration, 850 Third Avenue, Brooklyn, N.Y. 11232.

*Current Report*, periodically published by Occupational Safety & Health Reporter, Washington, D.C.

# Chapter 12: Video Invasion

1. The Television News Archive (TNA) at Vanderbilt University in Nashville, Tennessee, is a unique, efficient, and service-oriented archive. Its main thrust is public access. Anyone, anywhere can use the facility by going to Nashville or by ordering audio and/or videotapes from TNA's *Television News Index and Abstracts*. Aside from news programs, TNA's public affairs programming includes some presidential speeches, political conventions, debates by presidential nominees, and the like. At present, their holdings are confined to the "big three" commercial networks: ABC, CBS, NBC. In addition to nightly news programs the networks produced specials on Afghanistan: interviews, documentaries, and roundtable discussions.

2. ABC, 1/6/80.
3. ABC, 12/28/80.
4. CBS, 1/11/80.
5. NBC, 10/9/80; CBS 1/31/80.
6. CBS, 3/5/81.
7. CBS, 3/6/81.
8. ABC, 9/23/81.
9. NBC, 1/14/80.
10. ABC, 2/21/80.
11. CBS, 1/6/80.
12. NBC, 1/5/80.
13. NBC, 1/6/80.
14. ABC, 1/8/80.
15. CBS, 1/1–8/80.
16. ABC, 11/22/83.
17. ABC, 2/7/80.
18. CBS, 1/16/80.
19. NBC, 8/4/80.
20. ABC, 12/26/80.
21. ABC, 6/26/81.
22. ABC, 1/26/82.
23. ABC, 2/3/82.

24. CBS, 8/21/81.
25. CBS, 10/2/81.
26. CBS, 1/14/82.
27. ABC, 3/22/82.
28. CBS, 1/6/80.

## Chapter 13: Is the Press Quietly Promoting Suicide and Other Forms of Death Chic?

1. Bill Abrams, "New Prudential Ads Portray Death as No Laughing Matter," *Wall Street Journal,* November 10, 1983, p. 31.

2. George Gerbner, "Death in Prime Time: Notes on the Symbolic Function of Dying in the Mass Media," *Annals of the American Academy,* January 1980, p. 65.

3. Undated press release from the College of Communications, University of Tennessee, Knoxville, for a symposium on April 5 and 6, 1984, about morbid messages in the media.

4. *Proceedings of the 1983 Convention of the American Society of Newspaper Editors* (Washington, D.C.: American Society of Newspaper Editors, 1983), p. 277.

5. Alexander Cockburn, "Death Rampant! Readers Rejoice," in Richard Pollak, *Stop the Presses, I Want to Get Off: Inside of the News Business from the Pages of (MORE)* (New York: Random House, 1975), p. 3.

6. Ibid., pp. 16–17.

7. Harold Blumenfeld, as quoted in *UPI Reporter,* July 24, 1980, P. 2.

8. Lil Junas, "Tragedy, violence photos dominate in news prizes," *Editor & Publisher,* February 23, 1980, p. 17.

9. See Sheryle and John Leekley, *Moments: The Pulitzer Prize Photographs.* (New York: Crown Publishers, 1978).

10. See *Moments in Time: 50 Years of Associated Press News Photos* (New York: Associated Press, 1984).

11. Wallace Stevens, as quoted in Susan Sontag, *On Photography* (New York: Farrar, Straus and Giroux, 1977), p. 204.

12. Nora Ephron, *Scribble Scribble: Notes on the Media.* (New York: Knopf, 1978), p. 62.

13. Roy Peter Clark, "The Unoriginal Sin," *Washington Journalism Review,* March 1983, p. 47.

14. William Robbins, "A brilliant Student's Troubled Life and Early Death," *New York Times,* August 25, 1980, p. A20.

15. Peter H. Bizen, "When a youth takes his life," *Boston Globe,* January 6, 1973, p. 9.

16. Unnamed Associated Press reporter, "Teen jumps to death after favorite TV show is canceled," *Boston Sunday Globe,* August 26, 1979, p. 9.

17. Greta Tilley, "A suicide at age 16," *Greensboro Daily News & Record,* Februry 7, 1982, as reprinted in Roy Peter Clark, ed., *Best Newspaper Writing 1983* (St. Petersburg, Fla.: Modern Media Institute, 1983), p. 26.

18. Unnamed United Press International reporter, "Teen-Age South Carolina Twins Die in an Apparent Suicide Pact," *New York Times,* June 12, 1981, p. D14.

19. Barry McDermott, "The Glitter Has Gone," *Sports Illustrated,* November 8, 1982, p. 94.

20. William E. Geist, "A Veterinarian For Race Horses Is Found Dead," *New York Times,* August 4, 1981, p. B3.

21. Michael Madden, "Death of a jockey," *Boston Globe,* December 19, 1980, P. 53.

22. Chris Hall, "Ex-Brewer's Mixed-Up Life Ends in Suicide," *Worcester Telegram,* August 20, 1980, p. 17. See also John Powers, "Danny, we hardly knew ye," *Boston Globe,* September 12, 1980, pp. 53, 61–63.

23. Unnamed Associated Press reporter, "Former teacher of year commits suicide," *Bangor Daily News,* April 19, 1984, p. 24.

24. Patt Morrison, "She Had 'Good Life' but She Chose to Die," *Los Angeles Times,* January 24, 1980, p. II-1.

25. John Andres, Anne Mackay-Smith, and Scot J. Paltrow, "Alan Saxon's Death Sets Off a Search For Gold Firm's Assets," *Wall Street Journal,* October 12, 1983, p. 1.

26. Mary Murphy, "The Life and Death of a Soap-Opera Actress," *TV Guide,* March 12, 1983, p. 3.

27. Michele Kamisher, "Why Suicide?" *New England* magazine in *Boston Sunday Globe,* April 2, 1978, p. 28.

28. Marcia Chambers, "Life and Death of a Campus Drug Dealer," *New York Times,* September 5, 1982, p. 1.

29. Jack Hart and Janis Johnson, "Fire Storm in Missoula: A clash between the public's right to know and a family's need for privacy," *Quill,* May 1979, p. 19–24.

30. Ronald Kessler, "Drug Arrest Turns a Promising Hill Career Sour," *Washington Post,* May 22, 1983, p. A1.

31. William Raspberry, "Sympathy For Those Like Us," *Washington Post,* May 25, 1983, p. A25.

32. Ibid.

33. Glenn Collins, "Study Finds Family Bears Brunt of Social Change," *New York Times,* October 6, 1984, p. 48.

34. Typescript of "30 Minutes," September 15, 1979, p. 5.

35. Frederick C. Klein, "Teen-Age Suicide Toll Points Up the Dangers of Growing Up Rich," *Wall Street Journal,* May 14, 1981, p. 1.

36. Blaine Harden, "Young, wealthy . . . and mixed up," *Boston Globe,* September 18, 1981, p. 43.

37. Unnamed Associated Press reporter, "Houston Suburb Institutes Antisuicide Plan," *New York Times,* October 14, 1984, p. 34.

38. Alfred B. DelBello, "Needed: A. U.S. Commission on Teen-Age Suicide," *New York Times,* September 12, 1984, p. A31.

39. Glenn D. Weimer, "Deaths have pulled us together," *USA Today,* February 27, 1984, p. 10A.

40. See William K. Stevens, "Youth and Violence: A Look at 4 Lost Lives," *New York Times,* January 25, 1981, p. 40.

41. Sheila Rule, "Many Runaways Found to Have Tried Suicide," *New York Times,* January 22, 1984, p. 27.

42. Jane E. Brody, "The Haunting Specter of Teen-Age Suicide," *New York Times,* March 4, 1984, p. 8E.

43. Nora Sayre, as quoted in a book review by Alden Whitman, "A helpful examination of indirect suicide," *Boston Sunday Globe,* February 24, 1980, p. A8.

44. See, for example, Eileen McNamara, "A question of morality in suicide," *Boston Sunday Globe,* December 28, 1980, pp. 21, 28; George Esper, "A suicide destroyed two lives," *Boston Sunday Globe,* December 20, 1981, pp. 50–51; and Frank Deford, "Kenny, dying young," *Sports Illustrated,* March 9, 1981, pp. 30–34.

45. "The injured athlete's friends," *Boston Globe,* April 27, 1981, p. 10.

46. Dan Cryer, "Suicide and euthanasia: Christiaan Barnard tackles controversial subject," *Boston Globe,* April 16, 1981, p. 43.

47. Derek Humphry, "Choosing to die: A society called Hemlock thinks it's your right," *Boston Sunday Globe,* October 19, 1980, p. A2.

48. Dr. John D. Arras, as quoted in Glenn Collins, "The 'Right To Die': Is It Right?" *New York Times,* April 25, 1983, p. B8.

49. Edwin S. Shneidman, "The mystery behind suicide," *Boston Sunday Globe,* April 15, 1979, p. A13.

50. Joseph Williams, "Young Suicides—Tragic and on the Increase," *New York Times,* April 25, 1982, p. 10E.

51. Dennis A. Williams, "Teen-Age Suicide," *Newsweek,* August 28, 1978, pp. 74–77.

52. Robert D. McFadden, "Besieged Robbery Suspect in Upstate Suburban Home Frees His Journalist Hostage and Shoots Himself," *New York Times,* November 19, 1976, p. B3.

53. See Ron Rosenbaum, "Turn on, Tune In, Drop Dead," *Harper's,* July 1982, pp. 32–42.

54. Judy Foreman, "Brush with death changes life," *Boston Globe,* May 2, 1983, p. 39.

55. Ibid., p. 44.

56. Richard H. Stewart, "Near-death experiences," *Boston Globe,* August 24, 1984, p. 27.

57. Kenneth Ring, "Near-death experience: Researchers probe meaning of phenomenon shared by millions," *Boston Globe,* October 8, 1984, p. 33.

58. Elisabeth Kubler-Ross, *Living With Death and Dying* (New York: Macmillan, 1981), p. ix.

59. Elisabeth Kubler-Ross, *To Live Until We Say Good-Bye* (Englewood Cliffs, N.J.: Prentice-Hall, 1978), p. 13.

60. Laurie Johnston, "Artist Ends Her Life After Ritual Citing 'Self-Termination' Right," *New York Times,* June 17, 1979, p. 10.

61. Ibid.

62. Ibid.

63. Ibid.

64. Jo Roman, *Exit House* (New York: Seaview Books, 1980), p. 13.

65. Ibid., p. 21.

66. Ibid., p. 28.

67. Jo Roman, as quoted in Susan Jacoby, "Hers," *New York Times,* July 3, 1980, p. C2.

68. Henry A. Bailey, Jr., "'Objectivity' aside, reporter steps to the rescue," *Quill,* December 1982, p. 38.

69. Ibid.

70. David Gelman, "The Most Painful Question," *Newsweek*, January 16, 1984, p. 72.

71. Patricia Koza, "Coalition Cites 'Proof,'" (Worcester) *Evening Gazette*, January 26, 1981, p. 16.

72. See David P. Phillips, "The Influence of Suggestion on Suicide: Substantive and Theoretical Implications of the Werther Effect," *American Sociological Review* 39(June 1974): 340–354.

73. Ibid.

74. See Edward Bunnell Phelps, "Neurotic Books and Newspapers as Factors in the Mortality of Suicide and Crime," *Bulletin of the American Academy of Medicine* 12(October 1911): 265–266.

75. Ibid., p. 266.

76. Emile Durkheim, *Suicide: A Study in Sociology* (New York: Free Press, 1951), p. 141.

77. Leon Nelson Flint, *The Conscience of the Newspaper: A Case Book in the Principles and Problems of Journalism* (New York and London: Appleton, 1925), p. 209.

78. Henry B. Hemenway, "To what extent are suicide and other crimes against the person due to suggestion from the press?" *Bulletin of the American Academy of Medicine* 12(October 1911): 254.

79. See Phelps, "Neurotic Books and Newspapers," p. 309.

80. Ibid., p. 311.

81. Ibid.

82. Ibid., p. 298.

83. Dr. Jerome A. Motto, "Suicide and Suggestibility—The Role of the Press," *American Journal of Psychiatry* 124(August 1967): 160.

84. Dr. Jerome A. Motto, "Newspaper Influence on Suicide: A Controlled Study," *Archives of General Psychiatry* 23(August 1970): 143.

85. Ibid., p. 144.

86. Ibid., p. 146.

87. Sol Blumenthal and Dr. Lawrence Bergner, "Suicide and Newspapers: A Replicated Study," *American Journal of Psychiatry*, 130(April 1973): 469.

88. Phillips, "The Influence of Suggestion on Suicides," p. 347.

89. David P. Phillips, "Suicide, Motor Vehicle Fatalities, and the Mass Media: Evidence toward a Theory of Suggestion," *American Journal of Sociology* 84(March 1979): 1150–1174.

90. David P. Phillips, "Airplane Accident Fatalities Increase Just After Newspaper Stories About Murder and Suicide," *Science* 201(August 1978): 749.

91. Judie Smith, as quoted in Jane E. Brody, "The Haunting Specter of Teen-Age Suicide," *New York Times*, March 4, 1984, p. 8E.

92. Silas Bent, *Ballyhoo: The Voice of the Press* (New York: Liveright, 1927), pp. 66–67.

93. Phelps, "Neurotic Books and Newspapers," p. 299.

94. See Philippe Aries, *The Hour of Our Death* (New York: Knopf, 1981).

# About the Editor and Associates

**Bernard Rubin** is professor of governmental affairs and communication at Boston University's College of Communication and Graduate School of Arts and Science. His doctorate in political science was earned at New York University. Before joining the Boston University faculty in 1959, he taught at Brooklyn College, Skidmore College, and Rutgers University.

Dr. Rubin's professional positions have included consultantships with the Agency for International Development, the United States Air Force and other government agencies. He was chief of research design for the United States Information Agency in the late 1960s and taught international relations courses at the Naval War College (part-time) in the 1970s.

His interests in First and Third World developments have led to numerous fieldwork and lecturing trips in Southeast Asia, East Africa, and Europe. In 1975, he founded Boston University's Institute for Democratic Communication (IDC) to concentrate on constitutional First Amendment-grounded media issues, and he headed IDC for seven formative years.

He is the author of numerous articles on domestic and international politics. His book-length works on politics, mass communication, and public administration are *Public Relations and the Empire State* (Rutgers University, 1957); *Political Television* (Wadsworth, 1967); *Propaganda and Public Opinion* (Xerox Educational, 1972); *Media, Politics and Democracy* (Oxford University Press, 1977). He has also been editor-contributor of IDC's *Big Business and the Mass Media* (Lexington Books, 1977); *Questioning Media Ethics* (Praeger, 1978); and *Small Voices and Great Trumpets: Minorities and the Media* (Praeger, 1980).

In 1983, Dr. Rubin founded Associates in Research for Public Reporting to encourage practical scholarship on relationships among politics, government, and the mass media of communication. The organization brings practitioners and practitioner-scholars together to structure and carry out long-range research vital to the continuance of a free and responsible society.

**Caryl Rivers** is a professor of journalism at Boston University. Her most recent book—a novel, *Virgins*—was published in 1984 by St. Martin's Press/Marek and is being made into a feature film by 20th Century Fox; it will be published in Great Britain in both hardcover and paperback editions. In progress is a book entitled *Future: Feminine: How Women Are Re-Shaping America* (with Professor Bernice Buresh), which will consider how American institutions are changing as women form a "critical mass"—in politics, business, the arts, academia, and the sciences. Professor Rivers is the co-author of *Lifeprints*, a book about adult women based on a National Science Foundation study. Among her other books are *Aphrodite at Midcentury: Growing Up Female and Catholic in Postwar America* (Doubleday, 1973) and *Beyond Sugar and Spice* (Putnam's 1979). The latter, is a comprehensive look at research on feminine development, was selected as a Book-of-the-Month Club selection for Fall 1979. The book's co-authors are psychologists Grace Baruch and Rosalind Barnett, both of Brandeis University.

Professor Rivers writes frequently for newspapers and national magazines. She was Writer-in-Residence at the *Washington Star* in 1976 and writes regularly for the syndicated column "One Woman's Voice" and for the *Boston Phoenix*. Her articles have appeared in the *New York Times Magazine, Ms., New Times, The Nation, Saturday Review, Mother Jones, Rolling Stone, Redbook, McCalls,* and other publications. She was a finalist in the national competition for excellence in magazine journalism sponsored by the University of Missouri and the J.C. Penney Company for 1978. She was cited for an article written for *Womensports* magazine, "The Girls of Summer." She also received the 1978 award as outstanding magazine writer for the New England area given by the New England Women's Press Club.

During her five years as a Washington correspondent for a number of papers and magazines across the country, Professor Rivers covered Capitol Hill and the White House. She has also been a television commentator. She holds a masters degree in journalism from the Columbia University Graduate School of Journalism and an A.B. in history from Trinity College, Washington D.C.

**Cecelia Tichi** is professor of English at Boston University, where she is a member of the Graduate School faculty, with special interests in American literature and culture. She received the Ph.D. from the University of California, Davis, has been a visiting professor at the College of William and Mary, and has lectured at Columbia University, Harvard University, and the University of Tennessee. She has served as consultant to the United States Information Agency and has traveled to Israel under the sponsorship of the U.S. State Department. In addition, Dr. Tichi has been a board member of the Radcliffe Institute Society of Fellows, has served on the editorial board of *Studies in American Fiction*, and has been a member of the Council of the American Studies Association.

Dr. Tichi is the author of numerous articles on American literature and culture, appearing in such journals as *American Literature, Early American Literature,* and the *William and Mary Quarterly*, and has published a critique of television news broadcasting in the *Christian Science Monitor*. She is the author of

*New World, New Earth: Environmental Reform in American Literature from the Puritans through Walt Whitman* (1979), which explores the ideology of environmental change in America. She is an editor of the forthcoming *The Harper American Literature* and has just completed a novel, *Crash Course*. Currently, she is at work on a book on American culture and technology from the 1890s through the Jazz Age of the 1920s.

**Ralph L. Rosnow** is Thaddeus L. Bolton Professor of Psychology at Temple University in Philadelphia. A graduate of the University of Maryland, the George Washington University, and the American University, he previously taught at Boston University, in the School of Public Communication, and at Harvard University, in the Department of Psychology and Social Relations. In 1973, he was a visiting professor at the London School of Economics and Political Science.

He has written extensively on the psychology of rumor and gossip and has been a consultant on rumor-control strategies and on litigation involving defamatory rumor. His book *Rumor and Gossip: The Social Psychology of Hearsay* (with Gary Alan Fine, 1976) was republished in Japanese in 1982.

Professor Rosnow is the author of numerous articles and books in social psychology and has also written widely on the methodology and philosophy of human subject research. Much of this work was supported by grants from the National Science Foundation and the National Institute of Mental Health. His books include *Experiments in Persuasion* (1967), *Artifact in Behavioral Research* (1969), *The Volunteer Subject* (1976), *Paradigms in Transition* (1981), *Essentials of Behavioral Research* (1984), and *Understanding Behavioral Science* (1984). He was general editor of the *Reconstruction of Society* series published by Oxford University Press, and he serves on various editorial boards.

**Marianthi Georgoudi** is currently assistant professor of social psychology at the College of the Holy Cross, Worcester, Massachusetts. Her main interests include attribution theory in social psychology and philosophical-epistemological issues, particularly as they pertain to dialectic theory and contextualism. Dr. Georgoudi has also worked closely with Professor Ralph Rosnow (Temple University) on theoretical topics in communications research, rumors, and gossip. She has contributed a number of articles in European as well as American professional journals in the above topics and is currently co-editor (with Prof. Rosnow) of an upcoming book on contextualist understanding in behavioral science.

A native of Greece, Dr. Georgoudi holds degrees from the American College of Athens (B.A.), the London School of Economics and Political Science (M.Sc.), and Temple University (Ph.D.). She has previously been visiting assistant professor at Temple University and has also been a full-time faculty member at Bennington College.

**Roger Manvell** is a University Professor and professor of film in the School of Broadcasting and Film in the College of Communication, Boston University. He holds a Ph.D in English literature from London University and a D.Litt in film studies from Sussex University, the only senior British doctorate in the subject so far conferred in the United Kingdom. He is also an Hon.D.Litt of Leicester University, an Hon.D.F.A. of New England College, and an Hon.D.Litt of the University of Louisville, where he was Bingham Professor of Humanities in 1973. From 1947 to 1959 he was director of the British Film Academy, the British equivalent of the American Academy of Motion Picture Arts and Sciences.

Dr. Manvell has written (with Heinrich Fraenkel) several biographical and other studies relating to the Nazi Third Reich, and he is also the author of numerous books on film history and television and a contributor on communications and other subjects to the *Encyclopaedia Britannica*. In addition to scripting documentary and animated films, he has written many radio and television plays and documentaries for the BBC in London. His latest books include biographical studies of Hitler and Charles Chaplin; a comparative study, *Theater and Film*, *Shakespeare and the Film*; and, most recently, *Image of Madness: the Portrayal of Insanity in the Feature Film*, co-authored with Professor Michael Fleming, with whom he has taught classes at Boston University on psychology and film.

**Tenney Kelley Lehman** is executive director of the Nieman Foundation for Journalism at Harvard University, which she joined in 1967. She is also editor of *Nieman Reports*, the foundation's quarterly. Her columns. "From the Editor's Desk," frequently focus on world press freedom. As a member of the International Press Institute and the Inter American Press Association, she has observed at firsthand the media in such countries as Norway, Switzerland, Sweden, England, Canada, Greece, and Kenya. Her prior experience includes affiliation with radio station WEEI(CBS), Boston, Massachusetts, and WING, Dayton, Ohio, and she has been a copywriter for advertising agencies in Boston and Dayton. She is an alumna of Brandeis University and of Northeastern University.

**Deac Rossell** has been the film coordinator at the Museum of Fine Arts, Boston, since 1974. He has also held the position of Lecturer in the College of Special Studies, Tufts University, teaching film history, since 1974. A former associate editor of the *Boston Phoenix*, he was photography critic of the *Boston Globe* from 1973 to 1975 and film critic of *Boston* magazine from 1980 to 1984. He has written for *Esquire*, *American Film*, *Cinema*, the *Boston Review*, and many other publications. A contributor to the anthologies *Arttransition* (ed. Virginia Gunther) and *Questioning Media Ethics* (ed. Bernard Rubin), he is a program consultant to the Munich International Film Festival, and programmer for the 31st Annual Robert Flaherty Film Seminar. He lives in Boston with his spouse Mickey Myers, an artist, and is working on the first history of American independent narrative filmmaking.

**T. Barton Carter** is a communications lawyer and a professor at the Boston University College of Communication. Former head of the Law Division of the Association for Education in Journalism and Mass Communication, he has authored articles on defamation, copyright, and legal rights of access to the media. His chapter on legal aspects of video is due to be published this spring in a new International Association of Business Communicators book on nonbroadcast video. He is the president and majority shareholder of Tanist Broadcasting Corporation, licensee of radio stations WFAU/WKCG in Augusta, Maine, and maintains a communications law practice in Boston. A graduate of Yale University, the University of Pennsylvania Law School, and the Boston University School of Public Communication, Mr. Carter has worked in the legal department of the National Association of Broadcasters.

**Walter C. Clemens, Jr.,** is professor of political science at Boston University. He is a member of the International Institute for Strategic Studies, the American Committee on East–West Accord, and the International Studies Association. Dr. Clemens studied at Columbia University, where he received three degrees, and also at Notre Dame University, the University of Vienna, and Moscow State University. He has taught at the University of California, Santa Barbara; the Massachusetts Institute of Technology; and Boston University. He has lectured throughout Asia, Europe and Latin America.

Dr. Clemens is the author or co-author of many books, including *Soviet Disarmament Policy, 1917–1963; Khrushchev and the Arms Race; Toward a Strategy of Peace; World Perspectives on International Politics; The Arms Race and Sino-Soviet Relations; The Superpowers and Arms Control; The U.S.S.R. and Global Interdependence;* and *National Security and U.S.–Soviet Relations.* He has written often in the op-ed columns of the *Christian Science Monitor, New York Times,* and the *Washington Post,* and his articles have appeared in U.S. journals such as *Slavic Review* and the *Journal of Conflict Resolution* and in many foreign journals, including *China Quarterly, International Affairs, Review of International Affairs, Das Parlament,* and others.

Dr. Clemens has received major fellowships from the Ford and Rockefeller Foundations, the Smithsonian Institution (Kennan Institute for Advanced Russian Studies), and NATO. He has been Senior Visiting Scholar at UCLA's Center for International and Strategic Affairs and Fulbright-Hays Lecturer at the University of the West Indies, Trinidad and Tobago. He is currently working on a long-term study entitled "Mutual Aid versus Exploitation in World Affairs."

**Robert H. Montgomery** is the acting director of the School of Mass Communications and Public Relations, College of Communication, Boston University, where he is also a professor of marketing communications in the undergraduate and graduate programs. Prior to joining Boston University in 1977, he owned an advertising agency in Cambridge, Massachusetts; had been director of advertising and sales promotion for Nashua Corporation (New Hampshire); and was manager of corporate advertising for Borg-Warner Corporation (Chicago). In addition to his academic and administrative duties at Boston University, Dr. Montgomery has served since 1979 as a consultant to the governments of Portugal and the Azores, advising on development of United States market opportunities. He has also served as a marketing consultant to three U.S. presidential candidates, specializing in the establishment of message and media strategies for reaching specified campaign target audiences. He was awarded the Doctor of Commercial Science degree by the Applied Research Institute, London, and he received the MBA from Western Reserve University. Dr. Montgomery has been the author of many articles about commodity investment finance, with emphasis on foreign currencies and precious metals in the forwards markets. His books include *Public Relations for Public Schools* (1958); *The Campaign Manager's Handbook* (1972); and *Advertising Management: Business-to-Business Communications* (1984).

**Anne Rawley Saldich,** an analyst of the dynamics among media and politics, writes and lectures about communication, specifically as it affects the functions of government and the press. Her book *Electronic Democracy: Television's Impact on the American Political Process* (Praeger, 1979) was the basis of a course she taught at the University of California, Berkeley, where she also gave courses in American government and international relations. Her articles along similar themes have appeared in publications such as the *Columbia Journalism Review, Change, Newsday, Vital Speeches of the Day, TV Quarterly, CATV, TV Digest, InterMedia* (London), *1'Année 2000* (Paris), and *Irish Broadcasting Review* (Dublin).

Dr. Saldich's public lecture at Stanford, "How TV Governs," was selected for reprint in *Representative American Speeches 1980–1981.* Her dissertation, written under the direction of Raymond Aron, is a classic of investigative reporting during turbulent times (Paris, 1967–1971). Based on 100 interviews with managers of radio and TV, with journalists, communication scholars, senators and industrial leaders, she documented President de Gaulle's systematic use of TV as an instrument of power.

In her conference papers, here and abroad, and in her articles on electronic history, Dr. Saldich has demonstrated that she is on the leading edge of research in that field. She has been invited by Vanderbilt University's Television News Archive to serve on a national committee that relates public communication to public policy.

As a Woodrow Wilson Fellow (1960), she went to the University of California's Department of Political Science at Berkeley, where she worked on her doctorate for two years. Her degrees are the Ph.D., honors, from the Sorbonne (1971); the M.A., high honors, from Wayne State University (1961); and the B.A., honors, University of Detroit (1958). Dr. Saldich is assistant editor of the *Journal of Economic Literature* at Stanford University.

**Loren Ghiglione** is editor and publisher of *The News* (Southbridge, Massachusetts) and president of Worcester County Newspapers, a company that owns twelve newspapers and one radio station. He has edited four journalism books, including *Evaluating the Press: The New England Daily Newspaper Survey,* for which he won the national Sigma Delta Chi Award for Distinguished Service in Journalism.

He serves as a board member of the American Society of Newspaper Editors, president of the New England Press Association, chairman of the United Press International newspaper advisory board in New England, and a board member of the Committee to Protect Journalists. For the past two years he has been a Pulitzer Prize contest juror.

Dr. Ghiglione is a graduate of Haverford College (B.A., 1963), Yale University Graduate School of City Planning (M.U.S., 1966), Yale Law School (J.D., 1966), and George Washington University (Ph.D. in American civilization, 1976).